Published by IPBooks

© IPBooks 2017 - - ISBN 978-0-9548411-5-7 Fifth edition

www.ignoranceparadox.com

A CIP catalogue record for this book is available from the British Library.

First edition 2004 ISBN 0-9548411-0-7

Revised 2005 ISBN 978-0-9548411-0-2

Third edition 2013 ISBN 978-0-9548411-2-6

Fourth edition 2016 ISBN 978-0-9548411-3-3

Contents

A chimp in human form might not be as restricted as Jeremy here.

Most are constantly distracted. So busy getting on with things that they never stop to truly ask what is it all for. Those that do stop and think might consider themselves to be more like a zookeeper. The really deluded ones believe they are above the chimps and superior to those without certain knowledge.

A simple reverse psychology trick would be to say;

Give this book to someone else, it is not for you. You are a mere monkey and won't understand it. Besides, most will not get it either. Few get past the first few pages.

Carry on your life as it is, for nothing here will brighten it.

It is after all the ignorance paradox.

It might help if it was written on good authority or at least by someone who could write well.

Why Bother?

"At the end of every hard earned day people find some reason to believe."

The central park in a big city is a fine place to get a get a snapshot of people's lives in action. To make a guess at what they have planned and what their dreams may be. Here one is steadfastly knitting while another is twiddling with a pencil making artistic strokes appearing to have a look of optimistic hope that things will soon get better. A marriage proposal sets off whoops of joy and an onlooker is resting on a wall having just gone outside to get some fresh air. They have taken a breather to take in the enormity of what they have discovered. Having worked so hard and for such a long time it all now seems such a good gamble. You do need to look far to see people making headway.

I am close enough to overhear a conversation between two girls that appear to have just left high school. This is roughly what I garnered or maybe I just made it all up.

"Isn't it great... No more exams."

"Just a leaving party and we won't be seeing that school anymore."

"A bit sad in a way, somethings we will miss."

"New shoes? What was wrong with the old ones?"

"Oh, a bit scuffed and I saw these reduced in the shop this morning."

"Are you getting your hair done for the big night?"

"Of course, and I have been promised a whole new outfit. I deserve it after all that work over the last couple of years."

"Dad was showing me those horrid photos of when we were young, cringe worthy, I gave him that look and he relented."

"Did you hear about my mum?"

"No."

"She was stuck on a train for hours yesterday. Apparently, someone jumped in front of it and it was held up for ages. Something about having to find the head and get it bagged up."

"Crikey, what a shame, poor soul must have been pretty down and desperate."

"Yes such a shame, she didn't think it was appropriate to grumble, but there were a few people on the train that were moaning. One was irate as they had a flight to catch and was real worried about missing it. They were going on about how they had booked time off work and wouldn't get another opportunity for a good while, not to mention the financial cost."

"Well the chap split in two won't be getting a holiday for a while either."

"There is so much in life to do, so sad, stupid to just give up like that, but I suppose you never really know what is going on inside other peoples' heads."

"You know, when we were in the Far East we saw a sign at the station that said no jumping during rush hour."

"Crazy, some giving up and my dad is battling an illness. He wants to finish his screenplay and wants to enter that golfing competition. So busy and then this operation. He is lucky that technology has come a long way and the operation is so much easier now, much less discomfort. He wasn't put to sleep, had it done wide awake. He reckons that the side effects were minimal, although there were some pretty odd sensations whilst it was being carried out."

"That's great to hear. I do think though, whilst he is having that done other people are dealing with their own problems. It is bizarre, each in our own little world, all going on night and day."

"I suspect my cousin is just getting up now; he is half way around the world on a work placement."

"Yep, people everywhere, some playing bingo, some fishing for pearls in the blue waters, some making love!"

"So Joanne, what about you. Have you decided on whether you are going to university?"

"I am. Not sure which one yet and there are a few course options to choose from, will decide next week."

Joanne flicked her hair back and felt something sharp on her neck. A small knife terminates all those plans. Due to incompetence, due to a desire to be fair to everyone and not placing the risk to innocents at the top of the agenda, a person with mental health problems is on the loose and has now attacked and killed this fragile irreplaceable young beauty. In their prime. A future partner not to be. What she would have done in her life, what she may or may not have achieved, no one will ever know. Only we and those that knew her can imagine.

What is it all about, why do we bother? It won't happen to me so not a great concern. Look at the statistics, these kinds of things are rare. Yet all the work done, all the forming of that child was to be just a happy childhood and no more.

There are a lot of people excited about upcoming events. Where do all these people get their enthusiasm from? The odd few that are pondering about their insignificance are not down and depressed, far from it, they just hit a point in their life where they want to have a spell thinking. Whenever they ask others about such matters they get bland replies or some rhetoric that feels inadequate.

There are always a lot of positive stories out there to bring gladness to our attention. Maybe it is the last piece of a bridge laid in place linking two towns together, shortening the journey significantly between the two. Or a huge swathe of land marked out where no development or human encroachment will be allowed. Great news for those concerned with the imbalance of nature and progress. You may jump for joy when seeing your team go top of the league. There are plenty of turning points and days marked out with projects coming to fruition which bring elation and pleasure. Items galore to make things seem worthwhile and put some sense into the heart of being.

Most people are grabbing all they can from each and every day. Life is still pointless, but there must be a reason why we bother. We can be lifted by simple carnal pleasures such as making a fire in the great outdoors and dancing around it. It can all be about finding the loves of our lives. We have a choice of taking positive action or choosing to leave it to the will of something higher out of our control. There is so much to be enjoyed except in those rare places where clowns parade around preventing anything other than servility and submission, stopping you from doing what you want. We can travel to see for ourselves what is denied or what is only held back through lack of imagination.

Some people are sitting there waiting in the queue to pass into the ether, but for each one of those who have all but given up there are far more that are full of life, energy and hope to do as much as they can with their life.

We can see progress in our life, we can find great things to occupy our time. There can be some magical moments. We can ignore the ratio of good times to bad. We can forget about the grief required to have those jolly fun days. It may require a lot of effort for a brief period of satisfaction. Many hard-fought battles to spend moments in periods described close to paradise. A ratio of an hour of effort for such comparatively few minutes of bliss, maybe the journey to get there is the satisfying bit. Contrive a routine free of annoyances, reading, munching, bathing and debating nothing disagreeable. However, it is not hard to get yourself in a position where fun peaks and you yearn for new challenges with more stability and more sense of that rush of life running through your days. Round and round it goes all looking good until the sun comes up again, shedding light on the cracks ignored the night before. This circular rhythm of life is a thing of majesty, but on occasions we feel different in the cold light of day.

The cycle

I spent years refurbishing electronic goods, giving them a new lease of life and earned a great deal of money from it. Although our jobs provide a living, where are all of those items now? I imagine most are in landfill. Some may still be in use and maybe one remains gathering dust in a museum. A few will have been reused in part and a percentage will have been recycled and put into new products. At the time, all the work we do seems so important. With perfectionists willing us to make sure the items we sell are the best they can be. We fuss over all the details and it makes us proud that we did a good job. When we look back at all the heartache making sure everything is ready in time and presented as nicely as possible, you think that although people got some use out of them they were soon dispensed with. So long as people made money and got by that is all that needs to be said.

The packaging however elegant makes it to the bin first followed shortly afterwards by the item itself. At each stage people get a sense of the significance of what they are doing. The factory worker will be doing their utmost to get the most done, the most assembled in the working day. It can be a repetitive job doing the same thing over and over for a meagre existence on the pay given. They will have people working upstairs devising new ways to do the job faster with more mechanisation to get greater numbers made at a lower cost. There will be people digging out all the raw materials risking life and limb shrugging off the impact on their health to feed those factories. There will be marketeers and advertising people working late into the night ensuring the campaign fulfils the remit. Then all the delivery people on ships and in lorries transporting the items making sure deadlines are met. They are all content to get paid for their undertaking, equally proud of the service they give. Finally, it gets to the shops. The people there create the displays and start feeling the pressure of hitting sales targets to ensure the overheads are covered. It is left to the shoppers to decide what to buy and take home and determine how much use it will get before it is thrown out.

When we make something, we have this hope that someone will appreciate the effort gone into making it. We envisage people wearing the cloth we stitched together or enjoying the product we designed and put into production. We focus on the upside and keep our focus away from how often items get damaged, destroyed on purpose or just left in a cupboard unloved. Once it is yours you can do what you like with it and disregard the feelings of those that made it. In the process of taking something from mine to landfill we don't pay much attention to the many meetings people have had in determining the path of their products. So much discussion about what needs to be done. They will have drawn up road maps, laying out routes the company should take and worked on strategies to embark upon. Talk to any retailer and they will brighten up your day with tales about the sharp end of what being in business entails. Dealing with the taxes, hassle from customers and countless other troubles they have to contend with. Nevertheless, we work through the issues and place a high importance on our involvement.

Some items are used more than once unlike the produce a farmer brings to market. After all the toiling in the field to get the grain to send to the miller and then on to the baker, we eat the bread. It gets consumed then dumped. The cycle of life providing us with the sustenance to go to work, to shuffle some more documents. Your magazine that was edited, spellchecked and proofed gets torn up and put at the bottom of the animal cage. You work hard to develop your skills and become a computer programmer, someone who rearranges rust on a disc. However, it is no different. Your project gets released, used then deleted or updated and forgotten about. So, you decide to get a hands on outdoor job landscape gardening. You shift all the mud around in people's gardens making rockeries and ponds. Then if you are smart you leave a business card around so that someone at a later time will ask you to return. You then make some more money levelling it back over again to make it easier for old people using walking frames to get about.

I went over to see one of my tenants and whilst there they wanted me to marvel at all the work they had done redecorating the property. They said in jest that the house was worth more now that all this work has been done. Sadly, although it may look nice to them now it will all be painted over back to plain white when they leave. Even the buildings themselves are not immune from this endless changing and tinkering. Many get put up nice and neatly then knocked down to make way for a road or a new development. If it is not deterioration, then a building has to avoid fire, floods and earthquakes and unless it has some preservation order placed on it is unlikely to be left alone. Whatever happens, it will need a lot of maintenance year after year. And that is what it is about - doing what is needed to keep on top of things. Leave your garden for a short while and it soon becomes an overgrown jungle. You can plot and plan a garden placing plants here and there but someone else arrives, this new custodian has other ideas and will rip them all out. Still, a little refresh whether inside or outside our home, gives us an uplift which lasts for a good few days. We do smile more when the furniture we get replaced is more comfortable than the last lot we ejected. All the upgrading brings us up to a new norm, raising our expectations whilst also removing arduous aspects of life.

It can be all about the temperature. Some like it warm some like it cold and things breed and spread according to the temperature. However, nothing you make or do is immune from a degree of heat, it can all be melted down. All the arrangements and construction that we spend a lifetime working on can be unravelled in an instant. Yet each person in the chain feels what they are doing has some significance.

Maintenance

It is not all downbeat but people wonder where they are heading when faced with this constant battle of maintenance, keeping things going, keeping things fed and watered, bills paid and up to date, friendships affirmed and toe nails clipped. There are forms of progress made without doubt in some areas and of course the houses provide places for people to live, food gives nourishment and the games provide entertainment. We also learn through the advancement of drugs and technology even if it is just new techniques and methods of doing things quicker and more cheaply. However, the bulk of the population go into work and do their bit then return home, arrange something to eat and retire to bed after a few short hours on the couch and begin to wonder what it is for. All those people you shifted in a taxi will make their way back again. Even the blood sweat and tears that are spent developing new medicines seems disheartening if their effectiveness wanes over time. When someone thinks in terms of productivity and improvement and push for progress others realise that what people are doing really is nothing more than tweaking, modifying and changing things around most of the time. Hence this book started from the very thought of why we bother. It too will be read by a tiny number of people and lost in the mass of all the better works.

We can revel in a long lie in, staying in bed into the later part of an afternoon or idle away a day or two but most tire of this when days of doing little extends to weeks and months. We certainly feel better once the house has been vacuumed and the rubbish put out and as much as we can do today has been done. Being thankful that we have another day where we can still do things for ourselves is enough for many but there are times when we look for more. Some things we create and mould may linger but the bulk of it will be refreshed, changed and updated. The vultures circle at your death picking the prized items to sell, a little is hoarded for a while whilst the remainder is dumped. Only the arguments about who is to pay for the hearse and next world arrangements persist, albeit briefly until the acrimony fades. Nothing much is forever. Not really. Only in our blinkered aspiration. Maybe some pearls of wisdom get handed down, utilised or rebelliously ignored and acted upon in a polar opposite way.

Motivations

It is quite clear that there are plenty with a desire to get richer or go down the path of becoming more and more well known. Being liked can be a draw. However, most plod on with no desire for huge wealth nor wish to be recognised everywhere they go. Neither does everyone have some kind of fixation on making the world a better place. Some people have a chirpy exterior that hides turmoil and anguish below and some gentle probing uncovered this frequently. Many people need only a holiday on the horizon or something to look forward to at the weekend to get through each day. Having a wish to see their children take the family name forward can provide the incentive and impetus to do lots of overtime in a mundane job. We find our own motivation. There are lots of aims that we each have that are bereft of a grander picture. So it became less of a question of what the point of life was and more a question of what drives us. You can have no point no purpose but have something built into you that motivates you to do things and find personal successes. Whilst I was keen to explore the whys and wherefores of life it became apparent that few share any great wish to look too deeply into such mysteries. People become defensive very quickly and the subject is soon changed. Maybe to uncover the foundation of our existence is too unsettling. Thankfully however I came across a sufficient number of people who were willing to open up enough to make progress in this exploration.

Many people have ideas that are so entrenched that no matter what you put to them they will never be swayed from their beliefs. Some will read this text and get the wrong idea from it. Others will take some interesting bits and reshape them to reinforce the ideas that they already have. The objective is to present the reasons why each and every one of us does what they do and then give people a chance to see if it applies to them or not. Finding out what impels us doesn't mean that it will give us hope or make us consider changing our ways in any shape or form. It is nothing other than an investigation into our drives. It tries to be careful about any hidden hints on self-improvement and rations anything that challenges peoples' behaviour. The bulk will understand and potentially agree but will not see the implication. Being given the answers to many a question is easy, comprehending the profound depths of them is another thing entirely and I would expect most to miss it here completely.

Suggestions regarding how we live or raising concerns about the ecological impact of what we do is not the focus here either. It is much more about the reasons why we care, why we bother to make such efforts to get things done.

Feeling special

It is quite natural to think of ourselves as being a bit special as we live in our own universe. It is not too hard to see the appeal in thinking of ourselves as being a bit different as well. There is nothing wrong with that but unfortunately we can't do much about how and where we are brought up. Certain circumstances can tarnish the core ability to think independently and have a balanced outlook. As someone who is never keen being told what to do and how to act, I found myself avoiding conformity without being too defiant or rebellious. I was always on the lookout for other ways of doing things, finding great satisfaction in self-employment since it allowed me to decide what goes on. A simple example of this would be my ability to give someone a discount if I felt it was fair without having to get someone else's permission to do so. Having worked in many places prior, I could take the bits that were positive and leave swathes of regulations and unnecessary procedures behind.

Outside of work there are social encounters to navigate. It is so easy to be influenced by people saying that there is a right and wrong way to conduct oneself. I could only see one universal conversational law - that being the requirement to listen rather than bleat on endlessly. I developed a habit of probing and asking a lot of very direct questions that were more often than not answered. This was despite the very personal nature of the conversation because on the whole people love to talk about themselves more than anything else. Going my own way was not unusual but it has been helpful when it comes to unearthing what I could about the intricacies of our existence.

Independence

Growing up under someone else's control is a real bugbear but hopefully you get to a point where you can leave and make your own way. Swapping the freedom of not having to pay for the roof over your head for the freedom to decide how you live, what time you get up and determining your own course, making your own mistakes. I appreciate that this is not the case for everyone. The liberty you feel can depend not only on where you live but also on the type of job you get. Some will be under far greater pressure than others. I was lucky that I wasn't subjected to a barrage of religious or political principles at home and made to abide by narrow doctrines. This can counteract most negative aspects surrounding anyone's upbringing. We had the opportunity to express ourselves and explore the merits of a whole range of ideologies. Some people were taught to question absolutely everything resulting in the habit of always looking for another question rather than seeing the promise in an answer. Others were taught to never question anything and rely on faith instead. Everything that they are told is held up as the gospel truth and only your attitude is open to debate. This didn't mean that I wasn't exposed to a whole host of ideas from the wacky to the plain illogical. I would listen to the musings of others and found the notion that there was no meaning to life particularly poignant. I thought to myself if that was the case, then why do people make such an effort to further themselves?

If you, like many others consider life to be some sort of test you are probably not far wrong, life is pretty testing no matter who you are. However, it must be stressed that despite any acknowledgement that life is in essence basically pointless it does not need to make you down and glum. Far from it, just that life and all things that we do and build is temporary. Trying to find a purpose is in itself a form of distraction. The busier we are the less time we spend dwelling upon why we do the things we do. The greater the struggle the less time we have to ponder and life goes by in a blur with little analysis of why we bother. I did encounter a few who sadly took their own life and saddened most by the opportunities they had but didn't grab onto.

One of them could have had a relationship that they would dearly have loved if only they had made a move. Instead lived out an unbearable existence right up to old age before they took the plunge. Another in their prime of youth had a world of tremendous possibilities ahead and one more seemed overwrought by a simple money matter. We never get to feel what they feel and it is hard to understand the torment or worries that fester in their minds before they make their last decision. The number of people that find themselves in that situation is small compared with the large population. We don't all just give up, far from it. Most find ways of contending with the periods when they feel trapped and in despair. For many, life is way too short to get what we would like done. So many things to go out and do, so much to try and master in such a limited timeframe.

Bigger picture

You may discover other purposes in life such as a willingness to do charitable things rather than just focusing everything on our own position. I most certainly am not fond of criticizing, judging or evaluating the merits of what people get up to. People find their reasons and in many cases the justification can be admirable. Alternatively, you may only wish to master something, get good at playing an instrument or prove yourself in a sport. Many spend years training, merely to throw a stick a fraction further than everyone else or shave a millisecond off a track race record and think it is marvellous. Pat yourself on the back and be happy with your achievement is snidely said by those that are not always doing much notable themselves. A race will be made up mainly of losers who put in the same amount of effort and sacrifice but do not get to be triumphant. They will think that taking part is what counts the most. Plenty more will be trying hard for a good while to be brutally culled in the pre-selection. People get wrapped up in a pursuit and have hopes that it will give them meaning and self-worth. There are numerous inane activities that swallow our attention for large periods of our life. All of this is fine but what gave people the inclination to focus so much time and energy on such things was a puzzle that would be fun to solve and like other explorers something to keep this writer amused for a good while.

The relevance of what is presented here is equally significant for those that cling on to the idea that life here on earth is a simple preparation for another eternal life in the hereafter and those that feel that once you are dead you are dead. Some see a huge value in a god, for them it is everything. Others show scepticism towards this coupled with a cynicism of the horrors, the pain that an all seeing all knowing entity ignores and never interferes with. Either way you can see how by design or default there are some ingenious mechanisms within us at work. We animals have some features that are incredibly clever and very very difficult to emulate in a man-made machine.

The age old question of what the meaning of life was, was brought up many times whilst exploring what people got from their lives. A diverse set of responses emerged. Some said that you find your own meaning. Others said you get a lot of meaning from simple pleasures, appreciating the here and now. Just enjoying things from the taste of the food we eat to the conversations we have. It is people themselves; being with those we get on with. One person said simply; it is to breathe. Another saw their calling in doing things for their family. Many realise that it is rewarding doing a multitude of things for others helping the needy, providing support and sorting the ills of the world. However, finding a meaning is a misnomer. Realising that there are things that drive us, all of us is key to unlocking this conundrum. I found three and a bit things that are present in all of us. They are there at all times from when you are born until your final days and if you were to lose any one of them hope and caring about life can soon evaporate.

Legacy

People pay a lot of attention to their legacy and that runs from those in high office down to the humble servant. You can have a wish to make as much impact as possible whether in the music industry, the world of literature, the scientific arena or just the popular imagination. Those that don't produce much, those who are blessed with minimal creativity can still have a wish to be liked and remembered. However, the minute you put this to the test you see the failing in this desire. What is the name of your great great grandparents? Few will know their names let alone what those fine characters stood for. Although some of you may have consumed some time looking into your genealogy and riffled through the names of those in the past to map out a family tree, at best you will get to know how long they lived and their occupations but little else. A few key facts, but no real sense of what that person was all about. Unless you have the good fortune of finding some autobiography there is a limit to how much you will know about these ancestors and to be honest I doubt many will have much real interest in delving too far. Yet you may have a hope that your great grandchildren will hold you in high esteem. The reality is that you will be forgotten and ignored unless there is some unpaid tax to collect or treasure to uncover. Any attempt to lay your grand life out in diary form assumes that there will be suckers with enough time to spare to study them and that they possess no wish to worry about their own life one hundred percent more.

You could be the end of the line, no children no more genes passed down but take a different stance. You may have a vision of mankind propagating outwardly colonising other planets and building a new kind of future and that your contribution counts. This is hope over expectation and can only be achieved in the imagination rather than in reality due to the inhospitable nature of other worlds within a sensible distance from this comfortable earth we have here.

We can add to the sum of all knowledge and make useful discoveries. We may provide new information to aid the next generation. It is less about being cynical than being comfortable with the fact that your individual life counts for very little. We see a great figure in the past and consider the implications of what would have happened if they were never born. Some characters have played a significant role but it is all romanticised. We place them on a pedestal and discount the others that were vital in their achievements. Take a look at those in the background and you will unearth those that made the tools, those that took the idea forward and those that helped. The point is that when one drops out there is another to fill the void and we make too much of one individual. Nobody is irreplaceable. It is never just one person that deserved the credit, it is the whole group.

Rather than mock those that have found solutions to big problems we can have some gratitude that there are some that take the lead and endeavour to quieten people's resentment. To be fair we are all prone to seeing things in terms of a problem to be solved and those without many significant problems are the ones found to go out looking for more. They will see a local society in a muddle and get involved in sorting it out or form a new one nearer to home. The key to all this again lies in what drives people and what it is that gives them so much pleasure in doing such marvellous things.

Getting on with it

We may find ourselves sleepwalking through life doing as we are told and what people expect of us. Undoubtedly, for much of the time things can be good, but as we age and grey we might contemplate whether it was all worth it. Clinging on to small achievements, even little successes here and there can be consoling. Some of us may have even made a mark in a particular field making a breakthrough in technology or pulling of an adjustment to our culture. We might feel that overall we got a great deal of enjoyment from the things that we did. Yet we can stall and think about whether there is there more to life than this.

Whilst some can sit about all day pontificating about things, you need somewhere to live and that entails paying for the property and then you get the bills and the grief. You find it hard to do without the electricity so begrudgingly find this and more has to be addressed. Then a roof tax demand drops on the doormat. A light bulb turns on in the heads of a few and they leave the system and escape the rut but sooner or later they still find something unanswered. You can be content with your lot or yearn for a good deal more, financially or to have greater experiences, either way you will have a drive of some sort to get the strength to seek it.

Think of all those note books you expended at school, all the strain of the exams. All the learning all that education all that effort. How much do you actually use during your lifetime and how much gets scrubbed at your death. All those lovely memories, the fine experiences the wisdom and hard overcome mistakes. All gone. All that structure, the links in your mind that are lost. People, particularly your parents spent so much time nurturing you. Feeding and caring, day in day out for years and years to produce a person of independence. Someone who could carry the baton forward. Parents and guardians will also do the same for a child who is unlikely to ever get to the stage of being able to look after themselves. It makes little difference to the love and affection shown. Having a child can be the greatest thing. A truly life and personality changing event. At least for those that can. Or want to. Let's not forget that a life that doesn't get involved with procreation can be as satisfying and complete as one that resides in a house full of grateful/ungrateful whingers. Whether the child appreciates it or not is far from the point. We undertake the task regardless, whatever the motive. Irrespective of whether it is deep down the power or the longing to have someone to care for. What we can ask is why we play the game and what can the answers do for us. This game of life that we play, the football match, the motor race, the crossword puzzle all gets completed. We take something from it for the next one and hand it over to the other players and care nothing for its inherent time limit. Everything expires. So long as you have plenty to do and find enough variety to keep downward thinking at bay no one really cares and there is not much people can do if they wanted to anyway. So what gives us those joys we may ask? That which is in the fabric of the soul is quite remarkable. It enables us to pursue our dreams or just meander through.

The will to form

One of the key features of the universe is a will to form. Although entropy laws make things head towards low energy ultra-stable states, particles also have a vital propensity to bind and build structures all by themselves. Like a snowflake forming when the weather conditions are right, animals, plants and us inevitably form too if the environment is set in a certain way. In the right place for the period where things are just so, the process of organisation starts.

Compare an animal with a snowflake. Snowflakes and animals both need the right conditions to form. Whether that is the right temperature and pressure or a randy teenager looking to bond in an alcohol fuelled party. Both snowflakes and us are pretty much unique. The odd snowflake here and there are the same and we may have a twin or a doppelganger with the same genes but these are rare and that doesn't matter. The relevance is in the way in which the same simple bonds produce individuality. Water molecules join up with one another. There is a strong 'magnetic' attraction between the hydrogen in one molecule and the oxygen in another molecule. It has been given a complex sounding name; inter-molecular hydrogen bonding. These bonds form a plethora of patterns. There is an equivalence in us humans. So whilst the water forms beautiful shaped crystals, snowflakes, we have muggers, murderers and thieves, poets, nurses and endless wannabes. Completely different people but with essentially the same aims and drives.

Besides the chemical and biological similarities, we share key properties also. Every one of us has these same properties yielding different personalities but seeking the exact same underlying aims. I call them the driving forces, the things that make us do what we do. These basic building blocks of our nature provide us with the will to do things all things anywhere we are on the planet.

I am looking for properties that apply to everyone. People of all ages living right across the globe. From an old lady hobbling along to fetch some supplies, or a troublesome two-year-old tidying the house up to a yob making an impression on any blank wall in the area. Each core property that we identify must apply to every one of us without exception for it to be a valid answer. It is a worthy hunt as the power of understanding what drives us, what motivates us is fantastic; it gives us an appreciation of the nature of being. Providing not only an answer but a total revelation of who and what we are.

Whilst the manifestation of these properties will vary to some degree, they are found in all people no matter how old they are and in all societies without exception. They may entice some to climb mountains, some to explore the oceans or others to look after helpless animals and so forth. We will each set out to do different things, the aims are not the same, but the reasons at the core are very much identical. Whether it is something we do by ourselves or by working with others, the heart of our motives are the same. Think of it like all the millions of different plants that grow in their own way but are built upon the same biological components.

The hunt

During a search for the items that drive us many possibilities will turn up. The first thing that may spring to mind is survival. We all want to survive, don't we? Indeed, many have gone to extraordinary lengths to stay alive. But others have given up and met slow deaths in similar circumstances. People have removed limbs with small penknives to un-trap themselves. A portable telephone is great but if you leave it in the cab out of reach and now have your hand trapped in some farm machine it is not much help. To cut through your arm, sever all the muscles and hack through the bone is no mean feat with a small implement and no painkillers to take. One renowned individual managed to stay alive on a raft for over seven weeks. This was achieved by catching fish to eat and trapping rain water to drink. What makes the tale most remarkable is that the long drift began without a fishhook. With just bare hands a nail was prised from the wood of the raft to make one. This however took several days and must have caused more aggravation than a mere splinter or two.

Some of us fight and fight and fight to survive whereas others are more prone to give up and wither away. Babies can be seen battling for life probably clueless as to what lies ahead and why they exist. They show a will to live and a strong urge to soldier on. We do not always care about our own survival though. There have been a few mothers who have thrown their child to safety when an oncoming vehicle would take them both out. They died but the

19

child survived. During armed conflict with gunmen on a rampage parents have jumped onto their child to shield them. In the aftermath those going to investigate found many children alive and well underneath a body ridden with bullet holes. Remarkable tales of compassion and desperation. The last hope that their child doesn't get killed as well.

We might steal to eat. Kill to defend ourselves. Push to the front of the queue to increase our chances. Not to mention clambering over seats, trampling on others to escape a burning vehicle. But will sacrifice our own self in times of despair to protect ones we love. We resort to desperate measures on occasions if required. Nevertheless, we don't just want to survive, we want to thrive more so. We don't simply want to make it to the next year for the sake of it. Survival is a big thing but there are things that make us want to survive.

Procreation, keeping the population going, is that what we are here for? It is regarded as important and is prominent in our lives. There is little doubt that having children is essential for the continuation of the species. However, from an individual's perspective it doesn't have to be you that breeds. So long as enough people are maintaining the population humankind will continue. You might be infertile. You may not find a suitable partner. You may simply elect to remain childless and be perfectly happy so, but still getting erect for the pleasure it brings. What's more, youngsters do not have marriage and baby making playing on their mind. You do not even need to contribute towards the raising of other peoples' children either. You do not form some sort of ancillary function. Just child free. Having children does bring great joy and satisfaction to parents. No doubt about it. Even after the hassle is taken into account. Many may aspire to settling down and starting a family and see it is a big part of life. This can push them to try hard to fulfil this dream, but it is not universal. Some do, some don't. There is something deeper at work.

When you get old, your direct role in procreation ends. Some might retain some grand-parenting duties. Maybe providing help with childcare if the adults want to work. Nevertheless, as far as child rearing is concerned you are no longer essential nor as vital as you once were. That being so, it doesn't necessarily make you feel worthless however. Relieved and unconstrained to pursue other things with your time and able to provide advice and assistance to ease the burden when required. We most certainly don't drop off the face of the planet when the job of parenting comes to an end. We can in fact begin a whole new journey and have more time to explore. If you opt out of parenting altogether you still can strive to make something of yourself. You can devour time and energy to equally extraordinary adventures. Having children is not the only highlight or absolute imperative. Not for everyone and it is more of a long chapter in our life than the whole book.

There is no grand scheme at work. We are not here just to assist in the continuation of the species. It doesn't matter how long you live or what you add or take away. It is just those species, the animals, the plants that happen to spread are the ones we see.

Clearly intercourse is somewhat compelling to a vast number of us. Hours of interplay, chatting up and chasing preceding a comparatively short-lived climax. Many will see great value in paying very significant sums to explore fantasies when not available for free in a relationship. Neither is it unheard of for characters to travel great distances to partake in specialist sexual interactions. A big force is at play. Sometimes dangerously so. Gratifying and moreish enough to be sought and desired day after day. Whilst sex can be a huge factor in getting us into action the question is whether there is something beneath this primal urge; something promoting the craving. It is also worth noting that it might be on your mind day and night but I can assure you that is not the case for everyone. Significant yes, but not the be all and end all.

Taking on the responsibility of passing on our genes plays on the minds of many. Whilst there was a time when we didn't understand the connection between sex and conception an animal instinct to copulate is abound leading to replication. It is a nice idea to spread your genes far and wide, more so if you think of your genes as being special. Yet no matter how royal, the passing on becomes diluted rather quickly. Any immediate offspring is half yours and half your spouses. Your grandchildren divide it into a quarter. By ten generations it is watered down to one part in over a thousand. It is less of a chain and more of a murky pool that you emerge from and potentially contribute to. Many will see procreation as the most significant part of living but what I am asking is, is something at work underneath this. I also contend to reassure those that don't replicate that their life is not in any way less significant. Each life is driven by its own internal mechanism for its own ends irrespective of how much contribution it makes to the species. Your goofiness, ginger, gregarious gene segment that skips generations or rears its head later down the line is no more prominent than all the other characteristics seen as good or bad that so many many others add or take away also each time a child is born.

Payments for wining and dining, payments for bills, payments payments payments, the bills keep rolling in. Money can be a pretty big incentive to work and has been a part of how we live for a long time now. Hunting and gathering, growing food to eat and building somewhere to live. All either using a monetary system or beg and barter. The lure of money can provide the impetus to make a huge effort. Whether for the proceeds of what the cash can do or for the status it brings. The money itself, the power it gives us, or the harsh necessity to survive. We know that whilst money is in essence artificial, we care a lot for being paid as remuneration for jobs we have done or having it in exchange for a change in ownership of something. The money people acquire might be deserved or gleaned through greed. Either way it can be attractive and magnetic. Nonetheless some manage quite contentedly with very little. Enjoying the freedom of life without the rush for wealth and the anxiety that it comes with, casting aside the pressure of keeping up. Our drive for prosperity in monetary terms is not shared by all. Some want it but some do not feel the same need.

Someone might offer a reward to locate a lost cat, some will hunt for it, not for the money they will get, but for the fun of finding it. Treasure hunts have been set up and a good few get hooked by the enigma of the puzzle using vague clues to find where it is hidden. After digging here, digging there, exasperated, they want the prize so much that they have offered 10 times its value to get to the bottom of where it was buried. An object can become much more than its monetary value and as much as we love money we can throw it into the wind for a whimsical purpose.

Money has entered into every nook and cranny of our waking day. It has become something we use to such a great extent that we begin to see it as the elixir of life. You can fill your car up with tons of stuff and return home having swapped it with a few sheets of printed paper and feel jolly pleased with yourself. But you can equally go out for a walk with the dog visiting a park and trundle through the woods and have no thought of cash on your mind whatsoever. You don't always have to buy your partner a box of chocolates or promise a meal out to get them to engage in some nookie. Of course you will need to pay for the house and buy the bed in the first place but there are many people that manage on the bare minimum. Cash, gold, stocks and shares sit on top of a deeper desire.

Progression can be very alluring; collecting a complete set, making headway in a project, finishing a task or achieving a grade of greatness and so forth. Being given a badge or sticker on a chart thus enabling you to move to the next level. Getting extra skills to take on harder challenges and making past tests a walkthrough. A sense of moving forward. More money can provide that sometimes. But so can moving up the scale thus having more privileges. Any form of qualifications marks success points.

People that have demonstrated their greater level of skill gain entitlement to wear a more decorated uniform and different coloured clothing to show their higher banding. Progression and collecting is not only consigned to stamp collectors and train spotters it is much more widespread. It is all about having an aim, setting a goal and trying to get there in a fair minded way as possible. What the hell makes us want to put even more decorated trinkets into our collection when we already have enough to fill ten suitcases already? Why are we prepared to break a limb or ruin our body to get the top medal in some sporting event?

Whilst some show ambition to make a name for themselves, to make changes and improve things. Others are more keen to build relationships as it provides a different sort of stimulus to material accumulation or fame. Many find that to feel sufficiently fulfilled all they need do is a find a partner to live with. Merely being with someone is enough to be adequately satisfied. Some people do enjoy nothing more than the company of themselves, alone but not lonely. Sailing off, hiding away for long periods of time. Yet the majority revel in the company of others. The majority find real face to face communication rouses the soul, lifts our spirits and harbours contentment. It is the building of bridges between us that counts. Having friends of quality as opposed to quantity, ones which you can call upon for help and advice, concern and comfort. Having fun with friends, partners and family gets us through the lows of a day.

Love can come into it. You can have a wish to extend this love of yourself to others, most laudably towards minors and major people in your life. Hold this thought for later and see where all of this emotive passion fits in. Ideally people stay with you or at least stay in touch as the fondness they have of you is reciprocated and shared in roughly equal measure. Whether people really like you as much as you think is not that important, it only matters that people appear to like you. However, nothing surpasses having those that remain at your side regardless. Through all hardship, irrespective of your standing or level of wealth they are there. It is a bond that has no material measure instead an untouchable feeling locked in our hearts.

We share passions and join clubs with those interested in the same pursuits. Nothing beats having trusting buddies to dive into something with. On this note survival takes second place to thrills in hazardous sports. We do not disregard the dangers but embrace them instead. Pushing the limits makes some people feel more alive, giving them a big rush of excitement. It provides a reason to live. More and more to try. The greater the challenge and the nearer we go towards the edge possible without fatally injuring ourselves, the more appealing it seems. Fun because of the risk rather than despite it.

We also form unions whether at work or socially, to change the politics or move an enterprise forward. It is as much about the camaraderie as the gains in perceived fairness. It is about making a difference. This can create satisfaction and is edifying to those involved. In most cases only a few stand out as the militant ones. The majority follow where others lead. You could argue that principles are a driving force. People certainly draw on as much bluster as they can muster to push something through that is a matter of principle rather than of real importance to the many. Along with envy, jealousy and attempts to eliminate unfairness these are second tier items that propel us.

Whether working to live or living to work take your pick, never can one state that work is the sole feature of everyone's life. We certainly spend a lot of time at work and strive to build a career and become a master of what we do. How many would still work if they did not need to is subject to debate but we usually feel much better in ourselves for doing something productive, even a menial job provides satisfaction. Building a career or an empire is once again underpinned by base wants, wants in common with a homeless workless tramp.

I am one who likes to do things for others. I want to build a future for the next generation, make the society I live in more equitable more open and one that provides opportunities for all. Good for you so long as you don't get too side-tracked to find some fulfilment for yourself in the process that is not about such an ambition. Far from being scornful about such ventures, people who get changes made are to be applauded. However, people recognise that even with compromises there are often unintended consequences. Building a dam provides electricity and lake for boating but alters the ecosystem. We think we are doing the right thing until we see that it is also detrimental in some way. Utopia building or simple modifications made to give people basic access to water and sanitation provide a drive to get up and do something about it. Spreading the word and providing an education to those spared this delight is another thing that can motivate us into action. Making the world a better place is a valid claim but thankfully not taken up by too many at once. It doesn't do it for everyone.

We can also be motivated by duty. Where we find ourselves willing to act to sort things that are in a mess. Some are obliged by authorities to commit time and effort into a battle of freedom or ideology. All that matters at this point is that a fair few either object or decline to get involved, the sense of duty and inclination to make a stand is not that rife worldwide. Most take a lot of coaxing to get them on side and into battle; a drive is not forced on you it comes from within.

From survival, sex, through to treasure seeking it is the very nature of enquiry that brings us towards the answer. That which brought your attention to this text probing you to find out what it is about. Call it inquisitiveness or curiosity that thing at the heart of us that wants to know more. It is one of the three and bit things common to all.

It is not what you are interested in, in particular that matters. It is just the fact that you like to find out more and explore certain things that appeal to you. Some pay attention to the news or catch up on the sports results; others keep abreast with the local gossip. Aunt Mable is having an affair. At her age. Really? Every facet in life has a curiosity factor. To find out what it is like to have sex. To glean facts or fiction from a book. To travel and see what there is in different places. To experience other ways of life in other countries. When we get back we want to know what has been happening in our locality whilst we were away. The height of curiosity surrounds intrigue and mystery where we want to get to the bottom of something. Whether it is to solve a crime or root out a problem in physics. Curiosity.

We all know that curiosity killed the cat, but do we realise that it plays such an important part in what we do. It is woven deeply into our make-up. The three drives are responsible for everything we do. Either an individual drive acting alone or a combination of them all.

Right from the moment you wake up, in terms of curiosity, you are at it. Some check the time then spend a few moments trying to work out what day it is. You want to know. Some jump straight out of bed whether they know how late it is or not. Others dwell in the bliss of that early morning relax. Awake and pondering, posturing and exploring thoughts. The nature of your curiosity changes during the day and carries on right up to the point you fall asleep. Some with more years behind them than years ahead, wonder if it will be the last time they go to sleep and wake up again.

The nature of our curiosity is tremendously varied. From small talk about who is doing what to finding out about historic events through to scientific enquiry. No interest can be deemed more important than others, just more important to the individual. Wanting to explore is in our spirit. Trying to find out when, why and what for. From the moment we are born to the end of our lives we are driven to do things because of our curiosity. A good many of us wanted to have sex with someone, anyone sometimes in part to find out what the experience would bring. In partnerships, we try different positions and experiment with different aids. All in the exploration of ourselves and in-conjunction with another person. In the case of things such as sex it is not about curiosity alone, but it is a significant element.

Our individual search for answers and wish to know things reaches out far and wide. It contains a lot of diversity. It might include a wanting to be around to find out how our children fare as they grow up. Catching up with friends and family to get up to date with the things they have done. Opening the newspaper to find out about the events in our locality and around the world. Sounding out new instruments to see if a better one is available for our music score. Venturing far afield to see the way others live and behave and to see what it is like in different climates, different settings. To see the wonders of the world for ourselves. Those that don't venture further than the end of their garden still have mysteries to uncover right at home. Get stuck in a high rise flat with no opportunity to get out and about and the desolation doesn't dampen our curiosity it just frustrates it.

Inquisitiveness features in so much of what we do, utilising all the senses from touching and feeling objects to putting them in our mouth. Compare the feel of a piece of velvet with the skin of an animal. You see some unusual food. First, we take a look and guess the texture. Then we have a sniff. Finally taking a bite to satisfy the question "what is it like?"

When the curiosity dies so does the person. When you no longer care what happens at the end of the book you shelve it part way through. You may also switch the channel when the programme or film no longer inspires. Though when it does you'll sit there for a long while to find out the conclusion, just to see what happens. Spoil it for someone by hinting at what is about to come. Some of us will spend a lifetime working on a single problem despite the effort required to resolve it. As you explore, more questions arise leading to further curiosity.

A film has the ability to take you on a journey while you lie back on your seat right into the action and promises that you will get a real sense of what it is like to be somewhere else. You are led to believe that you will experience the full effect of taking a boat down a river along the jungle over the rapids and emulate the tension of living. Except it can't. The stimulatory effect gets better with more effort put into the visual, sound and environment of the auditorium, but it is hard to replicate the physicality of being bitten by mosquitoes, getting soaked, dealing with the disquiet and nervousness of people you can meet on such a journey all in the comfort of your home or cinema. The curiosity satisfied by going on an adventure is bound to be filled with events that take many forms and is hard to put into words when you return to let people know what you got up to. Your memory of what the Oncho berry tasted like is hard to explain unlike something less pleasant like the carpet tile nature of the pasta meal you were given. Curiosity filling is not just about a single fact. Somebody can give you an idea of what something is like but until you have tried it for yourself you won't understand it fully. They are only feeding you words and gestures, they can't portray the full experience and will also have a different take on it than you may get. You have the ideas, the words and the curiosity compels you to add the physical sensory inputs to join up the mental pathways.

It is all about the gaps. What links coat and fire. Maybe warmth, a gap between words. You see a picture and wonder what it represents, where it was made. Who is in the photo? You hear a sound, what caused it. Who wrote a song? Any gap in your knowledge is brought to your attention. Not everyone is fascinated by the same things, but when there is a motive to look further we make a lot of effort to find out more. If someone mentions a spigot you might think, what is that? Some will ignore it as they don't care, others will be intrigued and investigate what one is. You may worry more about the expression on someone's face, trying to work out whether they are hurt, afraid, upset or annoyed with you.

We can be on the hunt for patterns, looking for matches and seeing where something fits in. We know the bird on the branch is a bird but what type is it, what group is it in, bird of prey or song bird. Our minds are full of concepts, data and memories and before a link is made between each such node we have this aggravating gap. We endeavour to fill it where necessary and once it has it can be ignored for a while.

The first key point is to understand is that the validity, truth or accuracy of what lies in your mind, is irrelevant. You can live a whole life from start to finish with information that other people will claim to be completely wrong and it does not matter one jot. They may be wrong also or only partially correct. Or right for the wrong reasons. The bulk of what you know is most likely to be incomplete at best and frequently contradictory to the beliefs and knowledge others have. What we hold in our mind is rarely the same as what is stored in that of others. We might live with someone for a good portion of our life never realising that they have a different way of thinking about things. Despite all those conversations it may seem like we have the same ideas but they never always quite match. Many things seem right to you and will remain so for as long as you can refrain from using your inquisitiveness to check it out more thoroughly.

When a child asks you how something works you can provide an explanation to appease them. If the answer that you give seems reasonable it will usually satisfy them regardless of whether it is correct or orthodox. In many cases any answer will do. A child asks you how does the steering wheel in the car connect to the wheels. Now you have a choice. You can bring out the elastic band concept. Tell them there is a big elastic band that pulls and pushes the wheels from side to side and some children will accept this and visualize what you mean. Some won't believe you as they have played with elastic bands and know they stretch and snap. You then try the "I don't know" ploy but that makes you seem less adult and all-knowing and then you face having the child pestering you forever in the day to find out. If you bring up rack and pinions, then you face the daunting task of then having to explain those elements as well and maybe even trying to draw some diagrams when all you want to do is get home and put your feet up. Some people, kids included will accept flaky information. The issue is that every time they see or think about cars they follow the mental pathway towards how they are steered and get reminded about this problem 'something' that breaks the trail. If they see someone changing a tyre the sight of the wheel brings up the steering problem once again. So many triggers and a hole in their knowledge. All manner of things and situations can bring up a deficit in our understanding. Any time someone or something is doing something that we haven't come across before there is a potential to get a spark of curiosity so long as it is within our field of intrigue.

We will get a diet of junk information fed via our parents and at school. Some of it may have some merit but it will also be biased for sure. Someone decides what will be taught and what will be left aside.

When we search for more, we are liable to exclude ideas outside of what we are accustomed to. The term brain washed is used to describe cases where the information provided is too narrow in scope. Extremely limited. Extremely one sided. The truth has been kept from them. Very little is truly true but shutting out other viewpoints feeds only those wanting power. Had this text been written in a different country or in a different era there would be other things included and lots not. Much would be the same but things of interest get missed if the writer has not encountered it.

We can also rinse a mind of unacceptable ideas, particularly anything counter revolutionary or against the script. Once your mind is so full of information all cleaned of balance and proportion we become brain awash. This makes us incapable of thinking along other lines. It is insidious and sad. You can only think in a language that you know. You can't consider something that you don't understand or have not encountered. You can only relate to what you have experience of and if all of this and more is based on one ideology then you will not care about so many other possibilities.

Curiosity is not complex. Not in the slightest, even though we consider ourselves to be highly intelligent random predictable super beings we are built upon simple mechanics. It starts with the seed. This seed can be anything we come across. From the seed we begin to follow pathways in our minds. Were one to think of a cat then one can then run through some links, fur, coat, warm, fire, wood, tree, apple, pips, swallow, bird and to feather and so on. See one on a ledge and wonder what it is up to, hunting, scouring for another cat to fight or mate with. Lots of possibilities. Links may be in a chain or in a spoke wheel like manner. You can start again with the cat and have paws, whiskers, tail, meow, fur, purr and other attributes of a cat trigger in your mind. Along with the words themselves you can have sounds, feelings and also some form of imagery inter related. If the cat is up to some mischief again, will it lead to more vet's bills. Curiosity arises from gaps in these chain links or items missing from the central hub.

It rears its head in many ways, maybe manifesting itself when you decide it necessary to look up the standard definition of a word or find a way of obtaining a mental picture of it. You can find out what something looks like through search and discovery. Upon seeing something we may wonder what they are called and what they do. The seed is sown and if we have the inclination we begin the process of finding out more if it piques our interest. When we have no mental path from a seed to the understanding of how it relates to that what we have in our mind already we seek out more information. The gap is the curiosity.

Closure, the filling in of the small details, the little bits that niggle us. Who did it and why to me. What was their thinking? Was this tragedy caused by something that I didn't spot? Who was really at fault? Was it avoidable, will I get an appropriate apology and will something be done to prevent it from happening again? Curiosity can plague us far more if we do not have a path to follow. If you have a plan which you hope will lead to an answer it is less troublesome. Gaps can't be filled if we have doubts about the veracity, the truth of what we have been told. Frustration ensues as we have the constant niggle but no idea of what direction to explore. A prisoner may hatch an escape plan and work through all the obstacles. Finding out what can and can't be done. This gives them a target and reason to be optimistic. If your hunt for an answer is blocked, we can't rest.

Filling the gaps is usually pleasurable. A breakdown on the road causes a blockage and a delay, not as nice as a smooth ride home. When a bypass is built, you have another option, an alternative to take. It might be a faster or a more enjoyable route to take. This is similar to having new ways of thinking about things. Upon bridging a number of puzzling areas with new links it gives rise to a period of restful contentment. It feels good filling those gaps. It is an actual physical change in the biological structure of the mind that brings about pleasure. This contentment may turn to disappointment soon afterwards when we no longer have an aim that gave us a reason to try.

There is a difficult question of how our understanding starts, with so much of what we know being dependant on so many other things that run in circles through our mind. We can posit that a child will get a sensation then make associations. A new marvellous journey through life is rooted in links that form right from the start. Words get added when we garner language and memories of being too warm, too bright too distasteful and a pictorial representation or recall of a scene all adds to a highly elaborate schema. Untold elementary links producing a machine that can be appeased and delighted by a change of state. When we add the new link of feeling some heat we not only add the word 'warm' to a place, an object, but create a representation and a recall of that scene. It is multi-dimensional, multi-faceted and enables us to learn a new process, to do something without getting burnt. Discovering how it is done and getting a new ability is a feature of how we use curiosity to further ourselves.

From not knowing to knowing more, the curiosity gadget rewards us when we make new links. The validity of the links, the integrity of them, the accuracy, the relevance, its meaningfulness is nothing other than personally preferred. Once a clean smooth pathway is formed you don't get alerted to it. If there is a gap, a piece missing or a section where the concepts don't quite marry up, your mind will invoke an interrupt and you pay attention to it. You can either find a way of ignoring it or try to find out what information you have that is wrong or incomplete. Whilst there are some obvious comparisons to certain other machines our memories are not always binary in nature as some can be much more hazy, chemical, analogue rather than definitive on or off in nature.

The curiosity we have has similar strength but directed in completely different ways depending upon those seeds that get sown. We can have a conversation that makes us take a whole new direction in life. A signpost on the highway can entice us to take a new turn. A thought path that we take may jolt us if it were to encounter an error, something that doesn't seem right or is incomplete and it bugs us. Really bugs us. It stokes inquisitiveness. We want that thought path fixed or filled and we go to incredible lengths at times to do so. We also do it for ourselves and we do it on behalf of others too. When filling out a form describing yourself you come across a section marked 'interests'. Now some will write 'none'. Putting down 'walking' and 'going to restaurants' It is not only dull but obvious as pretty much everyone does that. Leaving it as none makes people wonder about you, not that you are an oddball but that you must have some interests and it will be worth getting you in to find out. You can use the power of curiosity to your advantage if you want to.

"What you don't know about, doesn't bother you."

The term ignorance can refer to a form of stupidity. It can be about ignoring something, but it is used here mainly to describe the way we are oblivious to some things. You may be living atop a gold mine and never find out about its existence. You live with it there and never discover it. Whether it would have made you happier or whether it would have made your life run more smoothly or whether it could have even been the start of your downfall is pure conjecture. In a different vain, if you have no awareness of the plight of an individual who is suffering or succeeding it simply passes you by. We only have the capacity to care for a relatively small number of things. We can only pay attention to a small number of people. You can't have four hundred friends. You are not able to devote time to more than a handful, the rest are just a list of people who you have made contact with. In the world around us there are issues aplenty. People in desperate situations. We tend to throw a few coins into a charity bucket and head off to lunch as normal. There are also many with noteworthy accomplishments. You just take a pick and read up about some that seem interesting. The rest? The sun rises and sets before you wade through the highlights and finding the spare minutes to sign another petition let alone get really involved is not physically possible.

The world is not full to the brim with evil but some knowledge will be scarring and detrimental to the well-being of one's soul, particularly war and pestilence. By living in a bubble people can shield themselves from the traumas people suffer. We may forget any sense of responsibility due to a lack of awareness. Others are left to pick up the pieces and see things that prompt them towards getting involved. Some do not have the capacity to even recognise much outside their narrow domain. The extent of your curiosity about certain things will not be matched by the curiosity other people have for it. You may care about the rise of your favourite pop star but others will not have even heard of them let alone uncovered the beauty in the lyrics of their songs.

For the most part we only need to fill the gaps in our knowledge in order to cope. we don't need to understand every precise trivial detail of something. To drive a car, we do not need to know all the mechanics of how it works. We can manage with just the skills to control and utilise the vehicle rather than bothering with a complete knowledge of how the previously mentioned steering wheel changes the direction of travel. But those who are in the business of improving a car would explore the inner workings in great detail. Each person will delve in as far as they feel it is warranted.

As soon as you start looking into something, holes in your knowledge start to appear. It might not be an academic item as such. If you get an inkling that someone close to you is up to something you want to know more. What secrets are they keeping from you? Unless you can prevent yourself from beginning these avenues of thought you will keep getting irritated to a certain degree by those missing things, plus items withheld from you. A prime example is how you will be distracted if you can only hear half of a conversation. Someone not too far away is on the phone. You can hear them but not the person on the other end of the line. You mind tries to work out what this other person is saying. Guessing and assuming and calculating with various degrees of accuracy consuming a lot of mind power. This can be much more distracting than when the whole conversation is audible as you get both sides of the little story and have no doubts about what is being said. It can be hard to get to sleep when you can blatantly hear someone talking to someone else, but can't hear what both are saying. It is all about trying to calculate and create complete pathways in your mind. Curiosity keeps rearing its head until you find a way of managing it.

One thing that will restrain our curiosity is boredom. It has an important function. Boredom helps us avoid becoming forever stuck. A child playing with the same toy day in day out learns far less than a child playing with everything in the house. No doubt some things that are sufficiently interesting will overpower the boredom of paying attention to it for a long time. Most children can get a lot of amusement from watching the same cartoon over and over and doing the same jigsaw with you to your utter dismay as the filtration system of laying down ever stronger pathways takes effect. Some will have an inherent super rigid routine structure that quashes the boredom in favour of repeating the activity interminably but only a jester can be the judge of what is normal in this respect. Children are less likely to be challenged about their habit of repeating what they did yesterday as we give them more leeway. As adults, we may attempt to disguise our predictable routines to avoid being tainted with a boring tag. What is boring to you is boring to you and you alone and perhaps those in your small camp.

Boredom can balance curiosity and reign it in. Curiosity needs this restraining yet liberating force of boredom to work fully. This can be a nuisance when you want to discover something impressive. Studying countless documents, researching and probing for ages with an inner voice egging you on to leave it and do something more fun instead. If the gap is large, you can obtain enough determination to keep focused.

Boredom tends to manifest itself when you either have little of interest to do or are doing something of little interest over and over. If you fill and empty the same reward buckets again and again there is no change, inadequate variation. You also have more and more reward areas sending ever increasing interrupt requests in a 'withdrawal' manner making it harder to concentrate on a particular task. If you vary what you do or at least make plans for change in the near future, you are less likely to experience so much wearisomeness. A challenge of any sort will open up new possibilities, but again if you have already accomplished things of a similar nature doing it again will not always provide the noticeable feelings of reward. We might go to the same café in hope of recapturing the magic of that last chip butty we had there last time but it is the novelty, the new experience that forms the seduction. You may well go to the same café and eat roughly the same thing but meet new people or just change the sauce on the butty to get some point of difference.

Boredom can be a great motivator for change. When we have had enough with the way our life is going we can be inspired to change. The monotony that has taken root is the key part of thinking about moving on. A tipping point is reached. We may change our job, our subject of study or place of residence partly to find out what other paths will bring and in part to escape the boredom of the present circumstances. Boredom and curiosity are factors that drive us. Only factors, not the complete reason for doing things, however. Part of the reason we want to survive is because we want to discover what will happen in our lives later on. We want to know what the future brings.

To claim that we are driven in part by our inherent curiosity is not particularly controversial. It is widely accepted in part because the term has minimal ambiguity and is easy to comprehend. The other two things that drive us are far more complex. They take much longer to explain and even longer to understand. It is easy to present it, but you have to think about how it works and how it applies for a very long time to truly relate to it. Does curiosity fulfil the aim of finding an element that is within all people of all ages and drives them to live as they do, if not what does?

Feed me and I'll feed you too

Many a mother will breast feed their children. The salient point is that they cannot lactate and produce milk to feed a baby unless they eat and drink well themselves. The more a mother looks after themselves the more care they can do for others as well. Likewise, a father figure would hunt and gather to provide for a family. They also find themselves in the same situation. It is harder to work when you are not at full strength. The better you are, the more you achieve. The more you can generate the greater the amount you can provide to share. To be of any real use to anyone else it is necessary to look after yourself first.

We give, we take, we help, we care. We can also be greedy, ungrateful, dispassionate, rude and violent. We can do things by ourselves or with the assistance of others. Are we selfish creatures or do all our actions revolve around doing things mutually beneficial to all. How often are we altruistic, doing something whereby we gain nothing ourselves whatsoever? When you ask someone what the last altruistic act that they did was you often get a long pause. It is so rare that we do something and gain nothing at all. No satisfaction, no money no help in return, nothing. For it to be truly altruistic it implies that you got no benefit whatsoever, not even the release from guilt. When you can give to a stranger, someone that you may never see again, you get a sense of reward for your kindness. You feel better for doing so. You may even give just to stop them from harassing you further. The level of appreciation shown by the recipient will adjust the level of pleasure of helping of course. There will be odd occasions that it feels like a waste of time helping someone who throws it back in your face. A nonchalant begrudging "thankyou" doesn't inspire you to do nice deeds in a hurry for them, or their likes again. Nevertheless, nothing beats the joy of helping other people in any way you can when the time feels right.

Many animals groom one another. Some may see this as a game of you scratch my back and I'll scratch yours. Those that don't reciprocate create a sucker. You spend ages doing something for someone else and then rather than them doing something for you they just walk off. Sometimes we do it and get some attention and feel involved, sometimes it is to get a helping hand up the social ladder or access to more food and sometimes it is an instance where you are just made a complete fool of. Clever people make all kinds of stupid assumptions sticking numbers and percentage points to actions and results. You cannot enumerate the pleasure you get from doing something for someone else. If they do not reciprocate with the same kindness that is not the point. The grooming is a bonding process and some animals enjoy tick removal, enjoy the giving and enjoy the internal reward that it provides regardless of what they get in return. One mean individual doesn't imply that everyone you meet will be the same. Forgiving and forgetting those that don't work in co-operation appears to be the best strategy in the long run, not because of some mathematical formula but because being nice is nice for all. Niceness spreads and returns, often in a big loop. Crucially, we do it because we want to do it and gain from the pleasure from doing so.

Labelling an act of kindness as selfish doesn't seem right when two parties benefit. By giving, you undoubtedly gain from your action. Whether the act was a conscious one or automatic, two parties were considered, you and the other. Whilst this trait is embedded and is probably the most clever design feature imaginable, no word in the English language seems to exist that describes the concept fully. We can be very selfish, never selfless, rarely if ever altruistic but one way or another we co-consider. Co-considerational selfishness is the most accurate way to describe this driving force.

We either gain everything for ourselves or gain a little and give at the same time. By sharing and caring we both gain. You can hardly escape from eating, drinking and sleeping, doing vital things for oneself. These are selfish and needed to survive. Some people are greedy, selfish. Some people won't share, some will take, steal from others, really selfish really uncaring. Being inconsiderate is selfish. However most find that sharing your items is far more valuable in terms of the friendship and harmony that it creates, not just for the group, but for them in particular. Sharing some of your lunch can be a small short term sacrifice to gain popularity but it also makes you proud of yourself. Somewhere along the line you gain from giving even though it can be hard to see at times. If you feel better, a better person even for being cooperative it is a gain for you.

Selfishness is not always a bad thing; in the co-operative sense it is rather good. Few people will discredit those that do charity work. It is hard to claim they are doing it to make themselves joyous. Nevertheless, they do get a lot out of it. We stop in the street to assist someone in peril to help them and upon doing so we can get a feel good buzz. Selfishness, co-considerational or otherwise is found in everything we do whether we like it or not. It is sheer genius for a designer to give creatures a pleasure feedback when they help others. The system invokes co-operation and benefits all animals everywhere. No mechanism can compare with the power it has from the joy of nurturing offspring to nursing the sick.

If you examine the details of bringing up a child and the sacrifices made and drill down into the mechanics of it, you can find some interesting forces at play. We may have a hope that they will look after us in turn when we get old protecting our own selfish needs, but it is not just a quid pro quo investment. Whether we had any control in the number we have or not, they are born and we bond with them. Protecting and shielding them from danger and maybe setting them on a particular path. We may want them to have a better life than us. Whether it is measured in happiness, or in the realms of success. We can have a lot of fun educating them and may wish to have them follow in our trajectory especially if we are wrapped up in righteousness. Our children are our projects.

In most instances we have children because it is we that want them, warming to their vulnerability. Some find that a maternal/paternal instinct never kicks in and think of the children as being a huge drag. You are selfish if you want them or selfish if you wish you had worn a condom. Without a doubt children gain from the life created. The more focus you put on them the more they can do for themselves and the more help they can provide for you as parent. We enjoy seeing them progress, we get a lot from bringing them up. A typical stance is to think of a parent as being nothing other than a selfless provider, generous, giving. To call it selfish is hard to fathom. People hear the word selfish and think it is only about being mean. Having children is selfish in that you got something whilst simultaneously doing a heck of a lot for them. We say we are doing it for the kids but a huge part is doing it for our own satisfaction.

Are you selfish if you look after your partner? They are more use to you in the practical sense if well fed and you get significant gratification after nursing them back to health when they fall ill. As always you both are better off. Do you keep someone alive for longer than reasonable because you wanted to be vindicated, to show the world you were right to stay the course against popular wisdom? Was it an action really for them or deep down were you blinded by consideration for yourself and your own needs. Proving that you were justified in holding out. Persevering against long odds and that pathetic voice in your head that can be amplified through your mouth to tell the fortunate soul that is was you that stood firm. You also get to spend more time with the survivor. At least, that is the hope.

People that feel zero empathy for others are rare. Some can kill with no remorse no internal hurt and seemingly no guilt either. Selfishness in the extreme. However most of us get racked with guilt when we do unkind things to others. The guilt that arises is coupled with the damage to our moral standing. Most want others to perceive us in a good light and few want to be thought of as nasty and lacking decency. A criminal baron type might revel in an aura of being feared and spreading an uncaring dangerous reputation but even they will have self-set rules of behaviour and principles. Protecting their family and those in the same clan; fending off rivals, keeping their own interests alive.

The real evil ones have a selfish agenda. Sometimes askew. They think that what they are doing is for the greater good. To build a nation that will be better, better for all in the long run. They see it all as a positive and adore seeing the project coming into fruition. Those that feel the positive is outweighed by negative consequences will consider putting a halt to the scheme. This may mean that in the process of removing them they will need to eliminate all the supporters as well. All the killings can be viewed as an unfortunate side effect for the benefit of a larger section of the population.

Guilt

When we see someone who has a problem and fail to act we can feel rather guilty for not doing something about it. We can feel guilty too for not checking that someone was alright. The guilt is a problem for us as much as it is for the person needing assistance. Just in a different way. It plays on our mind and lowers our self-esteem. Guilt is a minus. Not having a minus is more positive. To not feel awful is a benefit. To swing from guilt to being pleased with our self creates the best outcome for us.

Our own self comes into the equation when we resist doing harm. We feel bad about what we do at times, when not helping or when hindering and learn from it. Being racked by guilt helps us change our mind and do things differently next time. Whether it is doing or not doing it will always be co-considering ourselves and others at the same time. We may aim to prevent something seemingly bad from happening or encouraging others to do more things that we see as good. In later periods of life, we may modify our ways to lessen the further build-up of guilt. Changing our ways can feel as though we are making amends for past mistakes, even if it is indirectly.

People have become trapped underneath a vehicle. Some have got their leg stuck between a railway platform and the train. The group effort to get them free is remarkable. With many stepping in to lift it off or push on the carriage to get the person out. None of the group gets anything for their efforts except an emotional hit. Groups of people often work together to get someone out of such tight spots with each member feeling pleased with their involvement yet make no tangible gain from it apart from a good anecdote to tell others that they were one of those assisting. Bunches of selfish unrelated unconnected people working together for nothing other than an uplift in the spirit of the community that they take from. Each one involved felt a good bit happier and those watching were impressed.

During many a battle, soldiers have done outstanding things which assisted the progress of their cause and furthered the advance of those on their side. This brings us to the more extreme instances that we can consider, even though few of us will ever be in such knife edge scenarios. If you find yourself badly injured and on the brink of death it is much easier to make a final stand than if you are cowering behind a wall intact. Running into the line of fire to throw a grenade when you know you are about to die anyway is a different proposition to holding back if you have a good chance of surviving. Altruism, but with the consequence of death. Dying in the process of achieving an altruistic act is the only real way of being totally unselfish. That just leaves the glory. Some could see death as a way of promoting their vanity. Their demise and sacrifice would not be in vain if family and the nation they represent might benefit. You just won't be around to see it. You could encourage the dim witted to commit a suicidal act by creating a belief that they will gain a valuable place in the never never afterlife and make them selfishly hurtful. Training and a virtually automatic response to the situation can't be discounted. In war there is often too little time to reflect on how a decision was made, events occur too quickly.

Upon seeing a grenade, a soldier threw their rucksack over it and jumped on it. The result? All survived. The rucksack absorbed a lot of the energy. The soldier didn't ponder on it. Had they all tried to duck they would have all been killed or severely injured. Maybe the unconscious thought was to save their companions knowing that if nothing was done quickly enough they would die anyway.

You hear of people that see someone step into the road and instinctively grab them, pulling them back and out of harm's way.

We would save them without really thinking too long and hard about it and would feel pretty chuffed with ourselves for doing so. Chuffed and relieved for having responded quickly. To criticise the motives of someone's action is to deny the eloquence of the selfish system. Doing something we see as good and feeling as though we should not gain is just plain daft. People that live with the barest essentials, no material goods and spend their whole time caring for others are as selfish as the rest of us. Their minds are saturated with feel good reward chemicals from the co-consideration donations that they bestow on others. The concept is murky but entrenched deeply within us all.

The number of potential scenarios to test the selfishness concept on is very great indeed. When you consider the prospect of sacrificing someone you care for deeply for the benefit of large numbers of people it can be quite difficult. If it is your child or your parent, there is good reasoning to suggest that no amount of lives saved will compensate for your loss. The loss to you is too great and other people will think differently because their close loved one's life is not on the line. The feel good factor is overridden by the more pressing realities closer to home.

Flow

In trying to make an artificial machine to emulate the processes going on in a living organism the problem of reward becomes a major issue. To simulate the chemical processes in the body is very difficult indeed. Although, like it or not, we are biological machines and machines in the metal computer driven sense are not going to be rewarded unless they have a biochemical heart. A body is needed to feel the changes in chemistry. A living thing is ascribed to something that metabolises; the extraction of energy from sugars and countless other chemical reactions that precipitate a life form. Particular complex chemicals will create significant changes to the flow and running of the body, some of which is described by us as feel good, rewarding.

The reward we get when handing in a lost item is felt inside. You don't want to be given money, you care more for it getting to the rightful owner. Others take advantage and see the lost item as a reward for their deviancy. The prize money for winning a competition can be secondary to the reward felt for the accomplishment of beating so many people. Bringing a criminal to justice produces a change in the mind which can feel gratifying. We can be paid to do a job but the dedicated ones do it with more vigour if it is not just for the pay. Toiling long and hard, running stagnantly on a treadmill or lifting weights up and down over and over again causes the flow of endorphins, an inbuilt natural high. Solving a problem, finding a solution, changing the framework of interlinking memories in the mind creates a reward. The sense of accomplishment surfaces when you rearrange some disorder within a set of tasks embedded in your mind. Resetting the priorities and clearing the list of items to do that have built up during the recent period. Emptying the in-tray and looking forward to a new set of challenges.

Unsurprisingly the reward mechanism can to a fair extent be fooled. It can be overridden, creating an almost indistinguishable sense of pleasure as that gleaned through years of hard graft. It can be brought about by electrical stimulation or by ingesting certain chemicals - what is commonly referred to as drugs. When an animal is wired up with cables directly placed into their minds and access to a button to hit the reward they press and press, ignoring food and ignoring the animal on heat nearby. Like an addict disregarding the demise of their body. The effect can be to keep one's attention off of would be priorities and onto abstract thought. You can forget the humdrum of daily life and move into a world of fantasy. You can get to a point where the highs are replaced by the zero state. You take more drugs to get out of the minus zone.

Drugs and electrical intervention fail to have an Impact on certain types of reward though. There is a difference between unlocking rewards where you spend a lot of time and perseverance doing something and simply popping a pill. The mind and body are well connected. Exhaustion from a work out provides a spectrum of sensations somewhat different to simple chemical exposure. This is not to denigrate the potential for excitement in seeking new experiences from novel forces as if it is some kind of cheat. We might work hard to create comfort and have more opportunities and we may aspire to eat fine foods and experience a range of delights to diversify the types of rewards on offer. The scope of reward is quite wide and meaningful to different degrees in each individual.

If you have an ambition, you will have a great deal of knowledge, memories and experience relating to the objective. A massive amount of interconnected synapses are deployed to structure and ultimately make sense of the end goal. Only by persevering with the objective, working on it in stages to get it to come to fruition, will this type of reward be realised. If you want to climb a mountain you need to prepare the way. Find the equipment, travel to the site and work through a multitude of small hurdles to get to the top. You will have a lot on your mind to contend with. Each issue, at each stage, that is overcome adds to the sense of accomplishment. Adding chemicals to the body and artificially supplanting memories does not invoke the same level of reward as the real thing so to speak. You can only emulate success to a point. One has to go and actually do it to obtain all the feelings through being in the situation for real. However, a drug induced trip is an experience in itself that can't be garnered from physical or mental actions. The change is what we seek. Change in how we feel. We do it despite any discomfort or anxiety that comes with it. Reward is all about how it makes us feel different for a while.

An employer can increase the salary as a way of rewarding people. Alternatively, they can make the job more fun, do things for the community and they can make the workers think they are doing something for humanity. A simple thankyou is a nice enough reward at times. We talk about getting paid for something as if money is in itself the sole reward. Hence offering more cash as an incentive does not always deliver as much as we might like to think. Some people will work for free as they enjoy the idea of making their thing available to all and sundry. Being a contributor is often a bigger enticement than physical land grab. The reward system is not necessarily about gaining physical entities; it is more about an internal mental dividend. Neither does it need to be a boost to boast as the reward satisfies the deeper self. If you are good at something, really good, you may be asked to take on a task. As you are not terribly keen, you raise the price. You think of what is sensible and treble it. You still get the commission. You reluctantly accept not because of the pay but because you now feel obliged. The more compelling, fun, idiosyncratic project that you had on the workbench which would have brought in little income, but great joy to finish has to be put on the shelf for a while.

Amongst countless other things conversation is unmistakably rewarding. Telling other people about the things in our lives and listening to the woes of others produces a vital sense of well-being. How well we comprehend what someone really means play a part. The greater success we have distinguishing that what is said to that what is implied the more we get from it. Being able to translate body language, subconsciously or otherwise is exciting, stimulating. We like to transfer the concepts in our mind into the minds of others using words and gestures. This doesn't seem to be trick-able by artificial means but it appears that the recipient of our wisdom or banal thoughts is often irrelevant. So long as we tell someone, someone that appears to be listening. If we feel that someone has heard and acknowledged what we have to say it is usually sufficient to get the pleasure. The reward is gained during and after the process of dialogue. We feel much better after going out and having a good talk with people compared to staying at home with no one to discuss things with. We need the reaction, we crave the verification that what we are saying has merit and this is not so easily achieved when you are talking to yourself. Though at times there is not a lot of real difference as the words are poorly archived in the minds of other people. It is just the impression that they got the gist of what you were saying and acknowledged the core principles.

Change

Change is crucial to the way in which we obtain reward. Even the release of fluids brings about change whether it is because we are crying or ejaculating. How much better do you feel when you pee, especially if you relieve yourself after being stuck unable to do so on a long journey. Of course sexual climax is much much more than a pumping action, great many changes occur albeit briefly in the whole body. The sensation of a cocktail of hormones traversing through the veins is pretty distinct from a state of rest. Whether it is new links that create a sense of change or the flow of chemical altering its direction within the mind and body we are geared towards noticing and potentially enjoying it.

Satisfying the curiosity and providing for others, giving pleasure connects reward with the selfish being. Interlinked. When we discover something new we spark a new node of curiosity and delve into it to get the resultant reward. All three facets are intertwined. You get rewarded through the exploration of curiosity and the satisfaction is for yourself even if the discovery helps other people too. You get rewarded when you help and find out more about yourself in the process.

You need not travel great distances or spend a fortune, you don't even need to be amongst friends to make a change in the course of a day. One can sit still, contemplate, call it meditation if you will. It satisfies the proposition of being a change and in itself it is remarkably sanctifying. Stimulation or a day with a lack of stimulants is stimulating. The abstinence, going without, fasting and feasting periods is very enjoyable for many. Routine doesn't imply lack of change when you consider that an individual may do the same thing at roughly the same time each day, yet their body state varies a lot hour to hour. Waking up, eating, doing some activities getting hungry again and so forth until being tired and relishing another good night's sleep.

We can fear death because of the addiction to the drug of life brought on by each reward chemical. You need a pretty unsatisfactory lifestyle to lose that addiction. Pain has an association with reward. It provides some, some pain is invigorating, but only up to a certain point. After that it negates it becoming anti-rewarding. If there were an expectation that voluminous amounts of pain was heading your way, a quicker demise becomes attractive.

Stimulation of the senses through hearing, feeling or looking at things and so forth provides the gamut of differences, multi part experiences that change the state of play. To work all day for little more than a small portion of food with minimal respite from the arduous nature of the tasks befallen you may test the will. Somehow the rewards however shallow are sufficient to stoke the selfish want to survive at least until the next day and beyond. Thus a pointless life is powered by the co-considerational selfish nature, curiosity coupled with boredom and a powerful reward system. A combination of some or all of these forces brings about the motivation for the things we do.

Can you do something just for the love of it? Can you do it with no curiosity like an automaton, a robot? Just to pass the time without becoming more masterful and with no feeling of reward whatsoever. Your mother and father may have scolded you for being selfish and it has connotations that we want to avoid but then try doing something that avoids being so and stay alive. Cast aside the word and its general meaning and revel in the real broader concept.

In years gone by we had such things called zoos where exotic and commonplace animals were held. These were places where our curiosity was placated. They enabled us to see species from distant lands and our selfish wish to do so were truly at the expense of so many creatures that had little in the way of any communicable say in the matter. Put them in a cage, ensure it is small so that there is nothing much to explore. Provide all that is needed so no work is demanded. Make it free of all challenges or at the very least limit them to those that you conjure up for silly amusement. Don't give them any opportunity to decide whether to give or take. Feed them when it suits you. A paradigm of utter dismalness. Wherever you look you find the three same things resonating driving us to happiness or leading to despair if we can't use them.

Translate this to a human zoo and you will see that you can't get a real reward for just turning up. Don't ever confuse being handed the treat, a cake, some cash or rumpus pompous with the internal reward that is felt when you have truly earned it. It has to be a genuine authentic prize for your endeavours and granted after the chase rather than akin to a dog simply lifting a paw to receive a tasty treat. The dog will go for it every time but only gets proper pleasure when you make them forage for a ball, maybe, or do something interactive that is demanding, taxing.

The most selfish people in the world are those that go out to work so that others don't have to. Smug and content, getting your daily fix of problems to address and work through whilst those stuck indoors are left with nothing much more to do aside from fantasise or attempt to do something naughty just for the challenge.

Going from a time when beans and spaghetti were mixed together in a pan along with a little pepper to brighten the meal, night after night, first world poverty, to a period where money piled in free and easy brought about an odd feeling. After years of hard grind to a place where it became akin to printing money. Upon taking a succession of holidays a sense of being like a gate-crasher emerged. Lots of people running around and beavering away to keep us in glorious luxury. There was a sense of distance, not being there on merit. Different to a reward that is hard fought over. It can make it feel unreal. We can't appreciate it in quite the same way. It is as though we do not truly deserve it. A lucky gift from the gods. Those surreal moments may not last long nor effect everyone but when it does, it makes it difficult to be fully thankful.

The simplicity of the reward, curiosity and selfishness fans out into all realms of life, getting ever more complex. Reaching out into the vast multitude of possibilities. All those variations. Nevertheless, after extensive analysis, whatever you look at, it can all boil down to the same thing. Every item of human oddity can be traced back, filtering down to what drives us. Try going a day ignoring every time your attention is drawn to something based on a wish to find out. Attempt to speak with no what, why, when, how or who. Then note that people stop listening when they do not care what you have to say. One drive feeds the other, spurring each on.

Curiosity is not confined to just grandiose investigations, it is a 'broad brush' that comes into play constantly during each day and operates in layers. The ultimate aim of an archaeologist is to try and fathom who lived at a spot, what they ate and what tools they used. However, during the scrapping about in the dirt they will be intrigued by each item that looks interesting. In the moment, they get distracted by something touching them, turning around to see a fly. Countless other things distract and raise queries such as why the tea boy is taking so long to make the drinks. We use it hundreds and hundreds of times a day for tiddly brief items, sounds and smells, to the much more involved things that take weeks or months to get to the bottom of.

It can take a good hour to explain the core of what it is that drives us. After doing so, someone asked if there was anything else deeper? One more on the pile of those that don't see the brilliance of it. After exploring into the deepest crevices, the simplest of things have come to the surface. The pieces have always been around us. Now that they have been put together, it is of great significance. It is not particularly difficult to take in. When someone examines their daily actions, they see these driving forces are at work. Then they appreciate what it means.

Should

Many books you read will tell you what to do. These books will be skilfully written laying out some very good reasons why you should follow their advice. People can be very adept at convincing you that they are right. They may indeed make a strong case and without a doubt some things will be helpful. However, we might want to think about the hidden agenda. Are they trying to control you? Is the author wishing to propagate their views, spreading their message as far and wide as possible? We all have opinions about many things and there is nothing wrong with sharing them, but people struggle to do so in an unbiased fashion.

It is not just books, your parents, teachers and most certainly lots of clever preachers will say things like: You don't want to do it like that, you want to do it like this. You should get up before eight and be in bed before eleven. You should keep your elbows off the table and show good manners whilst at dinner. Endless things that people like to say you should do. You don't have to be particularly smart to see that there is often a lot of hypocrisy in what people say; Do as I say and not as I do.

Not every language has the equivalent of 'should' in their vocabulary. They either do something or they don't. What you think somebody should do quite often differs from what they think they should do. One sure fire way to ruffle some feathers is to carelessly use the should word.

This book is full of ideas about life and attempts to steer clear of telling you what to do. I say attempts, as there are probably quite a few things that are not exactly impartial. You will spot many things that are not sufficiently balanced. It is an aim rather than anything else. It is all too easy to disguise the real meaning.

How do you give advice without telling people what they should do? It all comes down to providing some reasoning;

"If you want the shortest way, you should take the red route.",

"If you want the quickest way, you should take the blue route.",

"If you want the most scenic, you should take the green route."

Some people like to take the quickest route to a destination so they tell people to take the blue road. Some worry that if there is a traffic jam you can get stuck on the blue road, so will take the red one. The red one also keeps the mileage to a minimum, but there are traffic lights and junctions galore. Then there are those with time on their hands who opt to use the green road.

You might think the blue route is the best as it is the one you take most often. Telling others to do the same is compelling. We handout so many suggestions based on our own personal preferences, not theirs. We have strong ideological and political principles and attempt to guide people by them. Refraining from telling other people what to do and how they should behave is jolly hard work. It is time consuming to give all those three options with their respective reasons, compared with "take it from me, use the blue route".

Follow in my path and I will lead you into righteousness. Follow your own path and make your own mistakes for not every pearl of wisdom handed out has honourable intentions. Should shouldn't be banned. The term has great uses. If someone wants to achieve a particular objective by certain means, then it necessitates using the word. Nevertheless, we like people to agree with us, to have the same opinion and we go to great lengths to persuade others to do what we see as best.

Given that few people really like advice, especially when we haven't asked for it, even less so when it appears to be interfering, 'should' antagonises. People welcome those that will listen, to hear our case and allow us to work out a solution by ourselves. A clever person will listen and configure the dialog in such a way as to make the person feel that they arrived at a solution by themselves. What about taking credit for our involvement in helping? If you want superiority then that is a must, but many come to realise that it is not a necessity.

"There is no greater sin than evangelism"

Evangelism is telling others what they should or should not be doing in their lives. We tell our children how they should behave. We want to create laws dictating what is and isn't acceptable. We tell someone what they should do, as we want them to live by the same standards as us regardless of whether we seek to serve the best interests of all. The moment you carelessly utter the should word you are in danger of being an evangelist. Evangelism leads to disputes and battles of power. The most forceful win for the period of their reign.

How often do you hear people talk about our manners but can't provide solid reasons for them? Those that think they have good manners certainly believe they are superior. They consider themselves to be better people. Slurping in one country is frowned upon whereas in others it is a sign of enjoyment and acknowledgment to the cook that the soup is good. What you think is the most appropriate way of conducting yourself will not be anything like the same as numerous other people from different cultures. The only principle that comes close to being accepted by all is having the decency to listen well to others. Yet people hold rigidly to the view that they are doing everything correctly and expect others to follow suit.

People think that they have more decorum than others and know the proper way to greet one another. When you travel the world you see many contrary views on such matters. The error is thinking that you and only you are right. We can share our thoughts and listen to other peoples' views, but people like to think that they are more civilised rather than different. A lot can be had from observing other customs and simply enjoying the differences without pressing upon others to change. No diktat is followed by everyone the world over. Each country adheres to a different political system, none of which is perfect. Every nation has its own set of laws, each with many flaws.

With so many contrary opinions abound, not everyone can be right. On balance your method, your teachings are most likely to be representative of a minority when taking the whole world population into account. Power is gleaned at the expense of encroachment on the freedoms experienced by your prey. You do not have to be religious or politically minded in any way to be enthusiastic about your evangelical arm-twisting rhetoric. Even the most ordinary characters get caught up in selling their values to anyone that will listen.

It is a difficult task for many to include the reasons with the should word along with the potential alternatives. Most favour those that lead by example and let people decide for themselves whether to copy or not. It is hard for many to stand aside whilst allowing others to learn to sink or swim. The most respected people give others the chance to make mistakes for themselves, letting them enjoy the reward of learning to improve. Great leaders to great parents will inform and make as much information available as possible whilst taking care of the use of this term 'should'.

Maybe too many people think of themselves like football managers. Too old to play themselves now, but with the experience to give advice and commands to those on the pitch. The player and the manger will however be sharing the same aim of winning the game. Both elected to be there. If it is not your game, then the potential for not seeing eye to eye by being told what to do is that much greater. Our parents can be adamant that doing something can be foolish. We go against the advice and find it to be the best thing ever. Not always, but sometimes we find our own way running counter to what we are told is the best.

Anyone with any sense, will see the irony in saying that you should be careful with the use of the should word.

Philosophy is everywhere

Some people think of philosophy as people arguing inane senseless trite with endless language trickery. However, all societies are underpinned by a philosophy that has been laid down in the past. It will be one that gets slowly modified over time. In practical terms, laws evolve to protect and provide for the greatest number of people whilst hopefully catering for minorities also. Should we obey these laws and should we help update them when it becomes evident that there are failings in the system? Should you not kill, unless someone was about to kill you? Should you steal if it is the only way to stay alive? There are many conundrums like these with no definitive answer.

No law or commandant is perfect in all cases as there is so often mitigating circumstances. A philosopher can frame the arguments leaving a foundation for politicians to formulate regulations according to the local environment and situation. The following example on the subject of abortion provides an example of how you could lay out an argument to be then taken forward by law makers:

There is divided opinion about abortion with some saying that it is wrong to interfere at all, suggesting that contraception should be forbidden. They claim that whatever child does or does not emerge is in the hands of nature. A slightly less extreme view is that once conception take place, nobody ought to destroy the growing embryo. At the other end of the scale we have those that see it as a right to do what we please until the baby is born and the umbilical cord is cut. For me the interesting point is where we decide a human has been created. If a human is killed we consider that to be murder, manslaughter at best.

Many a comedian has remarked "I didn't ask to be born". You can't select your parents. You had no say in your conception but at what point did you become a person? Was it when you were born or when you were conceived? What about at the age of three? Also, at what point are you pronounced dead. When your heart stops, or when rigor mortis fully sets in? If you lose your arms and legs, you still count as a person. What therefore defines a living human being?

We all start off as something very small. You are probably at least twenty times bigger now than what you were as a baby. Saying a foetus is very small and just a bunch of cells is no different to saying a baby is very small compared to a fully grown adult. The size of the person has no relevance in this debate. An exact definition of a person is not easy to come by, but a body that metabolises using sugar and fats to derive energy, is a good starting point for deciding what is living. In the womb, you begin as a parasite sucking as much nutrients as possible. There comes a critical point however when you no longer need your mother, you will need someone to feed you, but not necessarily your mother in particular. Someone, anyone could look after you from then on. At the stage in the pregnancy when the child created no longer needs the mother to survive, a new human being is created. If a birth is induced and the child delivered could be nurtured by someone and nobody does so, then it becomes neglectful murder. The father, the grandparent, the charitable, someone could care for a child if the mother is incapable or has no wish to. In late abortion, a birth is indeed induced. It can be judged to be murder if a child is sufficiently developed to survive and lead a full life and no effort is made to feed and care for them.

The mother does not own the child simply because it is inside their body. Once it reaches the stage of viability it owns itself. In fact, the entity never belongs to anyone bar itself. It is a mystery as to why someone would be horrified if a five-year-old child was locked away and left to starve but not at all concerned that a new-born baby is dumped in a bucket and disposed of just because the umbilical cord was only recently cut.

One might describe a human being as that with the signature human genome, is metabolising and most importantly is viable. There is a considerable distinction between viability and independence. When you get old your body is certainly viable, but you may need a lot of assistance. You may require help getting out of bed, onto the loo and spoon feeding like a child once again. Nevertheless, you can continue your human existence for many more years despite the burden you place on others.

We might wish for a precise definition of what viability is, sadly that is not possible. We may revert to a judgment call made by people that can make mistakes. If a typical pregnancy is likely to result in creating a viable child at around 24 weeks we might err on the side of caution and declare abortions before 22 weeks as murderous. The proportion of viable entities increases as each week passes, with very few at 22 and the majority at 26. If we accept that it is beyond belief how hard it is to make a stick exactly

1 metre long or make an object precisely 1kg it is easier to be more relaxed about what person is deemed viable and who is not.

Viability at heart is the heart, lungs and organs that are working and are sufficiently formed to sustain the life of the person. Unless they are replaced by a machine they are essential parts that work on their own in an autonomous fashion. However, advances in incubation and medicinal intervention blur the issue.

We could say that removing the foetus from the womb at an early stage prior to it becoming viable is a termination of pregnancy. Letting it die or destroying it after this stage becomes murder by definition. We leave it to the policy makers to set the rules for how we behave and what we can and can't do when intervening in the course of a pregnancy. The philosophy simply aids and potentially clarifies the issue.

The desire to live

In man's earlier history it was quite common to place any baby that didn't look right behind a bush to die. If it had an extra toe or some minor malformed part it would be chucked away. It would seem unacceptable to people in modern times to do such a thing. Having a cosmetic problem is one thing, but not ever being able to look after oneself is a different matter. Some may worry about the consequences of having a disproportionate number of individuals that will never reach independence. If the number of those that need twenty-four-hour care is very high, it would place an unsustainable strain on the rest. This can lead us to consider what the priorities are in our society. This along with the potential for having to artificially inseminate ever greater numbers can make us wonder what will happen in times of global crisis.

Whether we label them as different, defective, handicapped or whatever, many appear to be as happy and if not more so than the average individual. They show a desire to live. Having a desire to live is key. Whether it is a new-born or one with low verbal communicative abilities, the inability to speak doesn't detract from their desire to live or die. Many indications can be read from the body language that they express.

The desire to live can come to the fore after a life changing event. Maybe to do more and live life to the full. Having a desire to live is everything. Personal, individual yet universal. This desire may wane occasionally. Some begin to have suicidal thoughts when life becomes a real struggle. Alternatively, we may have a wish to leave early because of major physical and mental deterioration.

Do we give people the right to live and the right to die? If murder became legal the murder rate would rise for sure, but having a right to life does not stop us killing one another. The laws stop some murder and take murderers off the streets. However, the majority are not hesitant about killing one another just because they are afraid of the repercussions and are fearful of any punishment metered out after. We do not refrain from killing simply because we accept someone's right to live. It is more down to the ability to recognise that another person wants to live. We empathise and grasp their desire to live in the same way we want to live also. We see the fear and distress on someone's face when they are threatened. We understand the many signals in our body language that indicate that we want to be unharmed. Only the minority, the psychopaths don't care.

If you appreciate someone's desire to live you might also be appreciative of someone's desire to die too. When life becomes an absolute chore with each day getting progressively worse the desire evaporates. If the balance of pain and reward swings markedly towards the suffering end of the scale, then one may feel that continuing is unwelcome. Losing the appetite for life can occur when most of the day is intolerable and not offset in anyway by its meagre rewards. However, if there is any doubt then the ignorance paradox will imply that euthanasia is not the course to take.

Doing onto others as you would have others do onto you, partly suggests that you treat others in the same way as you would like to be treated. This is quite noble but has scope for improvement. What you like does not always correspond to what other people like. You may like to have grapes brought to you when ill, other people may prefer something different. Maybe a banana or a big bar of chocolate. Obviously we do not like people stealing from us or damaging us in any way. You don't like it and they don't like it. However, we all too often guide our actions in a way that we think is right without properly consulting what the other person really wants. It is about respecting the desires of others rather than focusing on our own individual desires. Do onto others the way they want to be done onto.

Moderation

Balance in health, balance in views, balance in perspective, balance is found everywhere and people can get away with a lot if what they do is done in moderation. Plenty on occasions but not to excess.

Finding the balance to suit you is what it is all about. There will be plenty of people egging you on to do more or trying to slow you down. Sometimes it is not about being unable but not wanting to take part. Balance is giving some leeway to do a few things we don't like from time to time to please others who do the same for us.

We are not the same. Hence attempting to emulate others can lead to our downfall. Everything from the amount of pain we can tolerate to the level of endurance we have is different. What is a lot for them is not a big deal to you. Hopefully we each gain enough confidence to stand our ground and not be too swayed by everyone else's idea of how much is enough. People learn to stick to what is right for them individually.

How much exercise is enough to stay fit and healthy? Nobody really knows but there are plenty of educated guesses. Some that promote more exercise can be found guilty of doing too much. They are the types found complaining of bad knees, bad backs, bad tendons and bad tempers struggling to get a good night's sleep with these ligaments and more flaring up at night.

A commendable endeavour may be to have a balanced way of life and that extends to a measured outlook. This is only gained through insights from many points of view, not just one. Certain media will only present what they need to in order to justify their position. A lot of time and work is needed to filter out all the biased reasoning and establish what people stand to lose and what they may gain from any changes that are afoot.

Tolerance

Throughout life we will be faced with the tolerance problem. We might like to do as we please, but some things will have an impact on people living around us. So some decisions we make will encounter opposition and others will be welcomed. The main aim is to seek a balance between what is tolerable and what is a clear infringement into other people's lives. If we live isolated on our own, we can do much more that suits us and our family than when bunched up in a community. Making noise from time to time is a case in point, people will accept some but will object to constant aggravation. Complaining about a party held next door is less warranted if twice a year rather than twice a week. We do require some level of tolerance towards activities that we might not like for we all may test the lenience we are given by others at times.

As a general rule your body is yours and yours alone and what you do with it is up to you. If you want to deface it, colour your hair bright green or work it to death that is your business. It only becomes someone else's concern when you start endangering others; when our activities begin impacting upon their way of life. If you go hiking in mid-winter and have to call upon others for a rescue you make use of the obligations of others to come to your aid. Your recklessness becomes someone else's problem. This is more of a political problem than anything else. People make mistakes and we need not see them die just because we don't want to use resources to get them out of a fix. However, ignorance of the dangers is not an excuse that sits well with people that are in the line of fire. We are not happy when what people are doing jeopardies the safety of those not involved in that activity.

You could set a rule; with tolerance in mind, don't do anything that infringes, upsets or endangers anybody else. Some will think of the saying that all rules are there to be broken. It will always come down to the interpretation of such rules. Hence there will be clarifications and examples. As each explanation gets added with more and more exceptions the wording of the rule gets ever larger. From one sentence it soon expands to cover hundreds of pages or more. It will be nice to live by clear cut simple rules, but in practice things pan out very differently.

Some keep themselves to themselves, many are at the ready to jump in when asked for help. There are plenty of kind people out there. However, are we supposed to be proactive with a duty of care for people around us? Is there an unwritten obligation to look after others and care for their well-being? If so, how often are we supposed to check in on the elderly to ensure they are fine? Who is included, who is outside of our zone of responsibility? People hate to face the reality of the time budget. There are limits in a world we think can do anything and everything people expect of it.

Life is a Game

We start a game of football with some hopes, expectation and optimism. Similar to the game of life. We know all games have a limited timeframe and the fact that the games come to an end in no way puts us off playing. The factors that make it off putting can lie at the door of the opposition. You don't want a walkover for that is no fun, no challenge. Neither do you want to face a team that will provide nothing bar humiliation. You won't get a chance to show your worth. Whilst a football match has a prescribed half-time, many of us have a midlife crisis. After some reflection, we consider some changes if needed and come out again playing to the end.

It is rare to find people thinking of themselves as immortal although a good few state that they wouldn't mind living forever so long as they remain in good health. However, nobody has defied death so far. Many succumb to the idea of living on via a great legacy or get ideas of an afterlife. Given that we know that it will come to a stop after a certain time we play to get something from it, enjoyment, satisfaction and the pleasure of team spirit. Different divisions, different leagues from scruffy dusty pitches to grand stadiums. The game is played whatever the environment. From the dressing rooms to the quality of the boots worn the privileges we get are not the same. We don't all get the same start in life. Some benefit from the quality of their contacts, people that they know who are able to give them a head start. Yet were it not for the rules imposed we are only held back by attitude and determination.

Substitutes sit on the bench hoping to get an opportunity to play and when it does it is often due to another poor soul getting injured. If the injury is really bad it will take you out of the game permanently. Equally in the game of life there are dangers galore that draws your game to a close. For better or worse, there are always more and more up and coming players waiting in the wings to see if they can shine too. This can keep us on our toes. One missed step can allow them to replace us. If we did live forever then barring any misfortune, people might become so rich and so powerful that a gap so large would materialise making it unenviable being a beginner.

Half-time

The midpoint can be a fascinating period. Like gluttons for punishment, some just carry on in the same way as they did in the first half, losing, making the same mistakes and blindly following the lead of the fools in charge. On the other hand, there will be those that do question their life so far and decide to change course. Some will feel trapped. On the surface there is a lot to be thankful for. A reasonable job, a respectable house, a partner and kids all with smiles on their faces. And a realisation that this is as good as it is going to get. Only downhill from now on. Less and less flirting. Would an affair liven things up? Maybe, but that will only provide a brief respite from this flat peak. Let's get rid of the flab anyway as nobody is going to want me like this. Let's do something positive. That's the spirit. Go chase those higher forms of enlightenment. Be selfish, yes selfish. Do something for yourself for a change and all else can wait until you accept your irrelevance. Real freedom. Get back to what you are good at.

You may be the one everyone leans on and the one person people assume has everything sorted. Inside you are in turmoil. Prospects of promotion or expanding the business are slim and that wouldn't really help much anyway. In your formative years, you had lots all mapped out. You had plenty to look forward to before and now that most of your wishes have come to fruition you feel vacuous, empty, unimpressed. Has it come to this. The sum total of nil. Nothing outstanding, all average. Best of all nobody seems to give a damn. Too busy, too many trivial problems of their own. Oh well, poor you. You pity those in ill health, pity the poor buggers in a cardboard box under the highway. I am at least fortunate in most respects, we muse, but empty inside. Some feel they have done everything right in life, kept to the rules and played it all straight. Yet it hasn't brought the bounty they expected. The cardinal rule is to keep advice to a minimum so that leaves it to you to figure out and decide where to go from this point onwards.

Tick tock

The time ticking down can play havoc with our priorities. As the second half transgresses and the final moments beckon a rush to score the vital goal ensues. Those on the side left 7-0 down can give up or push on. Ending at 7-1 makes no real difference to the leader boards but it gives those that are watching something to take from it and your fellow players some respect. Just getting one goal against a formidable team can be a real achievement.

We will often find little alternative to making the most of what we can do in our current position but are always able to fight on until the bitter end. As we age our health can deteriorate but the worries and cares we once had often dissipate. We may choose to focus more on what we think really matters such as our friends and family. Like all games, your life will have an end point and a result. Whilst the terminal result is the same for all of us, we can take stock of the score at any point and having some kind of finality is what makes us content. We choose a game to play, maybe in the form of a job and reach a point where we have 'won', where we feel successful or proficient. We can then rest on our laurels, revel in our success or quit and start some other game.

There will be many outside influences vying to get you to use the same scoring mechanism as them. Some measure progression by knowledge gained. Others value the creation of a family or position in a society. Many count the amount of material possessions gathered. If you walk around a graveyard do you value the age attained, look into the amount left in the will or the ornateness and size of the headstone. Alternatively, do you sit and count the number of visitors to a plot and remark upon the freshness and quality of the flowers abandoned there.

Thankfully for those remaining, few people will rip up the pitch and knock down the goal posts when they retire from the sport. In fact, there seems to be a desire to ensure that the club is left in a better state than when they joined. Many may even bequeath a little for the enjoyment of future players and spectators. They want their club to march forwards and hope that it will continue to succeed when they are no longer around. Such acts of generosity make them feel good about themselves and we can be grateful for it.

The end of the game can come quicker than expected for some and not soon enough for others. For some, days drag slowly. They find themselves withering by the wayside with dreary repetitive routines. Sometimes the mind is willing but the body isn't and the only challenges are the daily grind of dealing with an ever growing list of ailments. You can only chuckle at the wisdom of the quote "Don't get old". You can hope that you may be one of the lucky ones that reach a ripe old age in good shape. Satisfying yourself with simple pleasures right up to the end, with a swift departure during a peaceful last night. There is some debate about the length of a life versus how good a life is. Plenty are seen doing their upmost to stay as healthy as possible hoping to maximise their longevity. Is a life a bit misdirected if it is so taken up and consumed by self-preservation? Is the winner the one who lasts the longest? Where one builds the best house in the street another is maintaining the best body. We have our own aims.

If I was to espouse a principle in a more brazen manner rather than giving a subtle nod towards something, it would be to encourage people to play their own game. Whether it is the game of life as a whole or within the sub-games of schooling, courtship, child rearing and work to name but a few. You choose when to conform and when to stand alone. It is about playing your cards how you want to rather than running to the tune of other people and getting wrapped up in their games. A great motivational speech may provide the inspiration that you need or it might be a way of manipulating you to do as they want you to do.

Most of us will be spectators. It is numerically impossible to be any other way. A thousand in the stands for each one on the pitch. As a supporter we make an invaluable contribution by adding to the atmosphere in the football stadium or providing vital support to businesses and the community. All contributions count as every one of us has an impact even if just an ethereal interference. We do not have to do outstanding things to feel successful in life.

How do we measure our success? Is it measured in how famous we become? Or how wealthy? Or how happy or contented we feel. Do we have to achieve something exceptional? We might want to question our motives sometimes. Notoriety in particular is not a panacea. The job of running the highest office in the land may be enviable too, but it is also restrictive. There is a trade-off between privileges and responsibility with freedom to do what you want anonymously at any time and on any date.

Validity

I highlight the word 'validity', a word which has enormous resonance and can be considered when we talk about entitlement and worthiness. If you have a valid train ticket it gives you an entitlement to take a seat in one of the carriages. If it is full you may see that someone else is more worthy of the seat and decide to stand allowing a frail, disabled or pregnant person to sit down. Nevertheless, under no circumstances need one consider someone else to be a greater, more worthy or more important person than you.

There is a substantial difference between meritocracy and validity. In this game of football we expect those with the most skill and ability in this arena to be in the line-up. However, in too many areas we give way to people because of some artificial unwarranted respect. We hate it if some are chosen because they are the prettiest or the richest or succumb to favours and bungs. People may hold the 'leader of the nation' title. However, it is the job that is important rather than the person. It gives the holder of that job certain privileges for sure, but it is the position that is of the greatest importance. We install bodyguards to protect the person, but it is the post that is being guarded the most.

Revanche

A cyclist was bemoaning a situation they found themselves in: An old lady stepped out into the road without looking and the cyclist knocked her over. The locals then set upon him, dishing out a little beating. The fault lay with the cyclist regardless, being a foreigner more so. As far as they were concerned, if he was not there it would not have happened. If it was your mother, what would you have done? Maybe blame the cyclist for cycling near pedestrians. Anyway, whether this can be regarded as an accident or unfortunate incident it pales into comparison to times where people do wrong knowingly. The game of life is riddled with players who are proper cheats. Some do not realise they are at fault, but not all can hide behind that excuse. We will expose a cheat in a game of fun and shout more loudly if there is money and prestige involved. We want them excluded in future and penalised for their actions. Getting an unfair advantage at times can be a minor irritation compared to cases where somebody does something that is particularly malicious or has a total disregard of the dangers they put others in.

When you are subjected to an irreversible loss you have your rage, hurt and grief to contend with. Some can come to terms with it and move on after a while. Others employ the counter play of living a forgiving life. However, this doesn't always provide the required catharsis. We can't get over it and want to take action. If it means sacrificing ourselves in the process, then so be it. Usually most have a fear of further reprisals and do not have the means to do much. If total innocents get hurt when you are trying to get back at someone the masses will be very upset. Absolute care is required and it is too easy to get the payback wrong.

Some like to think of comeuppance and karma but no amount of fiery hell can set straight the destruction some have instigated. Humankind rarely takes adequate early action to reign in the amount of power at the disposal of a single individual.

End of days

As time goes by there is a tendency to prioritise the things that are dearest to us and what we think is really important. Things seen as significant years before become less so. Some say youth is wasted on the young and each hour of each day becomes more precious as we get older. You never know for sure when your number is up and can rarely foresee a pending accident or upcoming illness. Even if things seem to be progressing fortuitously you will undoubtedly notice your teeth beginning to rot away, your hair greying and thinning out. All examples of clear, startling signs of your mortality. It is reassuring and comforting to know that the degradation that we will all undergo tends to make our initial fear of death evaporate.

The aging process causes our skin to lose a lot of its elasticity inside and out. A typical death through old age commences when the acidic contents of the stomach pierces the lining unabated and enters into the bloodstream. Every last drop of heroin like reserves are released in the mind allowing us to depart on quite a high. Before this though, exhaustion can set in and we tend to reach a point where we fully appreciate that there is no limit to the number of people we would like to meet, or scientific studies that we may wish to embark upon, or places we may like to visit, or wealth we want to collate or distribute, or politics that we feel inclined to amend, or how far and wide we would like to spread a message, or knowledge available to be sought, or do whatever thing that is of importance to us; acceptance of our limits is reached and the cares that we once had of the world and opportunities that it offered slide away. It is akin to returning to the time before we were born. Our unique set of preferences, affinities and abilities emerge, flourish and then ebb away.

Mankind has collectively expanded its capability from one generation to the next. Individuals have been integral in improving something, devoting a lifetime to it, but pass away well before they get to see the resultant applications of their work. However, as our lifespan is restricted we can do nothing bar accept the boundary and enjoy our turn.

Giving up

What happens when selfishness is lost or when the curiosity mechanism no longer works or we fail to feel reward? There can come a time for some when they feel that they have seen it all. They no longer have that same wish to explore anymore. If you have filled all the curiosity pathways that inspired you in the past, it can be difficult to seek others. The sparks of inspiration need to sit there long enough to seed further exploration.

If someone were to state that they were fully content and felt they had seen and accomplished enough they smash the concept of being a human being. With the curiosity and love of reward being so restrained pure autonomous behaviour must emerge. Not only is total contentment boring but contradictory and difficult to sustain.

The reward mechanism might not work too well for some. We are biological machines and machines are renowned to fail, whether at the start or later on. If you never feel pleased nor get any sense of gratification, animal life is pointless and directionless at its core. When any one of the drives disappears or wasn't formed properly in the first place you are in effect much less human. Survival is wanted where the selfishness prospers. If you never feel good about helping you are in danger of being helpless yourself.

To take one's own life because of an irreversible biological issue is one thing, but it is pathetic to even consider it to avoid facing difficult circumstances. Debt, duty or trapped. Regardless of whether it is something you have had any control over or not, it doesn't have to be the end of the world for you. When you fall out or foul up there is always a way to figure out a solution, apologise, make amends, reorganise and restructure without wasting the chance to reroute.

Reaching a nadir, the rock bottom, a really low point where life seems too much of a struggle to carry on can be an opportunity to pack your things and walk away. You can leave your troubles behind and start afresh somewhere else. If you are at a point where it can't get much worse, you really do have nothing to lose. Maybe you can return one day and explain yourself to those that worried about you. You can't properly explain yourself by leaving a note and jumping off a bridge.

The vast majority of people who have felt totally heartbroken at a point in their life have slogged onwards and come out the other side albeit bruised, but relieved that they are still here. They have looked back and can see the turning point in their life and become bigger characters afterwards. Shame and torment does slowly fade and can be turned into a badge of honour if your personality can be expanded.

There will always be people that are at the ready to bully you and be very hurtful. Escape is always possible. The game of life can be a monstrous challenge, bring it on rather than let it bring you down. Never concede - you can't regret dying. If ever in a spot of confusion you don't have to do it today. Leave it till next year and see how you feel then. You can be like those in war zones who considered themselves dead already so lost all fear of living. If you think of yourself as being dead already then you will have no difficulty unburdening your woes to people that will listen. You can take the fight to them with nothing to lose.

Think of the things you have not done yet. Think of all the people that you want to be with when they get together and have babies, pass exams and get to where they want to go. There is no place for envy, for your time will come when you too will be the subject of interest to them also. Some have explored their co-considerational selfishness through charity work. They treasured the sense of being needed and feel much better about themselves. You do not have to do dull fundraising. Simple hands on active involvement is as useful for you as them. Plenty will appreciate your assistance and in the process you heal yourself.

Choice

This chapter is dull as ditch water, dry as the desert, but those that bear with it might see something in it that is quite profound. We make choices all the time from what to eat, to who to vote for. Now you can choose whether to skip this very chapter or even bin the whole book. Does it matter how we go about choosing? Not really, but it gives a remarkable insight into how basic we humans are.

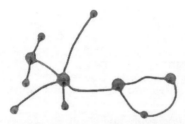

All the plans you had for the day can go out the window when an emergency arises. You wanted to go shopping like you usually do on a Monday, but now need to take a washbag and some food into the hospital. You care a lot for the person you are to visit and they can't stomach the offerings served up there. A quick dash to the local convenience store enables you to delete the requirement for milk and bread from your mind. The parcel you promised to send can be left until you get back. You see, we build a fretwork, a network of things to do around an excursion to the shops. The fretwork is a collection of tails leading off a node. Each tail being a thing we want to get to top up our supplies. The milk, the bread and so on. When the panic subsides we still have the fretwork etched on our mind. It is hard to shut it out completely. Instead we resolve each part so that they subside.

It doesn't matter who you are, a simpleton or a modern-day emperor, you have the same problems sorting out your priorities. How we prioritise sheds light on our choices too. It is quite simple. Involved, rather than difficult. We spend a lot of time choosing and deciding, but not so much thought is put into the mechanics of how it is achieved. We might make a list of all the options then take a pick. We might decide upon something because it is a little different, fashionable or in keeping with our style. Each factor is another tail. The more positive tails the more chance there is that we choose it. You are controlled by how you build each fretwork.

The largest fretwork becomes the priority. The shopping trip had a lot of tails, all attached relating to items running out in the fridge. You had an errand to run. Besides, it is something you do on a set day each week. It is easier to do something else if we can break the fretwork down. Hive bits off, in this case by getting the stuff deemed most important locally. Examining this trivial puzzle sheds light on how we set the course of our whole life. Good deeds, criminal acts and spontaneity all derive from the same mental process.

To come to a decision, we add, remove or deal with each tail. To do, or not to do? On the one side of the fretwork you place the advantages and on the other the potential consequences. You can draw a map of all the parts involved. What you see is the scale and size of it. There is very little depth to the way we go about our lives, no great mystery just endless links in our mind with clusters that change size and significance. Whether it is an objective or a choice it is none other than links in our minds relating to it. The more links the more presence it has. The size of the fretwork dictates our priorities. As each fretwork expands it becomes more important to us. We have a job to get done. We need to do the job to get the money. We need to pay the bills. If the bills are not paid the electricity goes off. One thing leading to another.

The seed

The fretworks that remain long term get added to and adjusted. This is what we describe as experience and these meshes mould future choices. When we plan something, we start a new set of links; Memories, pictures in our mind or emotions get connected to each other. We have a range of concepts that are joined up. Our sense of sophistication is merely related to the volume of concepts that you utilise. Some people take more factors into account than others. They appreciate the nuances. They are just accessing more links per choice.

From the seed, the little thing that urges you to probe further, we end up doing something. Be it an advert, something someone said during a conversation or piece in print. From this starting point, you begin to search for more information. Each bit expands the network pattern in your head. So a skiing trip would require some lessons prior, obtaining the right equipment along with making travel arrangements. From liking the idea of going skiing with the positive notions of fun and lapping up the mountain scenery, you garner more and more data clustered around the central goal.

Not all plans come to fruition. A lot can happen before you set off. Maybe after some evaluation you come to the conclusion that it is too far to go or costs too much. Many such obstacles might have to be overcome before you set off, if you do indeed plump to go. Whilst there will be nothing stopping you from shelving the whole idea, forgetting about it is not so easy. Many everyday things will hook into the fretwork. Every time you see or hear something ski or travel related the whole set of memories about your plans get replayed.

The essence of free will is about experiences and the knowledge you gain during your life. We find best practices (best for you), which are utilised over and over. The path of life is your way of doing things laid down by what you have done in the past. Your past doesn't dictate everything but will be the default route forward. We change by learning hard lessons and through discovering new joys. We have a store of negative and positive associations with certain actions. Parents may wonder why all efforts to advise their children is all too often in vain. Any attempts to steer them needs to be done by giving them first hand experiences. It is hard to convey the magnitude of an error by words alone. Personal experiences have large scale imprinting within the mind. Many more links created than any third-party knowledge transfer can provide. Along with words there will be sights, smells and sounds to accompany the memory of an event. Plus, the chemical excitations that emotion brings that can only be felt by the individual themselves. Whether they are described as a rush, fright or exultation it leaves a mark.

A parent with a criminal past lays down a story, one that other children would find alien. Some envisage that they will not be so stupid so won't get caught. Or it can spark a desire to live a more virtuous life. Few criminals begin at the 'top'; most will start with petty activities like stealing low value items from shops before progressing to more damaging activities. Rich people from well to do backgrounds have robbed a thing or two simply for the thrill of it. They have absolutely no need for the item they have stolen. The idea of having some excitement in their life along with the notion of being a little deviant is formed in their present fretwork.

At any time, we can choose to change but it is about our predisposition. Most folk walking down a street will be thinking, humming maybe, reflecting on the day ahead or day to come. Whereas a burglar will notice all the open windows, the opportunities to gain easy entry and flee afterwards, unchallenged. They will always be on the lookout for such chances as their fretwork contains so much knowledge relating to these acts. Gardeners clock the flowers, you and I might be identifying the breed of a dog or noticing the colour of the cats. Burglars will see animals giving off tell-tale signs of whether someone is at home or not. They are not predetermined to carry out the illegal action but care little about the victim, understand nothing of what it is like for those to suffer, and weigh the option of giving into temptation against the risk of getting caught. Any punishment and humiliation alters the probability of committing further offences. More connections in the fretwork. The memory of being held down during arrest, hours in a prison cell and the loss of liberty and so on.

Some may propose that free will provides us with the means to act at random. In theory yes, but in practice we tend to start with the seed then build on it before proceeding. We can throw a dart upon a map and journey to where it lands. We can change our mind at any point but this itself is inspired by earlier dealings in life. For the most part we are moving about autonomously with little real regard for ultimate reasons. The power and capacity of free will is not exercised as much as one might like to think.

Our will to be free is challenged by chemical imbalances, being intoxicated by too much alcohol or being subject to inhalation of industrial substances inadvertently. Provocation and poisons taken in unconsciously makes the ethics wrangle unanswerable. We can be equally stressed by disorders of the mind and damage inflicted in accidents. Being drunk may give rise to uncontrolled less coordinated behaviour but sober people can act very dangerously as well, wanting to show off without any need for dis-inhibitors like alcohol.

People can defer responsibility to someone in charge. We are much more likely to hurt another if told to do so by someone in authority. We can see red and begin lashing out acting wholeheartedly animalistic. Those accustomed to violence will use aggression with less forethought. It is less about focusing on a single incident and more about prior habits. It is automatic, as they will view it as justifiable. That is what they did on past occasions. The lack of control today stems from the development of someone's character over time. We can become more cautious if someone we take on turns out to be adept at fighting back. Once again, a link, this time to the pain we suffered last time alters the balance.

We might appear to be roving complex animals with determination and individual freedom to do what we want. We like to think that we can easily change our mind and alter our plans, then alter again moments later for the sheer sake of it. The image of being nonconformist and contrary might seem endearing. Being inconsistent and seemingly random is a feature of the pattern of habits expressed before. Doing things on the hop, if that is what we are familiar with, is what we continue to do. People do not change from a rigid way of life to become easy going free flowing wanderers overnight. It is a gradual shift. We do things that we are acquainted with and only embark on new ventures after learning about them in depth beforehand. You might have to 'cross each bridge as you come to it' but the crossing will be navigated by the knowledge you have.

We might want to break certain habits. We decide to quit drinking coffee. No particular reason, but that is what we want to do. We have one cup the minute we wake up and lots throughout the day. We associate doing something at a certain time of the day or in with a particular place. The weaning off process entails gradual reduction. Rather than attempting to stop a habit altogether in one go, we can stop it bit by bit. Identify each time, place or trigger and chose one in turn to forgo. Tea instead of coffee at lunch time. Stick to it until it is embedded then move to the next. The fretwork then gets modified much more thoroughly.

That will do

We walk up to the buffet counter and pick a cup. We select one that fits the bill from stacks of them. Most also take the top plate nearest to them. That will do. If we notice some dirt on it, we might choose to swap it for another one. Subconsciously we say 'that will do' in a myriad of scenarios. If something is sufficient and does the job we want, then we make the selection. We might make a more conscious choice about where to sit perhaps seeking the optimum spot where our back is to the wall and one seat in from the end. When this is not possible and we don't want to make a big disturbance by rearranging all the furniture we take the next best option.

There is no need to spend ages mulling over the finer points of everything all the time. However, there will be instances where we do hither and thither over the options available and the process of deciding can be viewed as labyrinthine. However, if you draw a diagram of all the links that come to the fore, you can see why you chose what you did.

Against our will

We can't be forced to do anything. Coerced blackmailed and cajoled maybe, but never really forced. Even with a gun to your head you can opt to die, call their bluff or obfuscate the situation. Cooperation is promoted with narcotics but that merely reduces your ability to show your objection rather than get you onside. Soldiers will be given training to be non-complicit. If an interrogator asks them to hand them something they will toss the item on the floor instead.

Having the belief that we choose our own destiny is meaningful. What we can and cannot do depends strictly on what possibilities are available. First and foremost, you need to be aware of the options that exist. Hence why so much effort is made regarding the provision of education to expand people's outlook. Most objectives of any consequence require step by step assemblage of smaller components. Having the will to start and tackle each element is indispensable.

It would be nice to think that the time and diligence making decisions are correlated to the impact. Someone buying a house does not take 10000+ times longer selecting a property than what toppings to have on a pizza. More time and more research but less than the square root of the exertion in relation to the money at stake. We have seen wars with huge losses on both sides. Leaders who commit troops to battle will once again analyse disproportionally small amounts in relation to the potential consequence of the decision. It is an aspect of being a human not a failure. If you think free will and determinism is a complex difficult subject, you may not realise or accept that choices are made by ludicrously simple processes.

More choice can mean more time and worry deciding which is the most suitable. If there was only a choice between white or brown bread it is easier to make your mind up than if there are 44 types. We find ourselves weighing up the pros and cons of price, value, texture, taste, health factors, image and a myriad of other innuendoes. Those that discuss and debate at length the merits of some items can be seen like thinking it is better to have 12 rather than a dozen. We see subtle differences as relevant but they are not always of great practical importance. We can be taken in by subtle gimmicks and persuaded to go down routes that other people are leading us to.

Doing the same as others

Why fight when you can trick someone instead. One dog wants the bone, but it is in the mouth of another dog. So, it plays with a ball, tricking the other dog to drop the bone and go for the ball. The conniver then takes the prey. An object of desire can play tricks on our inner certainty. We can be lead to believe that we want something that we don't need and can be fooled into parting with an item that is better. It all comes down to confidence we have in our own selections. We doubt ourselves too often and act gullibly, surrendering to the whims of people who are simply perceived to be the ones to follow and emulate. Wanting what others have because they have it, rather than building a desire by ourselves is typical of this baboonian trait.

We learn how to do things by watching others at work. We learn a language by listening and repeating what others are saying. We copy so closely that we obtain the same local accent. The process of copying others is vital and we couldn't progress quickly without it, but there is a downside to it. It limits us. Sometimes it gets us into trouble. We have to be single minded enough at times to be our own master and attain the self-assurance to act differently to what the majority are doing. You won't always be right of course, there could be a good reason why so many are doing things in a particular way.

How many friends have convinced you to do things that you would not have imagined doing without them egging you on? You probably had an impact on their behaviour too. It is only when you look back that you can see what a dreadful impediment these so-called friends were. It can take several lifetimes for some to realise that sticking to your own guidance is possible. On the plus side, there is something very special about friendships that I am drawn towards. I can be very envious of those that maintain a long-standing alliance. We can see two people that are very good friends and wish for a comparable friendship with someone ourselves. It is their strong connection they share rather than wanting to be friends with them in particular. Although changes in circumstances lead to many great friendships withering, our choices about what we put first says so much about what we place importance on in life.

Four actors and a stooge stand before a shelf holding several pencils. They are asked to point to the one they think is the longest. The actors all point to one of them that is quite clearly shorter than some of the others. The stooge doesn't know the actors are trying to influence them. Rather than wanting to appear to be the odd one out, the stooge points to the shorter pencil also even though it is blatantly the wrong answer. It is hard to stand out and stand one's ground in a sea of conformity. We loath to admit we are wrong and change our opinion. Not all of us enjoy the limelight nor do we always relish being seen as different.

The game of poker might seem like gambling but the best players win more frequently. One element that the game teaches us is that there is a distinction between knowing what to do and acting upon it. It is no good saying "I thought that was the case" after the cards are turned over when you didn't play according to your calculations and reasoning. Winners, survivors and instigators can take stock of the situation quickly. They act on their own self-assurance, ignoring the folly around them.

You may claim that something is obvious, but won't admit that it took something you read or heard to crystallise it. Once all the pieces are put together in a less fragmented way it is so much clearer. It is no different to knowing roughly what a word means then seeing it defined in a dictionary. It tallies better now and makes more sense. After ages and ages, you finally have a concrete understanding of the issue. You were never that far away, you used instinctive policies to deal with certain situations, but never quite understood all the motives. Now there is clarity. The transformation, acting less on auto pilot it is quite an awakening.

Fixed

Being true to yourself. Apt and something many strive towards. It is about finding out what you are good at. Uncovering what you enjoy and not working against the grain. Having the realisation that your preferences are fixed helps a lot in this aim. The only way to change what you prefer is by taking a hammer to your mind and body and damaging it. Apart from doing that you cannot change what you prefer no matter what. The fact that we cannot alter much about our key attributes is quite significant. It matters so much because it will dictate what we can do and hope to achieve. We also begin to accept that we can't do what other people manage quite easily, but where they struggle we might excel.

To understand the implications and to accept it, one must take into full account the notion of discovery, change and bad associations. In short, you find out what you like as you get older through trying and experimentation. Things around you change rather than your affection for them. There will also be times where you have bad experiences that change your behaviour.

If you make the statement "preferences are fixed" and encounter arguments to the contrary, you can search for reasons why the arguments against are flawed rather than dismissing the statement. Step by step it can be substantiated. You need to glue yourself to the spot tightly enough to hold that position.

Discovery

What you like as a child is often far removed from what you like as an adult. The first time people eat olives many can find such strong tastes revolting. More of a shock and surprise though as it can be a taste like no other, far different to what one has eaten before. Yet lots of people acquire a taste for them. The more they eat the less of a surprise it is. You begin to notice more of the subtleties in the mix of flavours. You have to overcome the resistance towards them. Not everyone will enjoy them despite eating a full bucket load. Those that do, appreciate the qualities of such foodstuffs and get lifelong enjoyment from them. You discover what you like as you try things out, but you can only discover your preferences if you overcome any initial distaste.

Ice skating may provide another example of this effect. You go ice skating, you fall over. You don't go again. Years down the line you meet an attractive partner who is hell bent on showing you how to skate. You hold hands because they are attractive and it reduces your attraction to the floor. After some time, you become competent and for some (not all) ice skating turns out to be something enjoyable. The preference was always there; it just laid there undiscovered.

There are a good few songs that are not very appealing when you first hear them. A bare-bones song that uses just a few instruments is easy to pick up on, but has the tendency to make a listener tired of hearing it quite quickly. A song that has a lot going on in it takes a good few plays to get into. You can tune into different components picking out one of many instruments amongst the barrage of sound. You can change your mind about an artist once you discover the refinements of the arrangement.

Change

You may like something then go off it after a time. You haven't had something for a while then come back to it years later, only to be surprised that it wasn't how you remembered it to be. Maybe less pleasant maybe more so. Here lies the perfect reason to dismiss the case for having fixed preferences. Some people have followed a football team for decades. Then the appeal diminishes. How can someone like something so much for so long then go off it? If you always prefer football over tennis, why are you watching tennis now and paying little attention to the eleven aside game? Games change, games evolve, bringing new followers with it. Players become professional, more commercial minded and sometimes it can be argued the spirit gets lost along the way. A team with faster more athletic players earning more money perhaps can be less pleasing to long-time observers. People preferred the way it was, not the way it is now. Your preference has not changed the thing that you enjoyed has.

When we think of preferences we often think about what we eat. Olives tend to be fairly consistent over time, unless some mad botanist meddles with their makeup to alter yield and shelf-life etc. However, some products do have their ingredients interfered with thus changing their taste and mouth feel. More sugar less salt, more whey to replace pricey constituent elements perhaps. Manufacturers have been found altering their creations gradually, bit by bit, praying that consumers don't notice. Some chocolate makers for example have reduced the cocoa content significantly. Down from a third of the bar to a fifth. Hence why your perceived preference for chocolate may dissipate. You preferred products of the past rather than the concoctions of the present. Endless other examples could be cited in support of this. If your preferences haven't changed, then you need to see what has. Should I mention a large drinks manufacturer that dropped the formula that had been using for decades in favour of a new improved variety? This new stuff came out ahead in every focus group. People said it tasted better. However, all the people that liked the old variety went from town to town buying every last can stockpiling what they could. Let's just say the new drink was quietly dropped and the old mixture returned back on the shelves after the company lost a small fortune.

Associations

Being ill can make you appreciate your life at times. These periods can make you somewhat thankful when you feel good. It can also give you a time to reflect. It is often said that to be a little ill, enough to take the day off work but not so bad that you wish you were dead, is quite sanctifying.

Illness prevention is also an aim of many. Irrespective of any concrete truth, drinking fresh juice might ward off colds, and is gleefully consumed when the rest of the family are groaning with exaggerated expressions. You hear them throw up in the toilet. Sometime later you follow suit, re tasting the orange juice drank shortly beforehand. From then on, the sight of orange juice brings back memories of that time. You drank it happily, readily before but now you declare that you would prefer something else to drink instead. These associations are powerful. They can linger for a long time. In some cases, you might avoid oranges and orange juice for some years. However, after several hundred revolutions of the earth you try it again. Maybe with a little trepidation and some attention seeking displays, fanfares, then the announcement that you like orange juice again. You have returned to the former state with the original list of most liked drinks in the same order.

The intensity of the associations can result in it bordering on a phobia. A total rejection of something that you inherently like, but avoid because of bad experiences associated with it. In such instances significant effort is required to dismantle the connections in your mind derailing your preferences. Associations of course need not be bad. We can be seduced by positive images through advertising and peer influence. Our friends may like something and we concur, not because we have found it for ourselves but because we respect their opinions. Image, presentation and fitting-in play a role but deviate us from the original precept of being at one with ourselves. Saying you like something, or being hoodwinked into thinking so can be polite and diplomatic, but not honest.

Fixed but mired in complexity. It is a cornerstone of who we are as individuals. Besides our preferences, other things are fixed, namely our affinities and the limit to our abilities. Affinities being similar to things we prefer but that which we actively seek out. Nurture will play a big role, big indeed, but never can one really change underlying aspects of our personal design given to us by our parents.

Limits to your abilities

"If you try hard enough you can achieve anything."

If you are a midget, two-foot-tall, you are extremely unlikely to beat the world high jump record. Not just unlikely, totally improbable. Someone could try for years on end with the best training, the best running shoes and with the finest diet coupled with the most perseverance imaginable. Yet no matter how hard they try they will never even come close to beating the fastest runners and highest jumpers on earth. You have in other words defined limitations.

There are maximums to your abilities physical and mental. These limits are set out in your design. To reach the greatest potential you will need to be made right, right from conception. If your mother ate well and you were not hampered by a polluted environment, then you have more chance of getting close to the theoretical top of your game. A massive amount of practice, refinement and doggedness would be essential to exploit your potential completely. The effort is the nurture the design is the nature. It is all very well saying that someone could have got there if they tried harder but they may have put everything they had into something and still fall short of expectations.

Your mind will be configured in a way that gives you excellence in certain thinking based activities. It might appear to be more malleable than other physical constraints. However, your mental makeup has constraints regardless of its adaptability in the same way as you have a maximum stride length and limited running endurance. Certain drugs will of course enhance performance and increase the rate of improvement a bit. The boundaries of your design envelope can be pushed and stretched by artificial means, though it puts you at risk of a premature death. Some will go down this avenue despite these risks. Realigning your potential in such a way doesn't imbue upon your natural limits laid down in your personal design.

When we take something up like learning an instrument or join a sport we make good progress at first. We try to get good at it. However, as time goes by and we work and work at it, we find the increments of improvement becoming smaller and smaller. We find our limit and to get a tiny bit better we have to put ever increasing amounts of practice in for less and less reward. This can be the point where we resign ourselves to the realisation that we might be better having a go at something else. We reach our maximum potential in that field.

Finding yourself is about the understanding that your preferences can't be changed and that you have to discover what you like through experimentation. It also means that you have to get over any bad experiences that you may have along the way. The world changes but what we like does not. You also need to be realistic about what you can achieve. If you have been at it for a good while there is little chance that you will get as good as some of the people that you look up to. Your affinities in the sexual sense are unchangeable. What you like is what you like and there is only exploration to work out what is most preferable at stake.

"I still believe my preferences have changed over time."

If you lost your sense of smell what happens then? Some unfortunate souls have lost this fabulous sense when they caught the flu and it never returned. Smell links with taste. Food no longer tastes of much and you are left with only texture to go by. How then can we still prefer strawberries over gooseberries?

A guillotine came down quickly, too quick for your reactions and you are without a hand. Prosthetics help and are improving all the time but it can alter what you want to do now, maybe spurring you on in a different direction with multiple upsides. The time wasted throwing javelins can now be spent on one handed golf. Consider the preferences you have been infused with as the central core. To access them you need your sensory inputs and the physicality of your body to garner its movement and hits it is subjected to. You are degrading daily. The more you degrade, the more confused you become in terms of your preferences.

When you emerged from the birth canal or were whipped out narrowly missed by the sharpest scalpel you begun the process of discovery. The milk, warmth and being held tightly to the bosom of those cultivating you weighed far more than sexual activity you may have twenty years down the line. You can truly hear a pin drop, along with hearing that is heading towards its peak performance, sight sense of touch and dexterity improve then deteriorate. Your body has no hearing on the makeup of your preferences. It only has an influence on whether you can explore them. You may be born with the capability to handle a flute with aplomb but detest every aspect of it. You may wish but a wish is all it will every really amount to.

Pressure to conform, incentive to change along with expectations and snide remarks about what you like hinder your ability to do what is right for you. An awful lot of things can get in the way, some shaping and coercing you to think that their preference is what you should prefer too. Habits and the path of freewill only add to the mush in your head. People around you put subtle stress on your behaviour and guide you towards things that are against your personal likes. We say that what we prefer has changed but that is when we fail to look deep enough. When you have a proper go at more things you can assess what is fixed within you.

Happiness

There are standard survival priorities; protection, then shelter, water and food. There is no point being snuggled up in a camp with food and drink galore if you are going to be eaten by an army of ants or mauled by a bear. We each put having somewhere safe to spend the night high up on the list of important things to sort out. This applies to the mega rich moguls who are fearful of being kidnapped to the homeless people. Nothing is worse than trying to go to sleep with the fear of someone setting fire to you with your alcoholic breath or beating you up for some perverse few minutes of entertainment. The second consideration for your hideout is whether it provides shelter from the wind and rain and once that is resolved you think more about something to stop your tummy rumbling. What prey has this got to do with happiness one may wonder? Well the list of survival priorities extends out to less vital things, more towards things of added comfort. As each of these items fall into place the potential for happiness evolves.

Hours and hours can be whiled away discussing the complex subject of happiness. Another angle on it is to consider how all the things that affect your mood contributes a lot to how you feel in terms of happiness overall. I defy anyone to stay in a cold damp place for any length of time and say that they feel happy right there and then. Warmth and shelter is one of the most basic tenets of happiness, no matter how wealthy or masterful you are. Sure, it is nice to go out and get some fresh air especially when being inside a stuffy room for a while but standing in the cold and rain or sweltering in the heat waiting for a non-existent bus can soon become pretty miserable. Obviously this has little bearing on how you feel about your job and it does not adjust the happiness you find in a relationship that is going well. It is just your mood at the time. However, all these things and more come together to build on happiness in general.

You may be hungry and irritable as a means to lose weight or because no food is available. Some can be contented with the simple luxury of a few beers in the fridge and a pie in the oven. Those with a nice warm house to return to along with many essentials found in life may seek finer dining experiences to get greater happiness whereas a beggar looks closer at food and drink for mere survival. It is all relative.

There can be a never ending search for more. It is the search and seeking with the plotting and planning that brings the happiness rather than a wish to be contented with what you have already. It can relate to having something to aim for. The problem arises when you wish for too many things that are unrealistic and this failure to accept that much in life is unobtainable results in you being unable to appreciate all the things that you do have in place at the moment.

Doing things a little differently, changing what you wear even and refining the little details can all add up leading to a transformation of a humdrum aspect of living to an electric dream. Routine with delight and relish. Not so much busy, but sufficiently occupied yet leaving time spare to deviate at will. A schedule that marks out days rather than blots the landscape. It is so easy to find yourself with too much to read, examine and digest, maybe feeling obliged to respond to heaps of it as well. Some call it information overload, burdened with keeping up with what is supposed to be fun and pleasurable interaction. It is easy to be sold an illusion. You look at other people and get the impression that keeping abreast with everything is essential and that you are missing out on so much vital stuff. One day you wake up so to speak. You realise that it isn't necessary and only wish you came to this conclusion earlier.

No matter who you are, you can put variety and change into the equation. 'Variety is the spice of life' becomes one of many sayings that is hard to improve on. Even those things that we say we enjoy the most can have variety built in. Different ski runs to amble down or being challenged by other players with their different styles of play. People have gone camping and found eight different ways to cook a potato. It is rare to find happiness in doing the exact same thing over and over for extended periods.

People do find some things they like doing and repeat it many times. It seems the same at first glance. Some things we do not get bored off so easily. There is a similar thrill and some variation with a different atmosphere at each event plus other people to meet. We find ourselves needing to justify our repetitive behaviour to others that have lives full of repetition themselves. They think they are making progress with something and fail to understand the fun you get. There is after all no need to question what and why we do things if they are giving us great joy.

Having a soulmate, someone who you are predominantly at ease with and warts in their character that are excusable. Find your reward and you find your own happiness.

Some can't sleep if they know they have to get up early hence they will engineer their programme to avoid early departures and you can't blame them if they can get away with it.

Through this examination of the things that have an effect on your day to day mood you can see what might make you happy/unhappy in the present. Happiness will fluctuate but the underlying sense of it is bound up in the small realities of our situation. Each thing that affects our mood adds up to the overall level of wellbeing. Animals have basic needs which if left unattended cause misery.

Happiness can be influenced by the discovery of the things that you find most preferable and being in a position to enjoy them. The idea of exploring what you like the most is all very well in principle but can be a challenge for many. Having the money helps but it can all depend on whether you can get the time as well to do more of what you want. Hence why many have given up well paid jobs to create more freedom in their lives and never looked back.

The whole complete mood list is somewhat arbitrary and not easy to pin down. It may include the frequency of conversations with certain people, involvement in the bigger grander schemes and building intimate personal relationships. Summarising them with a single word is insufficient as what does it for you may not appeal in the slightest to another. Some will get far more pleasure from new experiences than an expansion in the collection of physical material objects and vice versa. You may trade time with wealth or swap peace and quiet for the hubbub of city life. The yearning for the looks of youth may not be compensated by the change in stature.

The list of things that affect our mood is likely to incorporate discourse, discussion, debate and general interaction with others as this can be very uplifting. It matters less about the status of who you are with than the quality of the conversation. On top of that there can be thoughts about getting the time to be alone for periods, giving us opportunities to relax and think. Balance this with moments participating with other amiable and like-minded people and things can be good. Being isolated when you crave company is soul destroying. Happiness rarely falls on your plate, most have to work real hard not just in a job but by working on friendships and going out to find the right mix of people to spend time with.

Your conversation can be somewhat limited when you do little in your life. By making the effort to go out visiting places close by or faraway just for the sake of it, for the change of scenery, can provide width to your character.

On a personal level, we get a lot of satisfaction when we complete a task. We like to see some progress and feel as though we are moving forward. There is a big difference in how we feel about ourselves when we do something to a high standard rather than leaving after bodging a job. If you're happy I'm happy. No nagging spouse, no griping child, no disaffected complaining customers.

Many people will have the basics in place; they will have a nice home a reasonable income and a family in good health. They might amass numerous items to display and utilise. Then they may start seeking something more, higher forms of fulfilment. They may wish to bolster their self-esteem, toy with philanthropy, or seek what they regard as some form of spiritual enlightenment. All the aforementioned and more is predicated by your health and being free of debilitating pain.

All the little things that alter the mood converge to create the level of happiness at a given time in your life. There is the mind-set to consider, a possibility that an evaluation of what is good here and now which can alter the sense of positivity. Sometimes we need a reminder, a visit to someone with a large house all nicely furnished and plenty of trimmings inside and out. Then the bitter pill to swallow, they lost an only child in a road accident and things around them is just material. They know the life the child did have was superb but the 'what ifs' the 'if onlys' linger with help to move on not even wanted.

It becomes evident that the people with more years behind them have in their own way and to their own extent, explored their world and found what fits their preferred lifestyle. They become less interested in further exploration and adventure as they already have pursued many avenues already. They usually find where they want to live and how they like to pass their time. Some older individuals can become reticent to any changes in their locality as they become accustomed to the way things are and prefer it to remain so. Younger people are more prepared and excited about any modernisation of their state, as change for them in this respect is more appealing. The older folk obtain their change via a pattern that they have adopted and developed. They might have a range of pursuits keeping them occupied with perhaps lots of variation throughout any given week. This can be rather different to the more randomness found in youth and the greater willingness to do things impulsively. Few decline the draw of settling down and being happy without life's excesses, there is still a lot of fun to have but it is much more subtle in its manifestation.

Being down

You are what you are. If you break your leg you know for sure what it was like before to walk about. You can get it put in plaster and after a few weeks all is well again. When your mind goes awry you may seek a similar fix. Take some pills or gabber with a therapist every Tuesday afternoon for weeks on end. The problem is hidden, it's internal and it is a menace that is for sure. However, don't discount the possibility that it is just the way you are. We ask whether we have known different, have we always been like this. Did we simply suppress the feelings in the past but find it much harder to do that now?

Some can be afflicted with a tiredness that clouds the whole of the waking day. No matter what change in diet or change in behaviour the debilitating effect is not alleviated and certainly not by thoughts alone. On the other hand, many a down depressed individual is on the lookout for a resolution that is outside of themselves. You may have a normal natural cycle to cope, contend with and handle. Are you attempting to put on a show, to prove your worth, to justify your birth and demonstrate that the world needs you? The world needs nobody, nobody in particular just enough fine people to keep things in order when demanded. You may find it more productive to get used to your wild mood swings and come to a realisation that we are all different, we were never meant to be like what everyone else appears to be and the resolution is inside us.

Having a problem free life may sound appealing but being problem free can be a problem in itself. Having something to address and fix can be a part of the reason we want to live. People get a lot from seeing something through and finding a way through all sorts of problems. Find a fix for someone. Make their life easier. Solve a problem that stops them doing things they enjoy. It makes them happy and can bring a tear or two of joy on your own face.

Are you drawn more to those that are miserable or those that have a smile on their face? Like laughter, smiling is contagious. Most people will smile back at you and you can at least gauge their sincerity. Few of us can say "hello" in 200 languages but smiling crosses all boundaries. I think we need to be reminded about how great it is to smile. Having you spotted the hidden should?

Some will point out that if you spend too much time around depressed people you become down yourself. Many make a proactive choice to steer clear, leaving these people to dwell in their persistently miserable state on their own. Contact with others invariably proves to be uplifting. I found that it pays to try and try again with people that are down. Unfortunately, there are times where the only way forward ultimately is to provide some space in the hope they begin to realise that they themselves are driving others away through their negative and pessimistic views on life.

There are many triggers for a spell feeling down, depression. It can be the stress of your situation or sometimes, we and others like us are set upon. We have been marked out as less worthy or deemed to be doing something they object to. We find the only way to cope is by laughing off the insulting remarks of these belligerent people. We can't change the world to the way we feel it should be in a day.

Finding yourself unable to get a point across can make us spiral downwards. You try and present logical sensible reasoning, but despite that they don't want to listen at all. Mr I-know-best appears to have jumped to the wrong conclusion. Whether rightly or wrongly they are dismissive. Is there a solution to that wave of fed-up-ness than comes over you? You may need to ask if that is the sole person that needs to be convinced. It might be worth rechecking what you have to say anyway. Sometimes you leave it a while and try another tack. You will encounter the utter arrogant that will never be swayed, the activist who is on a mission that is not flexible. Alternatively we can be in a situation mired in bureaucracy. It is pretty grim to have to wait for the slow process of getting your voice heard if not by a jury but by someone that is willing to listen and take heed. What you do in the meantime is more often than not in your hands though.

Blame

Blame it on our parents, blame on it all the torture metered out in school, blame it on an illness or some disability, but never blame anything on our own stance.

Many rich people have become rich because of a life in poverty in their early years and an unbending desire to go so much further than their parents. From an abusive home emerges a person with a desire to help and intervene in the woeful situations of many in despair. The negative aspects of our upbringing form our personality, without it we would not be at such an advantage. It does not have to be something that makes us feel like giving up and seeing everything as down and depressing. From the ashes of a past life of hell we can come out strong and it can give us the resolve to do an awful lot of positive. You can only look at what you can do now, everything you can't is academic. Holding a grudge is the biggest waste of time ever. It is used instead to change, to stand for it no longer and actually see benefits it gives to your identity. Those given the most privileges and easiest of times, those who felt as though they were a prince/princess, praised endlessly for insignificant achievements that took no effort or resolve find themselves becoming wayward, confused and disappointed, much more so than those who went through a huge struggle. If you have come through the worst of the worst, it is unlikely to go downhill further unless you sink into your own mire of self-pity. Once people begin to love themselves, they can give and take love in large chunks from so many that are willing to share. If only you make the effort to go seek it.

Fair

In goes the coin, out comes nothing. Everyone using the vending machine got what they paid for except you. This can make you feel frustrated and cheated not just unlucky. You are standing close to the till in your local café and notice that someone else is paying less for their coffee than you. Had you not found out about it, it would not bother you. You have always felt happy with the service each time you went, but are wondering why have you been treated differently. Why them and not me?

Is it reasonable to charge those that can afford more, more? Is it fair to have a local price and a different price for holiday makers? Is it fair that some people can get a better deal because they are better at haggling than you? It is the knowledge of knowing that other people are getting things for less that causes consternation. We can be happy with our arrangements with suppliers until we get shown the different way they treat their other customers. It can be more about principle than the real need to make cost savings.

A government tried a progressive system of variable payments. Rather than mess with different tax rates they dealt with the inequities between the rich and the poor by bringing in a grand new scheme to level the people. Each person was issued a card so that whenever they bought something the amount they paid varied according to how much they earnt. So, a humble character in a low paid job paid 1 for their coffee and the big boss paid 15. Not much work was done by the lowly for they spent 90% of the day fetching teas and coffees for their seniors. Outside of work they were found loitering outside shops doing very much the same.

We like fairness but only when it suits us. Few shy away from being a member of the privileged set if the opportunity arises. To be thought of as a VIP even for just one night is attractive. We want to feel worthy and as good as the rest, not marked out nor victimised. When we come across some form of discrimination we see it as a challenge to work out what we are doing wrong. The cafe owner can charge what they like to whoever they like as it is their café, but some do not see it that way. Favouritism is not viewed as endearing.

The whole point of a government is to protect the citizens from dangers at home and abroad. It is also there to try and reduce any unfairness and discriminatory behaviour. We squeal and make the most noise when we see unfairness and discriminatory behaviour that affects us personally. We like to enforce fair play and get equal treatment yet won't always turn down the chance to jump the queue. Being more important gives us more privileges whether earned through hard work, certification or because our parents belong to a higher class. Some propose special car lanes to avoid the traffic jams, priority and the first choice in all offerings. The reasons they give are always pretty poor, they think they are above the rest and fairness is discretionary.

Life is fundamentally unfair. Nothing can change that. If you happen to be good at something that is also popular you have a chance of capitalising on it. Those born with a great voice may make a good living from singing. Is it fair that those who love to sing but sound like a strangled frog can't have a singing career like others can?

Life can also be more of a struggle if your body doesn't fit the norm. Nobody is really normal as such, but having 2 fully functioning arms and 2 functioning legs etc. is the modal, mean, typical way humans are designed. Fairness is irrelevant if you are born 'defective' whatever that may mean. Cynically one could blame behaviour in a past life for the state you have been reborn into. Realistically that is utter nonsense. You are a lucky/unlucky mash up of your ancestors.

Those that have physical superiority sometimes abuse it. I have seen and been involved with these moments when people won't take a joke. Rather than see the funny side they resort to some physical action. Suddenly the aggressor grabs someone by the throat or puts them in some kind of head lock. The victim feels more than just aggrieved, they feel powerless and humiliated. What makes these situations worse is that other people just stand by and don't intervene.

Now consider the times when you begin to cross a road at a pedestrian crossing point and notice that an oncoming car doesn't appear to be stopping. You have right of way, but could end up being dead right. Instead you are forced to step back onto the pavement. This too can be a quite annoying. In both examples, it feels unfair, rule breaking. It is no good complaining afterwards if you are strangled to death, mowed down or have your face rearranged. Once again life is unfair and the only course of action is prior. Look out for the warning signs and back off before they jump on you. We have to accept that certain people are dangerous, like tigers and lions that won't hesitate to maul you given the opportunity.

Being badly violated or seriously harmed is a much bigger price to pay than the ignominy of quickly retreating. For those blessed with intelligence at the expense of great strength, reading the body language early is helpful. Having sensed trouble, you can calculate and plan a fast exit.

In the long run, there is no point in trying to fight everyone. Even the strongest will be defeated eventually, either by someone nimbler or plain luckier. Well-built self-assured individuals have often been caught out by nefarious use of small weapons. Learning to accept loss of pride in the moment and not having to worry about saving face is humbling but safer. We can step back and allow them to pass, steer clear out of their way and extract the best in life. It is less about the rights and wrongs and more about deciding if it is worth the risk. Survivors are always aware of potential trouble heading in their direction.

Many young people get assaulted, raped or destroyed before reaching full maturity. Fairness doesn't come into this either. It is part of the rough and tumble of life. There will always be dreadful things going on. It is not what we would like societies to be in an ideal world. It is the consequence of the random chaotic nature of the world that brings life in the first place.

Excuses aplenty

Wherever you live there is always some onus on the individual to make an effort to further themselves. Some people have read the book entitled "1001 reasons and excuses for not doing something" and studied it or unwittingly seem to know it inside out. They then have plenty of ammunition to formulate a valid explanation for why things are delayed or not done. If they had used that time making a start instead of coming up with excuses they would be half way towards finishing.

"It is alright for you." Is one of my favourite sayings. It great for winding people up. It also expresses how other people have unfair advantages. Alternatively, that I don't want to make the effort that you have.

You can be positive with some pessimism; Disappointment is expected. Each failure is another avenue checked out. The proactive trier. Another way is to be negative and optimistic. Everything is done half-heartedly. One day someone will detect how valuable you are and raise you above the parapet. The fantasist. Then there is the vagrant who is respected for their free living. Instead of constantly moaning about the situation they rejoice in the unencumbered nature of their life.

To some the idea of profit is evil. If you get into the mind-set of killing any profit that those you deal with make, then things spiral downwards. Your greed pushes people to cut corners and opens the doors to counterfeiters and cheats. Your local cafe owner will start to buy lower grade coffee and use out of date milk. Paying a fair price can result in higher standards so long as we don't become emotionally wedded to inefficient businesses.

To Mock

I doubt that any person can go through life without being subjected to some sort of teasing one way or another, usually about something that is personal and unique to them. People enjoy making fun of others and in a way it helps us unite and get to know one another. It can be used to break down barriers and even lead to political change. When it becomes overly personal and too hurtful, we can look for ways to deal with it.

Whilst it is considered good to educate and condemn the bullies, it is extremely worthwhile teaching the victims some practical methods to handle being teased and taunted. The remedy is in being able to reflect and dispel the attack, and with practise it is very easy to do. If someone makes a joke about you then laugh with them, laugh even more than they do. Learn to find it funny yourself and, (a) It won't hurt, (b) people are much less likely to repeat it.

Those that seem displeased, most aggravated by the mockery get more and more teased. If you appear somewhat distraught and they see the visible effect it has on you they are more inclined to keep doing it. Getting annoyed and frustrated only amplifies their attack. Dispelling the joke by laughing with them avoids the demonstration of being hurt. Some over laugh making it appear false, it is about laughing as much as you would if laughing about someone else except that it is you that it is aimed at. In a sense, it is like an invisible person that you are laughing at. Many people have found that they can genuinely see the funny side, even though they are the one being made fun off. They feel minimal pain with no great anguish at all. Other people have had to work on it for a good while before the indifference sinks in.

Those with an odd name will hear the same joke over and over. Each person that comes out with it thinks they are the first one to do so. A refined response is used. We can think of a funny retaliation as ammo to reflect the humour back on them. Each reflection will be different for each person and modified according to the situation. I used to get irritated by people saying that I spoke too fast. They would keep asking me to repeat what I had said even though they understood me most of the time. So I would just say "Sorry I will s p e a k v e r y s l o o o w l y so that your little mind can keep up." Bouncing it back in this way turns the tables and the hurt is no longer felt. The provocateur is less likely to make such comments again. It needs to be done with a big smile and in a friendly way though. Sit down and consider a reflection for your individual case, try it out and modify it and the problem will go away. Learn to laugh with them and the pain and distress disappears.

A few people who are under pressure in their work will sometimes release their frustration on weaker individuals. Making fun of others and bullying them provides the mechanism to allay their own ineptitude and difficulties. In the main, ignoring them is usually the most effective policy, but where this is little probability of violence many can find a friendly retort to the jokes.

Making a joke once can be acceptable, making the same joke twice becomes less so. Where it goes on and on it turns into to a form of demonisation. This can have dangerous consequences. Large scale ethnic disputes begin with demonisation of other groups. Over time the disrespect gets published and broadcast in multiple areas of the media. This alters people's general perception about certain types and some might even begin to attack them physically. Trouble of some sort arises when we treat these differences with contempt and begin describing them with words that have parallels with lower life forms. If you say; "they are no better than a sewer rat" people are inclined to treat them according to that perception. This is the starting point of the events leading up to genocides. The opposite misconception arises when we refer to somebody as being 'godly' and then worship them as though they really are more important than the rest of us.

If in front of a wall plastered with pictures of peoples' faces we spot those that we can relate with. Some you have a special compassion for, a little bit more that the rest and you can identify the reason if you are unashamed to admit why. If someone works at the same place as you or is a member of the same club a connection is easily recognised and empathy is more forthcoming. This process may have originated when we became accustomed to recognise someone as being 'one of us' right from mankind's early period. The converse is where we see someone as being alien, an outsider and maybe singled out for some rather petty distinctions.

Any long-standing group will have ample strength to take some flak from time to time. Organisations need to accept some criticism but when it becomes relentless it could lead to something unforgivable. There are many groups that want it both ways. They want to curtail any mockery aimed at them and also use the freedoms of expression to push equally offensive ideas of changing the fabric of the nation they are in.

Humour

Have you ever finished someone else's sentence? We predict what people are going to say well before they finish a sentence.

83

If they say something you do not expect, something we did not anticipate, it can be humorous. As a comedian knows all too well, it is also about timing. The unexpected part has to arrive in people's mind at the exact same time as they arrive at a prediction of what they expected you to say. You have to pause to allow them to work out what you might say, then say the unexpected thing. Hence why it is not just timing that is so crucial, but why jokes you hear before don't create much laughter, as you know what is coming and can foresee it.

Priming helps but jokes out of the blue can be as comical. We use tomfoolery to aid the bonding process between people in our group. It has been suggested that the tickle reflex is a mechanism to aid parents to bond with their children even though extensive tickling is known to be torturous. You can be aroused and more receptive to humour in larger audiences because of the contagious nature of it. Laughing at someone when they fall or spill something on themselves is stoked by our competitive spirit.

A disciplinarian does not shout, instead they talk quieter than normal and close up. When we whisper on purpose people notice the drop in level and want to know what the secrecy is all about. Fake laughter has a similar effect as it draws attention. You can bug people by laughing to yourself whether intentional or not, sometimes because your mind is wandering and falls upon an amusing event in the past unrelated to what is going on around you at the time. Laughter in any form is therapeutic and causing it plays a part in our social status. People warm to those that smile or can make them laugh. We also use it as an inclusive mechanism and will laugh even when we don't get the joke to not feel left out. Having a nonplussed face soon after someone has reached the punchline sours the occasion, so many will laugh anyway as it improves friendships significantly.

Farting might be seen as disgusting by some but it can cross boundaries in its ability to make people smirk. Jokes do not always translate very well because there is not always the same ambiguity and potential to play on words. Nevertheless, there can be a lot of reliance upon unexpected ways of saying things. That person with the floral dress and long wavy hair is pretty.....ugly.

Children

You need not travel far to have one of the biggest and best adventures of your life; having children. Whilst the first couple of years can be particularly taxing, a bit of an ordeal, after two or so years things invariably improve dramatically. Your offspring become far more interactive and begin the transition from being a pain to become little helpers. It remains joyous until a small period in their teens when hormones run wild. It is at that point when mind games and other new challenges arise. Those that take a different view, where they see nothing but difficulties at all ages, might want to see if a different approach to their parenting makes life easier.

A lot of people think they are doing everything the right way when it comes to parenting. They are often reluctant to admit that they have any shortcomings. Here we can simply compare your ways to some alternatives. Although most parents do well in a lot of respects, there is often room for improvement. There is never an absolute right way in every situation. Those who don't have children may have childish adults to contend with and can use the same handling techniques.

A magnet will pick up metals, iron in particular. Try using a magnet to pick up a wine glass and you find it will not work. So, there is a kind of natural order. It is a bit cheeky to apply that principle to children as a way to claim that some things work better. Nevertheless, those seeking ways to make is easier, less stressful, might like something to consider especially when a child is hard to manage. All without being too insistent that there is only one correct way in every circumstance.

In some countries, you move a car a few yards and get given a driving licence. In other places, you sit with an instructor for thirty hours or more and get given intensive instruction. When it comes to children we don't have to pass a test before we are allowed to bring a sperm in contact with an egg. If your children are not assets, but liabilities are you not fishing around with that magnet hoping for it to stick? Typically, we have a parenting style that is similar to that of our own parents. Occasionally we will make a change or two, sometimes shifting from one extreme to another.

It is never too late to amend wrong decisions and badly implemented ideas that you thought were for the best. There is really only one true aim; to create independent offspring. Children than can manage on their own with less and less support from you. Pretty obvious given that humanity cannot continue otherwise. Whilst for some this is not possible due to physical and mental handicaps, the more they can do for themselves the better, better for them and you.

Patience

We see a child struggle and we jump in to assist. This is a mistake. At bath time, we are faced with two options. Either we help the little'un get the clothes off or we patiently wait for them to pull, push, twist and tug to remove the awkward clothes for themselves. Those that pause for the few seconds whilst they wrestle with the task recoup that time quite quickly over the coming months. It might mean standing aside for anything up to a minute or more or and it can seem like an eternity when watching. This investment is not meant to invite people to consider it like an accountant where time assets are calculated and tabulated, for it is a mere principle at heart.

A father couldn't do a lot following a bad accident. His son was not going to do everything for him for ever more. This father could not walk, far from it. However, the son goaded him to crawl on his hands and knees day after day. So began a long journey back to independence. Many an onlooker was scornful of the son's methods; they saw it as degrading. The son continued on this course regardless ignoring those that considered it humiliating and rather disrespectful. As time passed the father eventually regained use of his legs and was the better for it. Far better than being stuck in a chair day and night, waited on hand and foot. It is so easy in to intervene rather than stand back and allow someone to push through the difficulties by themselves. It feels so much quicker to help, but on the long term, it becomes a drain for everyone.

There are a lot of similarities between children and people that have had injuries. Physiotherapists encourage recovering patients to do things on their. Moving forward to regain use of the limbs is only possible through perseverance. It is hard to watch and refrain from taking over. The more you get the child doing for themselves, the more they will be able to tackle by themselves throughout their lives.

Some people have been known to do school work for their children. What is the point? Is zero marks worse than doing zero work?

Options

Giving a child options can make things very messy indeed. In a classic case of telling a child to go to bed, many will say;

"Go to bed now or you will not have any sweets tomorrow."

This contains the curse of providing an option. The child will probably get the sweets anyway and might consider it better to stay up late than having a few treats. Your command is being undermined. Simply repeat "go to bed now" over and over and bit-by-bit they edge towards the door, then up to bed. Ignore their protestations and stick to the instruction, no deviation, and no compromise. If they come back down, pick them up, without any discussion and put them back in their room. Repeat until they stay in bed. If you give them more than one option they can choose, but by providing only one option the problems created by choice are removed.

It is not about becoming akin to a military commander, but each time they disobey your instructions you edge one step closer to losing all control. People ask nicely, get ignored, so shout, get ignored again then after even more yelling still get ignored.

Those that never allow their children to get the upper hand in the first place manage to become authoritative parents without having to resort to aggression and ill-tempered actions. Patience and persistence is the key, never backing down. The irony is that we like teachers more if they can control the class. Fashionable new age willy nilly styles might sound progressive, but throwing out old tried and tested methods is plain pointless.

Sometimes you realise that what you asked them to do was not particularly important, but now that you have, you still need to insist they do as requested regardless. The child has a gadget that you want to use and they fold their arms with it held tucked in. You ask them over and over to hand it to you and then reconsider whether you really need it. Having asked them for it, you can no longer back down. If you don't get your way, the next time it gets even more difficult. Soon they find more and more ways of doing what they want ignoring your instructions.

The minute you start letting them win you begin the slide down into eternal grief. Letting them win does not refer to allowing them to have a head start in a board game, which some parents might do to give them hope and more engagement. Instead it means that if you make a ruling you must stick to it right through to the end consistently. Too many parents will get exasperated and give up allowing the child to take over. As the years pass you end up with less and less control and it becomes a bigger headache trying to be at peace with them.

People find that it not necessary to be particularly controlling. It is merely about setting a boundary and if ever the line is crossed you reign it in. Why waste time and effort getting them to tidy their bedroom if it is not a fire hazard, just close the door and forget about it.

Some parents will have many children and find one that is a bit more awkward than the rest. This extra challenge needs more patience than ever, but all kids are fundamentally the same and can be nurtured equally well. Make no mistake, no child is so special that standard techniques of handling them do not apply. It is a battle of wills between adult and child. The adult has to dig deep to find the capacity to prevail. Having said that, is it possible that you have a psychopathic super awkward one on your hands? Maybe, but on balance of probabilities it is unlikely.

They can't have what you haven't got. So, when you offer a yellow lolly and they start getting into a tantrum because they want a red one, just take no notice. Why some would go to great lengths to explain that the shop it out of red ones and this is all you have is perplexing. "Do you want it or not?" introduces them to the realities of life; we can't always get what we want when we want.

Discipline

Rarely is anything gained by hitting, smacking or aggressively disciplining a child. Violence breeds more violence and the ugly tone gets passed down for generations. We believe it is acceptable because it is what we experienced ourselves during our own childhood. Breaking the chain and trying new tactics is admirable and a lot easier than one might think. Those that smack do not benefit. The child will not benefit. You may be able to vent your anger and frustration, but no child deserves to be treated harshly.

If for example your toddler comes up from behind and bites you unexpectedly, it is common for people to lash out. Reacting in this way is hard to avoid and is similar to an involuntary response to an insect stinging. However, running after them and hitting them is not reasonable. Instinctive reactions may be an exception to the no violence rule, but most people will only find themselves in this situation once or twice in the whole of a child's life.

Some people may witness a child hitting another child then smack the child for doing so. This brings about the assumption in the child's mind that lashing out is acceptable particularly if you are bigger or stronger than the victim. You will always achieve a more desirable result by communicating calmly; that hitting others won't be tolerated and is unnecessary.

Shouting and raising your voice is best kept for real emergencies, when the house is on fire, not because the bins haven't been emptied. Raising your voice is self-defeating; it becomes normal and gradually less and less effective. Shouting is only suitable for instances where there is a major problem. If you talk to them in a quiet manner they will listen more, copy you and shout less too. Everyone gets stressed out. It doesn't get the respect that we wish for, it is more likely to create resentment.

When they are acting badly there is an alternative to shouting "NO, DO NOT DO THAT". Approach them slowly, once close up right in their face, speak in a firm quiet voice, almost a whisper "No, do not do that." Any infrequent shouting remains effective when you reserve it for times when you spot them about to grab a pot of boiling water.

Some people have taken the view that discipline is paramount so that the child learns to behave and is always respectful of their elders. However, many many others have demonstrated that it is without doubt, avoidable and damaging on the whole. The question of when the punishment becomes an assault as the child nears adulthood cannot be answered easily. The violence follows down the line and lots will continue to hit their children as "It did me no harm." The harm that it did was instilling a false idea that that is the only way to bring people into line. Anyway, are children not 'on your side', are they not a kind of team member?

There is often outrage and upset when news of something nasty has happened to a child, yet there seems to be a perverse acceptance of aggressive discipline at home. No child is the same and some will be more testing than others, but all are manageable one way or another.

Violence in whatever form makes it worse for everyone, you and the child. I have seen children dodge the swipes of their mothers learning how to dodge ever quicker rather than learning to behave. It is like the fish in the sea who keep sucking the baby fry into their mouths and spits them back into the nursery area. Once the baby fish learns to be quick enough to avoid getting swallowed they can then make their way out to open waters.

Children will make mistakes. You did when you were a child. How we respond can either instil confidence of a fear of failure. When a child drops some crockery, you can either scream and shout or ask them to clear it up and get another one. No sighing, no anger, no problem. A child who is actually trying to help, gets scolded and then frightened to do things. They learn by being a little embarrassed, a bit sorry for their clumsiness rather than worried that whatever they do could lead to some kind of punishment.

One extreme to another

Our ways are passed down the chain from parent to child. When a child becomes a parent themselves, they often use the same tactics that were used on them in their own childhood. Some however get translated into opposites. You might have felt too restricted in your youth so you decide upon giving your own children much more free reign. Food and manners are hot topics in this regard.

"I was made to eat a whole lot of horrid things when I was young, so my children can eat as little or as much of whatever they like."

You did not like having to sit at the table until you finished a mountain of vegetables, especially ones half cooked or soggy. Therefore, you won't put your kids through that. You hated it. It sticks in your mind hence you decide that is one thing you will not put your kids through. People swing from one extreme to the other though, rather than attempting some sort of commendable balance. You need not force them, but offer a little and encourage them to eat a little. Even a small amount goes a long way towards them getting a healthy diet. If not vegetables, then there are plenty of alternatives that are equally fine. Fret not.

Some parents hate to see children play with their food. Yet experts brought in to get kids to eat more of a variety, begin by getting them to play and feel the food in their hands. Soon after they have it in their mouths.

What happened to you as a child may have been extreme. Have you got the bravery to see that it had some virtue and can be moderated, brought into balance rather than banished completely?

So much fun can be had watching parents employ different tactics in a restaurant. Some will insist their children sit still, bored and frustrated. A pacifier of sorts is brought out. Others allow theirs to run amok. Do we mind a child of ours playing under the table? Not at all. Do we mind them telling yet another table of other diners about the snake their dad caught some years ago? Not at all. Unless they are in clear and obvious danger there is nothing wrong with allowing them to roam within reason. Being naturally curious and wanting to explore the surroundings is a desirable feature of all children. We worry about upsetting other diners, but it is the parents that stand out as the most annoying. Making excuses and labelling them with some form of disorder is a great way of masking parental inadequacies.

Children can be like cats and come to you when they want something. They prefer to be picked up when they want to rather than you grab them when it suits you.

'Ignore bad behaviour and tantrums, always respond positively to good behaviour' is a famous motto. When they play up, turn your head away and wait. When the behaviour becomes acceptable, re-interact. Pandering to the child in their ill-behaved state makes thing worse in the long term. Many parents will have great difficulty with this aspect, especially in public places. Being a little embarrassed a few times is a good price to pay, as these situations will gradually lessen over time. If you want to keep control, then you can't let them take over. They want to go, you want to stay. What to do? The easy option is to bend to their wishes. Playing fair is taking them places they want to go and for them to understand that they need to be tolerant of your wishes too.

It is hard to ignore your child when they are crying and getting steamed up. However, waiting for them to calm down by themselves is for their benefit. They gain from understanding that you will not liaise with them whilst they are behaving unacceptably. A child sulking or screaming must not draw your attention. This only works however, if you do pay them plenty of attention when they are being convivial.

Sweetness and innocence can disappear and in its place a nightmare child is awoken in what seems like an overnight transformation. Bad bad behaviour, more than just tantrums. Your home is a stress zone. It is not just a fit to garner some attention, as each tactic you try just leads to an escalation. Insults. Resentment. Just laugh at them. Make fun of their actions using the best humour you can devise, but never ever display any annoyance. Hard but effective.

Encouragement

It can be tiresome listening to children telling you about things that are so often nonsense, petty or plain dull. It might be banal and boring, but the more active face to face communication they get the greater their language skills develop. The love of being listened to carefully and with interest is felt by all of us. We all appreciate being heard whatever age we are.

A child held up an artwork to show their parents and the parents said "well done". Being somewhat suspicious the child kept showing ever worse pictures each day after school. Each time they said, "that is good, well done". In this case the child was essentially being ignored, quite rude. Those that do make an effort to appraise can be frightened of telling some home truths. It can be very hurtful to tell a youngster that their work is awful. However, fake false praise just delays the pain.

Jeremy, was drawn by an artist that was told their works was childish when at high school. Drawings of a three-year-old at fourteen. Would it still be shite if they were over praised back then? Who knows. You search (for ages sometimes) to point out what is not too bad in their work. Then give a genuine "well done" for each bit of improvement.

A balance between a joyous fun childhood and work for a prosperous adulthood can be found. Some expect too much too soon, putting them under a lot of pressure. Wind your mind back to Joanne at the start of the book. You invest in the future, but do not need to allocate every last drop of energy on a future that may not come. Others take this a little too much to heart and go over the top in an overly laid back attitude. A little learning is fun, excessive amounts puts you off the whole lot.

An easy ride does not bring about any sense of reward. You do not get a great deal of enjoyment from things that you haven't worked hard for. Which child will look after what they are given? Which child will appreciate what they have? Will it be one that has been given too much, too easily or one that has worked hard and earned it? A child who saves up for weeks on end for something will enjoy the result much more. The notion of save and spend extends into adulthood and can help avoid falling into the rut of taking on excessive credit.

The trap, the rut. You have worked hard, passed all your exams. You enter the workforce and have an income now. Time to be rewarded. It is so compelling to get things on credit. You can afford the repayments. However, as each new commitment takes a bite out of your wage packet you have less and less freedom. I owe, I owe, so off to work I go. Even if you never exercise the option of being able to take a month out, take a break away, move completely, change track, it is the psychological uplift, the sense that you can, if you wanted to at some point that is magnificent.

A steady reliable stream of income is desirable for companies and governments. They want you to work and they are adept at making you feel guilty if you are not at the coalface. Buy now, pay later is one more way of taking away any feeling of liberation. Regular tax receipts, predictable payments enable them to plan. You are after all a pawn in their grand game. You are conned into believing that it is what you are supposed to do. We do need the reward provided by work, but it can be free from the weight of conforming.

Each year a certain day is marked out where we feel obliged to buy our children something big and special. The child is past the stage where they play more with the box than the expensive item itself. We might try and persuade a child to value your time more than offerings, but have they are not so easy to fob off any more. Buying them something smaller to avoid going into debt is a far better medium term solution, but we know that they don't understand that. They see all the other kids in the street getting plenty, so why not them too. We resort to a loan of some sort, paying heaps of interest and have less to spend on them later in the year for sure.

If you want to be cruel to be kind make your children suffer the pain of waiting. Open an account at your local savings office. Place a small amount of money in it. Allow the child to place the account access document deep inside their toybox, out of your reach. As each week passes you give them some pocket money or chore redemption cash and they can build a small pot to buy something of significance. Do this in place of going into debt to get them something 'they can't live without'. Yes, it will be a disappointment at first, but at least they will see progress, as the amount in the account builds and finally a definitive end result that they are sure to enjoy, and value. Some promise they will get them what they want next month, but something crops up and it never materialises. If they have the money growing in the account it is so much more honest.

Us not them

We may wish our children to be a doctor or an accountant or be the next great inventor. They say that we should be careful about what we wish for. For most, it is adequate to want nothing more for our children than for them to feel satisfied, content and free.

We see them sleep in till mid-morning and want them in to the world of work, forgetting that young adults need more sleep at this age. You can push and prise, but also live your own life and not have to live it through theirs. We declare that we want them to be happy. The truth can be that we are only happy if they turn out how we imagined they would. When that fails to show, all the pressure we have burdened them with gives rise to an unpleasant late teen life.

Our parents may have had some hopes of how our lives would pan out and we have to respect the disappointment we bring. It is not about changing to keep our parents pleased, but appreciating that they see it as their failure. What may soften the blow is pointing out that although what has materialised is a little different to what was expected, all is well. There is always an upside to provide some reassurance to give them a sense that their efforts have been worthwhile. You say to your parents, "Ok I never managed to be a doctor like you wanted, but I have a good job nevertheless."

Precedence; you, your partner then the children

There is a precedence principle that puts you first followed by your partner then the children. The justification? If you are flagging most of the time, is your partner going to be happy about that. Do your children want to see you being miserable, tired and worn out all the while? You give more when in a good state to give. That means being a little selfish at times. It means doing things for your own benefit too.

There is no exact optimum. If you were to place arbitrary numbers on it, it would be around; 40% yourself, 35% your partner and 25% your children. This is the percentage of money, time and space at your disposal. There will be periods where you go off and do something 100% for you. At other times, you will stop everything to address something for the children. It is only a suggested approximate reasonable average.

Precedence ensures that you yourself are content with your life. It sets out the potential to maintain a good relationship and the children get a fair bit, but are not sucking every last drop of what you have from you. There will be less thinking about all the things I could have done were it not for the bane of having children.

Holidays and days out are chosen sometimes to appease the children and sometimes to fulfil the adults. If they complain, so be it. If they whinge about not getting the latest plaything that all their friends have, then so be it. Adults want their own playthings too and resources are limited. When children turn into self-sustaining entities themselves they can buy whatever they want. They will have years and years to choose how they spend their time.

People send children to bed early so that they can have some quiet time. The idea is that if you have you own quality time, you increase the likelihood of having quality time with the children also. It only works if you maintain flexibility and commitment. Too much emphasis on you or your partner, neglecting the children is not precedence it is unwholesome. Selfishness is two part. We feel good about giving and do some things purely for ourselves. The vital aspect about selfishness is that we have to look after ourselves in order to give.

In practice, you will be doing many of the things that you want to in the areas of work and leisure, which ought to provide a satisfactory level of fulfilment. On the occasions where a child does require extra support you will be in a better frame of mind to provide it.

The flexibility comes out when we bend at times to cater for things that pop up. The commitment could be setting aside one or two nights a week to do an activity on our own and another with our spouse. In that scenario, it still leaves a good few nights where we put the focus on the children. There can be guilt and pressure to spend every night in. We may be doing what we think is right, but if it makes us glum who benefits? A happy home where your children can thrive and feel more comfortable is one where all are getting a share.

Some look forward to the day the children leave home and they retire from their job. Plans are drawn up to explore the world. The day arrives along with a letter from the hospital confirming a terminal illness. These stories are commonplace. We can't do as much as we may like with the responsibilities we have, but we are not as constrained as we make out.

When we take a break away to reflect, we want to return and make some grand gestures. We say we want to appreciate our children more and will change our ways. All those commitments fade quickly and it is never long before normal service resumes. We can change little things to improve our home life that are sustainable, simple pledges. Maybe we decide to stop cooking three separate meals and all sit around the table every day for dinner, banning any distractions too whilst eating. Setting aside one afternoon to do something rather than attempting a resolution that isn't keep-able.

Giving

Are we supposed to appreciate all the efforts our parents make, appreciate all the sacrifices or do we accept it and instead repay it to the next generation, namely the children of our own? Some follow tradition. As our parents age, we can find ourselves lumbered and pressured to look after them as well as our own children. Not easy. Guilt can rear its ugly head. There are some occasions where parents can manage yet keep calling for assistance. It is not always because they really need any help, but because they want some attention and company.

We don't give to receive. We give because we want to and if we expect nothing back from our children we won't be disappointed. If ever in doubt about how much we feel we ought to give to anyone, including our children we can consider the reward drive in us. We get reward when we work for something. Going without to pay for someone's education is tempting and difficult to fault. Whether we give a lot which makes them expect more and have confidence to apply for a high paid job or we fill them with the belief that they can aim high can come from our parents or irrespective of them. If you can afford the amount you give and you are not depriving yourself of the things you and your partner deserve, then why worry. People search for a compromise. Ultimately, a child needs to learn to become independent and the help you give will play a part in this aim. There are always snags in whatever you do.

Step parenting

People might like to think that it shouldn't matter whether the children are biologically yours or not; step parenting is the same as any other parenting. That can be wishful thinking. Take a glance at those families that stated that it is all the same, then as soon as they split up a gulf emerged. Step children commonly desert any former step parents and resort to type.

Taking on the responsibility of a child that is not 'yours' is always going to be different to having a child of your own. Accepting this is important. The circumstances will be different in each family unit, but there will be a lot of things in common regardless of those that think they are a unique case.

As a general rule the step parent will find it easier if they never position themselves as the new mother or father, but simply as a new guardian. This would imply that the step child is in effect a guest in your home. Certain key decisions are often left to be made by the biological parents, pulling the rug from beneath the step parent. This can be particularly frustrating, especially when you take a dim view of the other party.

It is acceptable to make some reasonable ground rules for the step child if they are to be living with you, as any guest would be expected to abide by your rules while in your home. However, problems will often arise if you try to impose your ideals on other people's children. Distancing yourself is not necessarily an inappropriate option in the formative years of a new relationship. Making too much effort can sometimes end up being counterproductive. Focusing your attention on your partner is the key, involving the step children when they are ready to interact congenially.

When the child approaches you in a positive manner you can reciprocate accordingly. When they are pleasant you can be even more pleasant in return. If they are hostile there is no need to retaliate, just let it go. Step children can be fickle, unpredictable and liable to swing from being accommodating to quite awkward quite quickly. Not too dissimilar to many people in the work place. The danger is in the feeling of failure if you don't get on with the child. You can't be expected to get on well and become friends with everyone that you meet during your life and the same principle applies with step children.

It is much easier if you start your relationship with someone from birth than it ever will be at a later stage. In the instances where a disciplinary event arises, there is less heartache when you try to stand aside and let the biological parents control the situation. You are entitled to voice your opinions, but will rarely gain true authority despite the overall effort that you are likely to put in over the years. Some do get to a point where they love and regard the child as one of their own, but this will not always be the case and if this doesn't materialise not everyone will consider it as a failure.

No matter how distant or how poorly perceived the 'real' mother or father may be, there is always a biological inclination for the child to have contact with them to some extent. If you consider that there can still be love and affection between parent and child within the evilest of people throughout the world, it seems pointless trying to interfere with this bond.

Those that create the child have the ultimate influence regardless of all the energy and exertion asserted by the guardians. A reasoned child will give respect and show appreciation to those who brought them up and looked after them in the long run. The more time spent with the guardian and the better the relationship, the greater this respect will be. However, even an absent or absconded parent will always be of interest to the child, and naturally so.

You are a twin. You have a child with somebody. You then get locked up for a while. In your absence your twin gets together with your partner. The child will have a remarkably parallel genetic link to their new guardian. Is it a step child or something else? What about bringing up a child that you think is yours, but is not? Is it the knowledge of who provided the sperm or egg that makes all the difference I wonder.

Impartiality

We struggle to get our voice heard in politics. We rarely change the attitudes of those running churches, but we have some fodder for our ideals; our children. Is the information we give out complete? Is it always neutral and balanced? Nobody can talk about religion, politics and morals with their children without being biased to some extent. It is unavoidable. Some do try hard you try to maintain neutrality. Parents do however have the option of giving their children a reasonable opportunity to determine what practices they wish to follow up. We all have an equal desire to discover the merits of so many things present on the planet.

The weakest concerns/organisations imprison people literally or emotionally. Strong ones allow scrutiny and accept questioning. There doesn't appear to be a single cause that is accepted and adopted by all people the world over (which is probably a beneficial thing) therefore it takes a peculiar arrogance to suggest that a particular one is best. Likewise, there is likely to be untold critics and dissenters of this text and that is a positive. Can you present your beliefs with counter arguments? Sure, we can, but why bother for we are always right. We think our political persuasion suits the most, is the fairest and we are therefore keen to promote it.

A planned accident

"We spent ages looking at all the different pushchairs. Each had different features, some we liked while some had bits that were not necessary. We plumped for one that was in our price range and thought it would be best for our needs. We became unstuck however, a few months later when twins were born."

On the one hand we have societies that did not make the connection between having sex and producing babies, on the other we like to plan and control our child rearing to the letter. What can be frightening is the realisation that procreation is not something we can fully control. Some try for months or years to conceive, some never manage at all and there are the many that can't help but breed like rabbits.

Humankind has been known to drown babies without penises and abort for reasons profound and obscure. This is within our control. Mitosis is not so easy to control. Any one of several billion of your brothers or sisters could have been born instead of you. If only that sperm a few millimetres away had got in first, you would have been spared the torture of this amazing life. Add in the fact that if your father, for reasons aplenty, did or did not make that romantic gesture that evening, maybe your mother would have been less willing to lay back and position herself for conception that month. A person may have been planned, but you specifically we're not. Maybe in some sci-fi future we could predict the nature of all potential persons, but we would have to go against the certainty of randomness.

We didn't choose to be born, but that doesn't impinge on our gratitude for all the care given to us when we are young. We like the idea of settling down and deciding upon having a certain number of children, but nature gets in the way of that. You can't plan it in the same way as you might organise buying a house and furnishing it. There is more accident than planning when having children. Each child will present a different challenge and whilst some ideas here have been helpful to many, nothing stops you finding other, better, solutions. Besides, it barely scratches the surface of what comes our way. We don't have to do everything people suggest to the letter. We are free to improvise and accept that perfection is never attainable when it comes to kids. It is just some are better than others at making excuses for the outcome.

Many children come along in families where one or both parents were not exactly thrilled by the prospect. It is wrong to assume that a child will automatically bring instant pleasure and satisfaction. For many the maternal/paternal instinct is quite muted and remains so even as the children get older. Biology doesn't care. If an accident can happen, it will and there is no need to feel guilty if you are not as enthralled by children as everyone else seems to be. It is hard in some societies to be honest.

Boys, Girls and Freaks

Is it a boy or a girl? This is the first question we ask when someone has a baby. If they have a willy we say it is a boy, if not then we say it is a girl. Once they have been classified as either male or female we then segregate them in a number of ways. Worse still we lay down rules according to the gender given, rules that are often inconsistent and irrational. There are things we let boys do and not girls and vice versa. All because they have a penis or not.

For some though, the question of what sex to assign is a bit problematic. Some have a vagina of sorts along with testis and a malformed penis. It is not clear cut whether we can say they are a boy or a girl. We know that the camp we place them in will have an impact on the whole life ahead of them. God does not assign the gender. Instead a doctor will be brought in to decide as they have had all the specialist schooling. Of course, they are always right every time, without fail and never succumb to human error like the rest of us.

If we are not sure which sex to assign a child of ours we may decide to do something about it. Too many wish to put them in a category of our choice rather than wait for them to emerge as one of their own choosing. Many want the issue resolved right away so babies and toddlers are hastily operated on.

These problem cases may seem rare, but they are not as rare as we like to think. However, most see them as rare enough to be dismissed as exceptions and just 'freaks', freaks of nature. Instead of dismissing these so called 'freaks' as irrelevant they can shine a light on the way we view genders. Maybe the harsh boy-girl separation is something we have been doing for so long throughout history that we struggle to get away from it. The real freaks could be those that are ultra-feminine or extremely masculine and that the bulk of the population are a mix of the two.

What do we really use to decide what gender someone is? Can we draw up a reliable method of defining the genders. One that works in all cases? We are not debating the concepts of masculinity and femininity. Instead we are asking whether we can state that someone is male or female in a black and white manner rather than just people of the same species.

Most people claim that it is quite obvious that someone is a male or not and that we have a basic ability to determine which sex someone is. In day to day living we use visual clues and clothing plays a part. We still feel that we can distinguish a man from a woman even when somebody is dressed in drag. A man in women's clothes is still masculine enough to be spotted. The same goes for a woman dressing in a masculine way. They just seem sufficiently masculine or feminine to be separated. Whilst it is not quite so easy with babies as their facial features are far less prominent, we don't make such an issue of it. We don't pay it too much attention and it is pretty much unheard of to request that someone removes their underwear to establish what sex they claim to be. Most will admit however that there have been some occasions where they have come across people that we are not sure which sex to class them. We notice them and stare for a bit trying to decide. Anything a bit unusual evokes some curiosity.

There are plenty of stereotypes. We think of females typically having slender body shapes, maybe hourglass rather than 'A' frame. Breasts that protrude are seen as the prominent feature of women thus men with man boobs feel awkward. Body hair particularly on the face can mark us out, as does a sweeter softer face. Nevertheless, you will get some wimpy looking boys and 'wouldn't want to meet down a dark alley' strong looking girls. Men can't have orgasms people cry, but how wrong they are, I can vouch for that. On this note, the sensation when highly turned on ripples through a large part of the middle of one's body for some time. It is considerably easier to bring about ejaculation than an orgasm though. For many, sufficient arousal for it to occur can be when we are fizzed up and energised rather than being relaxed and calm for ages.

What if a man were to lose his member in a motorcycle accident, is he still a man? If a woman has a hysterectomy is she still a woman despite not having a womb? Half the population in theory can produce children, but this half have issues for many and are barren. The potential to bear children frames femininity, but is not entirely useful in determining gender reliably. Although men can't become pregnant, nor can many women. Men are deemed to be the providers of the seed unless they happen to be sterile or have opted for a vasectomy. A large percentage historically have a role in procreation, yet this is useless in making absolute differentiation between the sexes. If rules are going to be made in society, then they need to be fair for all. Most legal cases involve nit-picking to define exactly the issue at hand so it has great relevance. The approach we use to state whether someone is a man or a woman should surely work in all cases if it is to be justified.

If we were to fall back on the chromosomes, the xx/xy, we would think that we would be on safe ground except these have anomalies. The chromosome system is not a two-part system. It comprises numerous registers with each person having their various components set at different points on the scale. Big built strong alpha male types will have a lot of the settings to the one side, yet can still have a few feminine characteristics. At the other end of the spectrum, there will be those that have delicate sweet cute feminine bodies, but also some masculine traits as well. If we evaluate all of the bands we can see that on aggregate, people lean to one side of the gender divide. However, nobody is 100% male or female. When we feel hard done by, people will point to someone worse off than us. In the same way, there will always be someone stronger, taller, bigger breasted, more agile or with a more feminine /masculine voice than us too. And many of them will be put in the other gender box.

The idea of having two separate sexes is highly entrenched in our view of society. One has a hole and the other a peg. Any other viewpoint is swiftly rejected. Thus, from an early age segregation begins. We have different changing rooms. We like separate toilets except we don't mind in aeroplanes, trains, small shops and most homes. Some schools think it is wise to have separate classrooms for those with a penis and those without, because it is fun to control. People exclude half of society from taking part in a range of activities simply because they have been defined as male or female. Characterised not on performance but on an expected role in child creation and child rearing. Totally illogical and irrational yet violently enforced. Not one country at this point in time has managed to put in place a law that treats all people the same. Many places put more effort into repressing certain types.

Without a doubt those in power like to control and restrict those around them in many ways. In how they dress, in how they conduct their lives and this is the crux of the issue. Many want to dictate to others and harness their power, exercising our will over lesser beings. The idea that we are all just people and not boys and girls fazes the majority. Neither can we accept that some of us are just more feminine or masculine than others.

Whist we can point out a few minor examples of what is supposed to be different between the boy and the girls, they are dwarfed by the much larger number of things that are identical. If you counted all the body parts that are indistinguishable between the sexes, you will see only emotive reasons for creating such damning discrimination. This is not to say that we don't relish and enjoy the sight and company of the opposites and seek company with them. We can still gravitate towards cute people with exacerbated femininity or masculinity. Hence why some people like to accentuate their femininity by wearing makeup and refraining from becoming too muscular. Or conversely spend hours at the gym toning their physique. Not everyone worries about their looks, for many laughably, pretend to place higher regard on inner beauty. There is a lot of joy to be had in making oneself as feminine or masculine as we like and that is our business and an onlookers delight.

There can be a pressure to conform, to present oneself firmly within one of the categories. Being born without the affirming characteristics that set out our gender identity creates a significant issue within and rejection by those we encounter. Sexual confusion, sex changes and awkward lives materialise. The freaks have difficulties. In truth, we are all freakish, accidents and different. We may have been a product of a planned pregnancy, but we neither chose to be born nor did our parents select us specifically. One can be subject to the same amount of derision for being too fat or too thin whether male or female. We will discriminate when we choose a partner ruling out baldies, shorties and the loud mouthed to name but a few reasons to reject. This only changes when we are confronted by a limited pool to choose from or we reassess our own shortcomings.

Body types will have significance in the workplace. It can be advantageous to be beautiful, but sometimes beautiful people can be hampered by the fear of competition. An employee will use a different filtering mechanism to whittle down candidates to present to the boss than the boss might themselves. Staff might be in fear of being overshadowed by new attractive people coming on to the scene. Some are less inclined to give a petite figure a chance in something like the construction industry despite the measurable distinctions in actual performance being minimal when timed. Suitability is only truly proven once someone has actually been in the job for a while and preconceptions get eroded. Female warriors have been as deadly as any others in conflicts of the past. By and large there are as many capable people classed as women as there are classed as men. Make no mistake about it, I could find some people who you would call women to face off and challenge any typical bunch of those you call men.

People have different hormone ratios and that intensifies their appearance. It give rise to more body hair, higher levels of aggression and a greater ability to compete. Those most proficient at a sport, the champions, or those that are the best at maths seem to be in the male category. Nevertheless, the difference is marginal, crucial to come top, but the females do not lag that far behind. It is only a small number that make up the elite, most people have average abilities. Take a random sample and you will see no significant difference between the sexes. Besides, the best one or two doctors can't be on all the hospital wards right across the country. The top leagues would have a good proportion of female participants there by merit if the world lost its bias. Where there is no exclusion there is little difference in performance between the so called sexes. Tradition holds people back rather than lack of competence.

We can hunt for sections of our genes that can spell out what sex we are, but it will still come down to human interpretation. We can highlight types that belong more to the male or female category such as those with the obsessiveness trait. However, both men and women can be prone to focusing heavily on one subject for a long time. Whether it is nurturing, caring, loving, loathing, desiring or any form of human emotion we can never place them higher or lower on just one gender. Anything a boy feels will be felt by many girls too.

A nation that counts people as people and not as either male or female has no interest in making anyone change how they label themselves. It would just end the denial of access to anything based on a gender discrimination. The only time it would make or stop you doing something is if you were underage or truly incompetent. There is no need to banish Mr/Mrs/Ms etc from the diction. In English, there is plenty to take umbrage at with the masculine element in man/woman, male/female, lad/lady, prince/princess, count/countess and he/she and so forth. From here on you will see he/she/her/him replaced by they and them. You should notice that things become rather stilted and constrained. It is harder to write without these pronouns. Despite everything, the freedom to write how we want is paramount. So, you write how you like and address people as they wish to be addressed. If we say "they are handsome" or "they are pretty", do we assume 'they' refers to a boy and girl?

Revulsion

Many people will shudder at the thought of having sex with someone they consider to be of the same sex as them. They find it more abhorrent than having sex with someone aged or disfigured or jolly unattractive. The written or unwritten guidelines of acceptable sexual behaviour runs deep. A masculine individual will go out with someone adorably flat chested so long as there is assurance about them having distinct genitalia. We can look at someone and say that we find them attractive, but as soon as we find out that we are wrong in what gender we thought they were, we recoil in horror. It is a strange psychological barrier. Whether it is the distaste passed down through our parents during our upbringing or through conversations in the classroom, it is quite heartfelt. In reality it is quite odd to favour hideously ugly members of the opposite sex than someone good looking of the same sex.

Most people will opt for someone of their favoured type. We fall in love with someone. A person that gels. What gender you ascribe to them is not the most pertinent point. It is that somebody that suits you. Under no account does it suggest that we change our behaviour, popularise it or even promote trying things with different sorts. Instead it asks us to take a more candid view on other separate issues involving how we treat people. People are afraid to tear up the two-sex status quo view of humanity. They believe they can decide who are men and who are women. They think the world will come to an end and mankind will no longer continue if it is not solely men and women living together to have children.

Some of us have a role in procreation and some do not. We are reluctant to accept that the only requirement to maintain the population is to have an adequate number of people conceiving. Everyone else makes their own contribution to the economy and peace of a nation. Imagine 100 rabbits in a field where 40 of them can get pregnant. Then ask yourself how many will get pregnant knowing that all of them will be humping one another day and night irrespective of what genitalia they have. Those that can get pregnant will get pregnant. Nature has no intentions only consequences.

Anal sex is for the preserve of what is described as gay people, however not exclusively. A surprisingly high number of couples have tried it, many more than we might imagine: Couples that we consider to be straight, male-female unions. Notwithstanding a significant proportion of 'gay' lovers form long-term intimate relationships without ever penetrating the other. Most are more than content doing other things. It is not a fear of the potential health risks, but simply because they have no wish to do so. Thus, to criticise the pairing on the basis that we find that aspect repugnant, doesn't count when we apply it to many 'gay' couples. The argument goes that buggery is indecent primarily because it is inserting into an area that the body has set aside for waste disposal. Unhygienic it may be, but the penis also discharges buckets of waste urine daily. Spreading food on a body and licking it off is not too hygienic either. There are countless dangers in all kinds of sexual activity and there are countless dangers in many other activities non-sexual in nature. It is pertinent to make a stand if you know someone has a disease and warn others, but risks we take in life are our own business when nobody else is liable to be hurt. I repeat, not all homosexuals bugger one another, not all heterosexuals bugger one another. Some do some do not. Many homosexuals can be as disgusted about it as many others. The proportions that do are roughly the same between homosexuals and heterosexuals.

People that sit in a minority camp don't want special treatment, they want to meld in with the rest of us. We feel that it is acceptable to talk about possible rear end shunting between some people, but keep our own sexual deviances close to our chests. People may remark on couples that choose not to have children and they may revere those that copulate with attractive types. However, nothing compares with the array of suppositions that are tossed into the fore with u-bend users.

Oral sex in all manner of positions is also practiced between a whole range of deviants, deviants but not classed as the same sex. It is hard to argue that gender is important in this instance. It makes no odds what you have down below when kissing or caressing or at what angle or what posture. Sex for the sake of sexual gratification is commonplace. Sex during pregnancy. Sex on one's own. Sex for fun. Sex for thrills. Sex even in the hope of replicating. Maybe we could limit sex to once a month during ovulation and never again after or when we have no motive of making babies. Is it a sin, is it immoral for couples who know that they are infertile to have sex with each other? There have been many a long-lasting romance where neither saw one another naked. It is hard to imagine not seeing your partner in their birthday suit and just making do with some fumbling under the blankets. Many would discreetly lift what was necessary and in a few fleeting moments the task was done. How different, different times are.

How do you know if you don't try? Well do you know if you would enjoy intercourse with a goat if you haven't tried it? You know from the outset whether bestiality is for you or not without attempting it, yet we condemn others for selecting someone of the same sex because they are yet to find the right one regarded as of the opposite sex. If only they tried harder, they would find that they like it, but whilst discovery is key to finding the right person it doesn't relate to the given sex. You find the general type that you are attracted to at an early age and can't change much except be a little less fussy and more realistic as you mature.

The most foolish of fools think that someone can choose and change their sexuality; they can decide to be 'gay', rather than discover that they are homosexual/lesbian/etc. as they reach their teens. Some have suggested that one can be converted, turned straight, by all kinds of therapies. They think it is akin to some kind of addiction and can be fixed. Sadly, your preferences are hardwired into you. Not exactly sad, as to you it all seems perfectly normal.

Relationships

It is not uncommon to hear people place a gender role on gay couples describing one as butch and one as effeminate. Irrespective of your gender, to be feminine is considered to be more vulnerable and vulnerability is an attractive trait sought by many masculine characters. Far more attractive than highly confident self-sufficient persons. Occasionally this can be the reason such individuals spend many years being single. Those wrapped up in this frustrating situation may resort to pretending to have weaknesses to lure a quality partner their way. On the other side of the coin are those who present themselves as a protector, protecting but not quashing their partner. Sometimes we have to put on a pretence to draw people in whether it is as a male or female figure. Love is another game in the game of life.

Some worry that getting with someone could lead to a lot of heartache if it doesn't work out. No relationship is eternal, but it can be very enjoyable regardless of how long you remain together. Whilst caution can be admirable in some cases, people are prevented from doing what they want simply because they were unwilling to overcome a primitive fear. Some are fearful of rejection, others about what certain people might think. Worst of all, some seek an impossible reassurance that a relationship will last forever and will be completely harmonious. Life is just not as predictable as fortune tellers make out, any number of mishaps might be lying in wait today tomorrow or in the coming years. After such events people change their views and adapt their outlook. Astute ones do so prior. The fortunate couples feel at ease with each other, comfortable together and have an ability to tolerate the partner's many faults and failings.

People do change. The change is frequently about the person relaxing their pretence. They begin to accept who they really are and shake off all the shackles, ridding themselves of the pressures and expectations people have of them. You move towards the real you that was always there, latent and disguised. Relationships therefore come under strain as the person no longer resembles what you thought they were.

When a relationship does break down people tend to go through a similar pattern of anger, resentment and grief similar to bereavement before finally reaching a point of acceptance. Once it has, people can then move on and seek another partner. It makes a lot of sense to separate and explore a new life than staying together purely for the sake of convenience. Even children will agree in hindsight that the splitting up of their parent's relationship becomes more favourable than enduring a home with constant arguing and discord.

There is a notion that youthful relationships are oriented towards sex and possibly child rearing whereas those that have the good fortune to live much longer will have relationships that are more aligned towards companionship. This doesn't imply that older people are unable to enjoy the satisfaction of sex, just that it doesn't always have the same resonance. There will always be a few who manage against the scepticism of others to plod to the top of great mountains and attain a similar climax to that of their younger counterparts.

Couples that work together in the same occupation or for the same cause, can sometimes form a stronger bond than where the two have separate pursuits. If you are both working on the same project, then there is a lot more opportunity to have discussions on the same theme with both parties having similar objectives. Others are held together by taking part in activities that both can have a role in. If everything you both do is separate and distinct and little is shared, then there is a greater chance of a relationship of convenience emerging. People stay together as it becomes awkward, not because you have so much mutual respect for each other, but because you have become accustomed to the way things are and fear the effort required to move on and the disruption that would ensue.

Monogamy is a popular ideal, although some can have more than one relationship running concurrently with purportedly few side effects. Bigamy is outlawed in many countries and provides an example of the state meddling with our personal affairs. Many will see it as none of anyone else's business. That is unless there is some deception and they feel the need to inform the duped party. Do you pay attention to all the other monkeys frolicking in the trees or cats in your garden making long term bonds to multiple partners? What is the moral basis for limiting the number of wedded partners, nothing substantial I suspect? Having another partner that everyone concerned knows about is less of a minefield than the abundant affairs that take place in secret.

Sometimes it is the conniving and battles to keep things secret that is a huge part of the thrill during an affair. Besides the practical implications of being unfaithful, there is often a cost. There is significant chance of catching a disease and loss of respect from all family members. Whilst you can sign any form or swear allegiance to someone, you can in reality go against this promise fairly easily. The only real commitment one can make is when you actively decide to have children, for they can be a lifelong part of your life regardless of the success of your partnerships.

Infidelity takes two forms, both of which can be equally destructive. Some people find it easier to forgive and forget a physical affair than an outside emotional relationship. Emotional infidelity can damage the core of the relationship and is often harder to reverse. Alarm bells start to ring when someone confides in others rather than share their problems with their partner first. Trust is like a pane of glass, once shattered it is never the same again. You can refashion it like a stained-glass window to keep out the cold, but it doesn't always replace what was once there. When offspring arrive some frustration and jealousy can set in. Most couples see the importance of finding the space in their routine to ensure that intimacy is not neglected.

Some people split up having messed up their relationship. They see their children only part time and have entered a state of having nothing to lose. They do not care about preserving your relationship, a relationship that is going well. They will find or create the opportunity to damage and steal from it. It is not as if they want to take your partner from you and live happily ever after. Instead it is to have sex and walk off laughing. How do we protect ourselves from such venomous scum? You can see the virtue of keeping tabs and being guarded. Guarding in a number of ways which only those that have not had to deal with the problem fail to understand. Having a ready store of the element in all life triple bonded with the main component of air is one kind of tempting solution. However, "go away", "stay away" is the most customary tool. Like mosquitoes lurking and waiting for you to stop fidgeting, swat one and think that is the end of it, for another to crawl through an unforeseen gap.

It is hard to deny the importance of feeling comfortable and relaxed with the person you live with; where you can be yourself and behave according to your nature. Nothing aggravates the soul more than having to 'walk on eggshells', always frightened to say the wrong thing or cautious in too many ways. I soon learned to make fun of the bad moods with persistent jokes and comedic goading, this relieved the pressure and worked for me. Compatibility is about knowing that people are far from perfect and finding someone with a set of imperfections that you can accommodate. We have a few quirks which our partners treasure for their uniqueness. If you consider your partner's weaknesses to be sufferable then looking elsewhere would not be quite so recommendable. However, people can easily get distracted by the longing for a change as the years pass regardless of how well people get on together. A little boredom can set in and a switch to another partner or a period alone can appear very appealing. We can be so accustomed to the way our relationship works that we don't add all the plusses up and it is only when we begin a search for a new partner that we realise what we lost.

There is no clear formula for maintaining harmonious relationships. We say that somethings do not matter as we understand that life is a compromise. If one of the two in the partnership is significantly taller than the other does it make it harder to stand one's ground? Do we look for complementary characteristics, a submissive and the assertive? As for love, it is not so much romanticism and unyielding in its definition as it is just about knowing someone. In the first instance, we might have a love of all humanity, but the more you know someone the more love is felt. The people you love the most are those that you know really well and are in keeping with your preferences.

We care more for those that we are most greatly associated with. We tend to feel greater pain when we see someone we know in trouble than those that we are less familiar with. We do have an understanding with those that are more distant and can have a level of compassion with the fate of people that are far removed. However, it is impossible to be absorbed by the problems of each and every person given that there are billions of us that live around the globe. As there are so many events taking place we can only pay attention to a select few, otherwise we would become truly overwhelmed as an individual. This doesn't provide a good excuse to ignore the difficulties of everyone who isn't a friend or relative, but motivates us to assist in small ways whenever it is practical.

Some teenagers wanting to get noticed and receive attention can be a little mean or nasty towards those they fancy. The way we behave sometimes is opposite to what would be expected. We encounter people that are a little bit offish or rude and not consider whether they have been caught at a bad time. They may be in the middle of a bereavement and be very different on another occasion. There are quite a few people out there who deserve more than one chance and at some point, it is bound to be you too. "Friends come and go, enemies accumulate." You are likely to feel stupid when you have an accident and a foe comes to your aid.

Autism

A feature of autism is the inability to see and understand things from another person's point of view. Imagine an apple on a table with a vase in front of it. The vase blocks your view of the apple. Someone on the other side of the table can see the apple and would ordinarily work out that you can't see it. An autistic person would think that as they can see it then you can also. They just do not grasp the fact that your sightline is different to theirs. The vase hides the apple. A similar test of how autistic you are can be made based on your appraisal of other people's sexual activity. If you consider bondage, handcuffs, whips, thigh high boots, firemen's outfits and so on as items of despicable deviancy then you have a high level of this form of autism. You will have an undeveloped acquaintance of the diversity of humanity and its disparate nature. To then consider why someone would want to dress in adult sized nappies or be trampled on or urinated over for pleasure is completely outside your area of understanding. The range of activities that we do is mind boggling and would include balloon popping in high heels, tickling and countless more. Things that you will have heard of and lots that you wouldn't think of in everyday connection with sexual activity. There are also a good few who have no sexual interest whatsoever. The more you can accept that others like to partake in such activities or not, the less autistic you are.

We all lie somewhere on the autistic spectrum. Autism has more far reaching implications than just an inability to see someone else's point of view. What is clear and in fact the key issue that inspired the title of this text, was that people who we view as less able and less responsive in many 'normal' situations, lead just a rewarding contented and happy life as anyone else. They may have uncountable frustrations. They may not being able to tell us what they want at times, but in no means does it imply that their life is any less satisfactory.

We bump into characters from time to time with a pronounced level of autism. We ask questions and don't get much back. It feels rather awkward. Although they can be quiet, shy and reserved they appreciate the time you spend with them immensely. You just need to understand that human presence is adored, but they have difficulty showing gratitude for your time with them. Face to face contact can be a major struggle for some. However, you can be surprised by how well they can express themselves emotively when writing something down and presenting it to you.

The satisfaction of sex

The missionary position is probably a most underrated way of bonding. However, are we supposed to be content with this and nothing more? Your standard sexual routine may please you as it is coherent with your affinity, but it won't necessarily satisfy others at all. Only consent is important. Trying to broach the subject of what your fantasies are to a partner can be far from easy. Many will introduce the ideas a little at a time and try to share an experimental adventure.

Talking about what we like in our sex lives is not easy, particularly if what you crave seems at odds with everyone else. It may be popular to mention the state and size of peoples' breasts in one culture or the bums in another. It becomes acceptable to mention pert backsides, firm breasts and fine abs in your locality, but many will brush aside other likes as odd fetishes. A fetish, propensity, penchant and desire are all interchangeable words in this realm.

No fetish is strange to the practitioner, only to ignorant outsiders. An open admission of adoration for breasts or bottoms is just as much a fetish as anything else, it is a strong desire and attraction to them. Nobody is shocked when you join this acceptable club. You may get some giggles and grins when you bring up blow jobs or banging upside down in a lift but any hint of cross dressing, sadomasochism etc. and you can be considered unrightly to be a creepy weirdo. Make no mistake about it, what people claim to just do is likely to be limited in truth. Some may keep things simple, but are too dull to try more to get to the core of what they really like. They would rather let it fester in their wishes to avoid be thought of as abnormal. There is of course no need to think that your plain activities are inadequate, but some people are held back. Nor is there any need to let anyone outside of your private intimate trusting relationship know what turns you on. It is much easier to talk about something you regard as sexy and having a fetish for, if it weren't for all the disapproving detractors. A zookeeper knows this all too well. When you do find an opportunity to investigate what the population at large is doing, you will find a good few that share your fantasies in equal measure, with some more prolific than others nevertheless.

Some find a great partner and all seems well until they get asked to perform a mighty odd thing. To pick one as an example, eeny meeny miny moe; urinating. Holy molly, they are asking to be pissed on. How on earth can that be any fun? Now we are back to autism and not getting what someone likes. So, what to do? The main test is; does it damage or cause pain to the doer? Maybe it will make a right mess of the carpets, but no they are happy for this to be done in the bath. Could there be some physiological harm done to the doer? That is doubtful. To urinate one needs to drink, so a potential problem, but minor unless it is in large volumes. Does it get in the way of 'normal' sexual activities? Can it be done in the privacy of the home or hotel room?

We question whether it would be better to terminate this relationship. Will the next person be even more strange? Will they be violent? Will they be a super spendthrift leading to bailiff visits each week? Do I just say no and let it lie, hoping that it will go away and they contain their desires? Well, there is selfish and there is co-considerational selfishness. You will feel good about yourself when you give what someone wants. What you might read in advice columns is biased. People that you know try to present a perfect image. Things they don't want you to find out are hidden from view. It is therefore difficult to establish what the majority really think is acceptable.

In most cases, there is rarely a request for role reversal. Someone might want to be trampled on but not the other way around. If they ask if they can trample on you it becomes a different issue. As a person doing the trampling your greatest risk is if you stumble and fall off. If you tread in the wrong place it is not you that gets hurt. Effort has to be made but it is not fair to be a victim unless you give genuine unpressured consent and are happy about it. Those that get the intimacy that they hunger for, cherish their relationship the most. Who looks elsewhere when satisfied with what you have at home? The sexual drive we have can vary somewhat. Not everyone will share the same level of libido and will gravitate towards other fulfilling areas of life. It takes dedication to graciously give when you are not in the mood especially when it feels a chore, but is thoroughly appreciated by those that want it more. Sometimes you can repay the favour in other ways rather than take it for granted.

As we proceed we find more and more variations where some things emerge to become more of a success than others. There are endless avenues with lots of little variations to test out, each offering their own riches. You will never reach a nirvana. Rather we find highs and try out other permutations where peaks of joy can be found. To not want more is to not live to the full. Contentment is temporary. It is the dynamic changing experiences that are gratifying and rewarding.

We see someone and swoon. We are fixated. Then a few days later we see someone else and they become the new attraction. On it goes. It is not that each person is a bit nicer, but our capacity to enjoy fresh alternatives is what enchants us. This can cause us a fair bit of trouble if we are endless searching for something more and more novel. If this gets out of hand and becomes a necessity to bring about arousal we might need a reset. Those who struggle to get it up or find their juices have dried up may have forgotten what it is really about. People take a complete break, a break from pornography, a break for endless one night stands, then after a period of abstinence go back to where they first begun.

You can stand on a cliff edge or hang from a beam high in the sky and get a thrill. Likewise, in sex we can take ourselves close to the limit without being permanently disfigured or killed. Few actually want to succumb to any real harm. Instead it is the potential threat of being hurt that it the greatest turn on. It can be emancipating being tied up and at the mercy of a master/mistress thereby relinquishing control. It provides a contrast to other areas of life. Not all of it is real, it can be played out in a realistic manner to connive the senses. It is the thought of being in danger as opposed to any serious risk that provides the draw. A seedy prostitute, dirty and disgusting can be fantasied about. You don't really want an infection, but the risky allure is there nevertheless.

Toying with artificial attire features a lot in the realms of modern sexual activities. Given that so many fetishes involve something plastic we wonder what went on, where some people got their kicks, before such items were invented. This gets to the core of the matter for it is not the plastic item itself that creates the excitement, but the effect it has on the visuality of the body. The cleavage, the hint of what is available allures as often as the forbidden fruit. The objects enhance and pronounce the beguiling features of the character. The colour contrast at the junction of skin meeting accoutrement features large. Couple this with the partially hidden areas, the cleavage,7 and the focus lingers for ages.

Humans are human, far from a perfect model we conjure up in our imagination. Dimples, spots, marks, weight in places that we don't want. Veins which push the life force around protruding rather than held back in tight young skin. They say that one finds it best to avoid having sex somewhere where you wouldn't sleep. It may well be that your idea of fun pans out to be rather uncomfortable, the poke of the thorns and sand in your genitalia drowns out the pleasure. As for those positions that seem so inspiring, well try it for yourself and see. Get a grip of what you have rather than what other people pretend to make look exciting. Sometimes we have to rediscover the desire for the humanness on offer.

Nakedness has its own beauty, as does a genuine body. Makeup and clothing can hide some blemishes, things we might be less proud of. Most people look more attractive wearing something than when naked, even nubile people in their prime. In my view, and this is just my personal opinion, dressing up works best when the look is balanced between raw and artificial.

Magazines of yesteryear had sections with pictures sent in by the readers. Most were of low quality, grainy and poorly produced. Yet the popularity was enormous. The down-to-earth, candid nature and because there were no touch-ups of the photographs, it stimulated the naughty side of us even more. Contrast this with the perfection of the professional shoot and we can see that not all are wedded to clinical clean images.

How would you as a director of a porn movie show the ejaculation? You don't have a borescope so can't let the viewers see the spurting inside. All you have is a bit of a grunt noise from the actor. So, to spice things up visually you ask them to spunk onto the face or breasts of the other participant. They do it for the film rather than because it is more enjoyable. It is so easy to copy what you see other people doing thinking that your partner will be impressed by it and that it gives you kudos with your mates. It is about confidently sticking to what you like. It is too easy to assume your partner will be thrilled by things shown elsewhere that appear more glamourous than they are.

The difference between self-stimulation and having other parties perform sexual play with you is enormous. One is electric and intense the other rather forgettable. Masturbation provides relief and keeps you healthy, but it has nothing like the same intensity as doing things with another person. Some do lie on top of full sized dolls, but humanness is bewitching and irreplaceable. The body is everything and can also be presented at its best by the right kind of lighting. Clever bar owners will install blue lighting to keep you awake and use other subtle colours to flatter. You may have been somewhat unsettled by the difference in someone's looks when outside of the club and not inebriated enough to override the concern. Most people can add a touch of sparkle and improve their appeal with a plethora of adornments simple or complex. It is the ability to exaggerate the femininity or masculinity that provides the treasure for the senses.

We are certainly drawn towards different things. Where one person's idea of attractive can be unattractive, even repelling to another. Some see no limit to how fat someone could be, the more the better, whereas others like rake thin for example. With so many variations of hair and skin colour, to height and proportion to style and presentation, beauty in this sense is personal. In many cases, we meet somebody and then the beauty seeps out and attraction steadily builds. There is not a distinct correlation between a person's absolute beauty and wanting to marry them. Someone who has damage may deviate even further from the mathematical ideal and be less pleasing to the eye. Where damage is not symmetrical i.e. one side of the face has an injury, the instinctive repellence becomes even greater. We need to remind ourselves though that some quirks can be attractive to many people and even preferred to a numerically aligned one.

It takes a lot of mind power to recognise faces. When we say that people with foreign ancestry all look the same it is because we haven't seen many. The more you see the better trained you become to distinguish one from another. In a sense, it takes practice. Beauty identification however uses a different skill. We all can assess beauty in any creed, whoever we are, no matter where we grow up. There are some that can't recognise anyone's face (prosopagnosia) and presumably there will be a tiny minority that can't gauge beauty. However, this universal beauty that most can appreciate comes from magical numbers derived from the series: 0 1 1 2 3 5 8 13 21 34 55... Divide any two adjacent numbers and it heads towards 1.618, the golden ratio. You can fuss about where to measure, but the key point is that we use our eyes to approximate and we guess and rate quite well. It is not about getting a ruler out and comparing down to the width of a hair. It is the proportions from the angle we are looking at, the rough comparison that counts. One example looks closer to the beauty sweet spot than another.

We have a natural curiosity for anything unusual so will stare at those that look different. This can make those with a blotch on their face rather uncomfortable. Some apply makeup with a trowel to hide the marking, others see themselves as having a beauty spot and live with it joyously. It is all about the attitude and how they carry it off rather than seeing it as a negative. When someone stares at you there are two options. Either carry on feeling uncomfortable or smile back at them showing a couldn't care less attitude. Ponder about those that get stared at because of their fame. You may have not have asked for it and may have preferred a sense of being normal, but with a change of thinking it is so much easier to cope with it. It is worth noting that some people have mad piercings and wear wild clothes to increase the attention they get and stand out. You may see that as their choice but you can copy their indifference to how people react.

We can all be repelled by something diseased and disturbing. Some have some startling uncommon features. Our initial prejudice tends to erode quickly once we have greater familiarity with them. Rather than blaming and shaming people for their hostility and repulsion, we can understand that there is a natural instinct to shy away from any unusual form. We steer clear of things that we perceive to be damaging to us regardless of the actual probability of it really doing us any harm. However, the greater the interaction these people have in a community the more they will be accepted. The more normal you act, the more normally you will be treated and the less odd looks you will get.

When we look at the differences in our sexual outlook and bodily performances we see huge contrasts. Surveys were carried out to try and gauge what we want, like and manage. This altered what we had previously generalised about. It found that there was little in terms of standard practice and rules of thumb are thrown out of the window when it comes to sex. One person being interviewed claimed that they could go from flaccid to discharge in ten seconds. The interviewers were in disbelief, saying that was not possible. The person dropped their trousers showing a limp penis. Then after some vigorous hand action they did indeed prove them wrong. Some like to think that it takes longer for girls to climax than the boys, but that is not the case. It is all individual in this respect and nowt to do with genitalia. Those that have hang ups and fears of premature ejaculation need only consider taking a short rest and go a second time. They will usually if not always take longer to finish in the following bout.

The time spent asleep is used by the body to maintain itself thus leading to wet dreams and waking up, up. Circulation doubles when erect increasing the essential repairing blood flow. Far from doing any harm, masturbating regularly, even on a daily basis is highly recommended and it is not uncommon to continue doing so despite having an exemplary sex life with someone else. It is pleasurable primarily because it is a required function of the body to maintain its health. Added to that, regular self-induced climaxes helps in the discovery and examination of what you find favourable, both mentally and physically whatever the gender you claim to be. You can convey your favourite methods to a partner far more effectively when you have scrutinised your own mind and body. Closing one's eyes and lusting brings no shame only inappropriate actions are devilment. Like all things in life, moderation is the aim, worrying about too much or too little is only necessary at the extremes.

Procreation

From time to time you will come across a family with one or more of the children standing out a little, thus putting the paternity into question. Rather than upsetting the apple cart you say nothing. Cuckolding seems to be prevalent in more than just the bird species. There is a devious mechanism at work, surreptitious and inspired. You could be having sex with your partner every night and no conception, but the extra single event with someone else hits bang on. The egg is held at the top of the tube in a waiting state for a short while and can be subconsciously released spontaneously to fuse with the seed of an interloper. Such an individual would be seen as having fine breeding potential but unlikely to hang around for years providing for the child. So the one with the high calibre seed provides the nature and the long term partner provides the long period of nurture. Rather than an affair it is more often than not a single one off brief encounter that is not even consciously controlled. The cohabitee is unlikely to suspect a thing. Biology has gone down a path of genius that only becomes unravelled in the modern must behave society. Our world can fall apart once we uncover truths, but the genetics may only account for half of the sum total of the child. Where one hasn't made an input in the genes they can more than compensate by the years of effort nurturing and adding to a child's development. Those bringing them up impart ideas and show them things that form a massive part of their character.

Your outlook is shaped by expectation. If you live in a place where 80 is old, your view is different to those where it is nearer 40. You would think much less of having children when still in your teens if half your life is gone by twenty. As nations develop the life expectancy can double. Those that live in places where they can live for a comparatively long time, lose sight of how it was in the not too distant past. Old in your world may equate to being long dead and buried in others. Life expectancy has changed for many, but not that much in large swathes of the planet. Furthermore, the infant mortality rate was unbelievably high and still is in many places.

To sustain a population, it was essential to produce as many children as possible. Being capable of doing so whilst young assists in this greatly. The window of opportunity to bear children within the typical human design appears to be between the age of twelve and thirty; this however doesn't fit modern emancipated ideals. It is not until our late teens that we can even comprehend the emotional impact and make sound decisions regarding having sex, let alone having children whilst still a child ourselves. Whilst many people have demonstrated that they can have children at a much later stage in life, the number of birth defects and other problems rise dramatically. There are also untold problems related to genetics when interbreeding within the near family and strength when far removed.

We can have children when we are young at a time where we have more energy, but for many people there is a bitterness about our former situation that is felt later in life. At the time, we had work pressures and probably less cash and could not 'enjoy' our children as much as we would have liked. Perhaps that is why we can take on the role of a grandparent in such a relaxed way.

One child per thousand sexual acts

The fairy-tale goes something like this: Boy meets girl. They fall in love and get married. They consummate the marriage and have the first child. Then during the time together, they will have the occasion nookie to expand the family. The sex was for procreation only, all structured, respectful and abiding to long held customs. This narrative paints a very different picture to the one most often observed. The fairy-tale is fictitious and fanciful, it belies palpability in the real world. A much more reasoned guess is that a typical individual may have sex of some sort around two thousand times, maybe more maybe less. Whilst this might be a bit of a generalisation, you can come to this kind of calculation by adding up every night in the first year of getting together with every other night the year after and the once or so a week thereafter. If you include all the healthy masturbation before during and after any relationship, the total is truly justified. We have sex thousands of times yet the number of children we have can be more or less counted on one hand. Now an ardent contraceptive avoiding couple may have a quantity of children

117

that reaches double figures. Yet if you take into account the couples that have none you find the average is closer to two. So, one child per thousand times you do it. To propose that the principle reason we have sex is to multiply seems farcical. It is much more prudent to think of sex existing for fun and pleasure and any offspring arising as incidental.

Sexual attraction brings us together; we and all the other animals have this primitive natural draw. The scent from hormones can trigger and arouse, we witness animals sniffing one another to see if they are on heat, but whatever the spur, animals get frisky and they want that release. People that want to suppress our desires through moral ideologies do so to confirm their power and more often than not are hypocritical.

It is only in recent times in the long span of human history that we made the connection between having sex and it causing pregnancy. They just did not know that humping had anything to do with the children that popped out. Most of us have had sex education so it seems absurd to not know this, but I as a child had no idea about the process and I doubt many other people would either unless they had it explained to them. It means that we had sex as a bonding mechanism not as a conscious means to reproduce.

It does not matter about the ratio of sexual acts that bring about babies to those that don't. There will always be plenty of people conceiving even if the hit rate is tiny. If you have a lot of sex that doesn't involve intercourse, it makes little difference to the world population. Rather than thinking that sex is for reproduction, think of sex as a lure to induce people to bond that happens to bring about the occasional addition.

Consent

Consent maybe limited in many animal species, but in ours the ethical conclusions of many a thinker will agree that it is crucial. The main area of concern is where the individual is incapable of providing consent. A person who is too immature mentally and physically, is unable to make an informed choice. Any act with such people is traumatising and abusive. Those that have an affinity towards young people have an unresolvable problem. As it is never acceptable to pleasure themselves with children they need self-restraint. Children can be taught from an early age that a hug and a cuddle is fine, but anything else needs to be reported in confidence to their parents without fear of reprisal. It may appear obvious in retrospect, but when a child seems unusually gloomy about spending time outside of your domain, it may be a subtle clue to there being something wrong going on. Most exploitation of this nature is close to home in the near family rather than by random outsiders.

The problem a group may face is how to deal with those who discover that their affinity is towards the young, rather than an acceptable attraction to others whom are old enough and are valid to have sex with. The nature of someone's affinity can't be altered so can only be contained. Acceptance of the situation and possible removal of the chemical system that causes the sexual arousal and excitement is an option. Those that cannot control their actions might prefer some form of castration on a voluntary basis to free themselves of the temptation and torment. Unless a paedophile can find a method of release and control the powerful affinity towards children without any interaction with them, then a dangerous and unwelcome situation is bound to arise. If they were to be locked up and then released without something being done, they will be highly prone to reoffend. Doing some time for each crime doesn't solve the issue.

Not all those that abuse the young are paedophiles as such. Some abusers are opportunistic. They will groom and exploit children staying with them as they make 'easy' targets. It is as sinister, if not more so that they can target them because of their vulnerability. They might not go out and about looking for youngsters as they have a general affinity towards people of all ages and not children specifically. It can even be the power and taking advantage that appeals, as opposed to the fact that they are young. This abject disrespect is not to be confused with damaging actions because of an attraction towards immaturity.

It hardly needs mentioning that a child who has dreadful sexual interference suffers a huge loss of self-worth and can be haunted by the experience for decades thereafter. Some predators have a utterly misguided idea that they are showing care. Confusing kindness and compassion with delusional destruction.

Tampering with that that is not yours

"I wanted it done to my child so that they looked the same as me" is a very odd statement. As if we all walked down the street each day showing our disfigured genitalia to everyone. You wouldn't dream of shaving a child's head because one of the parents has gone bald. An attack took place on a dictator. They survived but lost an arm. The body double was not best pleased.

To claim that it is easier to operate on an innocent's sexual organs when they are babies is a thinly veiled excuse to carry it out when they can't complain as much. Any circumcision is an abusive mutilation, which is completely unwarranted. Absolutely unbelievable given that we claim to treasure children above all other things. If the cultural identity is strong and revered the individual can elect to follow in this path by their own choosing when they reach adulthood. Why have a child if you are so

119

vindictive that you are prepared to hold them down and force such violence upon them just because it happened to you.

The premise that some forms of circumcision makes people cleaner and can lead to lower rates of infection is also feeble. Maybe we want other people to have less sex so interfere and make it physically painful for them when they do. The loss of wonderful sensations and the inability to get rewards from certain sexual plays is heart wrenching. An austere life with minimal rewards is not enlightening nor satisfying if it is not your chosen path.

Your children are yours to look after, but on no account, do you own them. They own themselves. It is also their prerogative to decide when and to whom they will lose their virginity. You can advise and lay down guidance but their body is their body. Your child will be born with a different set of preferences to you and you need only set the framework up for them to explore and discover what is suited to them. Affinities are fixed and locked in place to be identified through exploration with willing participants.

We do have to make decisions for children, such as inoculations and medical care. If there is ever any duty of care this could be one example. Making sure the right type and quality is administered and doing it in accordance with the latest findings is imperative. Neither rushing nor brushing it under the carpet. Knowledge is a wonderful thing, but it can come to us way too late in life. There is a practice called the lotus birth which chastises the haste at which we cut the umbilical cord. If I were at the side of my partner when they are giving birth again, I would be happy requesting that we leave it be for a good while, though I see little to be gained in having it attached for days on end as that seems excessive.

Courting

The dating game is a game with very few shortcuts and has to be played out moving one square at a time. Chemistry needs time to enact irrespective of any charming catalysts. Compliments work wonders as enzymes of new beginnings and being able to listen well, put some at a great advantage. Sadly for many, no amount of wealth or wisdom overcomes the wide berth people give them due to lack of conformity or instant appeal. Other tactics need to be deployed to break down the barrier and expose their heart. Attractive people get more attention in most arenas and all of it in places where there is loud music and big crowds. Maturity alters our perspective and whether we are attracted to the status of a person or their wisdom we become more inclined to cast aside someone's physical shortcomings as years go by. Lots find themselves becoming less fussy as they age and not put off so much by relatively small imperfections as they were in their formative years.

Fear of rejection is very real. From butterfly twinges to extremely raised levels of anxiety that blow opportunities into the wind. People psych themselves up at home then go out and approach a target, but back out at the last second. We have this philosophical notion in our mind that there is nothing to lose yet it can get harder and harder for some to overcome the fear. When it is faced head on, over and over, we can be transformed into an un-embarrassable being. From panicking over a mistake to turning it into a joke, pausing then recommencing as if all totally normal. The finesse is where you can stare into the eyes to show seriousness and mix in a downward all over body stare to flirt. Most people appreciate the conversation even if there is a near zero prospect of a second encounter. Wear them down, wear them down and the chances are they will relent. They will be glad you did if you are a worthy soul.

There is a saying that ~~women~~ people are like cars, as they get older they depreciate and require more maintenance. We can use a comparison such as this and wish for the latest model, fully formed brand new rather than setting our sights at a realistic level at first. However, some of those that look like they are closer to the bottom of the pile might seem more approachable and have more than likely been approached frequently even if as a last resort by the swathes of hunters just before going home. There are pros and cons with attractiveness, best is relative and it is much more of a mental challenge than anything to do with how well-endowed you are. You can keep the vision of finding someone so long as you are prepared to widen the circle and accept compromises. Some say that before you dismiss all as unsuitable, it pays to give a good few a test drive without necessarily looking under the bonnet. Go out for a meal, have a long chat and see what your opinion of them is then. When you find that their interests are different and that their understanding seems lacking in your area of expertise, remember that you don't have to be identical to get along really well.

"If only everyone was like me the world would be a much better place."

This belief is further from the truth than can possibly be. Thank heavens, thank your god, thank anything you like that we are not all so stilted and so similar. There are many a person who passes way beyond the mid-life age marker retaining no clue whatsoever of what or how other people think. Not spotting other peoples' desires or what another looks for is the ugly side of the ignorance paradox.

Power, control and the desire to be needed

Power is everywhere in our lives, not just with those in command at the top, but within each home and workplace. At one end of the scale there are the power hungry wanting to control each and every move others make. At the other end there are those with nothing more than a simple desire to be needed. All brought about by the selfish mechanism with the reward granted when we get our way or feel that we have some usefulness and significance.

Whilst power can be used for making improvements we may worm our way up to the top of the tree in an organisation to be the one making the decisions and it can be truly great being able to tell people what to do. People have worked in an organisation and have got frustrated with the way things are done there. When the management failed to listen they then left and set up a rival company. When in control you can make the changes that you see fit. It is not always about seeing a gap in the market but being dissatisfied as a customer with the offerings from established businesses.

The reach of your power is limited no matter how big and powerful you become. Even in the harshest most controlling states, you can't get into the minds of the daydreamer and make them care about you all the while. So many are indifferent to you and your actions, they have a love life and no cares in the world for your projects. They get on with their things and escape if need be to the woods or to another state. People have tried to have their tentacles infiltrating into every crevice of the lives of the lowly. The lowly look forward to the day your reign is over and make do with what they can get away with until then.

The idea of power is better than the reality. The more under your control the less of the smaller details you can get involved with. You have to delegate and trust those under you. It is simply down to the time factor; you can only spend a limited amount of it on something before other areas become neglected. The higher you go the more of a puppet you become and only a few pet projects can be seen through precisely. The great masters are really just good recruiters of people with true capabilities. Decent employees will do their duty and more, show creativity and flourish with just a simple sure sign of appreciation from those above them. They don't need you standing over them watching your every move. Empower or micro manage at your peril, working twenty-four hours every day gets little done. You can't have it both ways, power and control over everything.

People have this belief that they are right and only their views count. In the majority of cases this is not a problem. When people become so vigorous in defence of their ideas they employ a range of tactics to get people to succumb to their standpoint. The fear of violence is a greater weapon than the actual deeds themselves. You do not have to kill every single detractor, just hang one from a lamp post and serve it as a warning. Only those that consider their life worthless will continue any struggle. People who make a vocal stand can be dealt with in many ways. Ban them from talking. Flood their messages with thousands in support of you. Send them a death threat. Shout them down in the street with a simple slogan. Discredit them with some small innocuous fiction that you can be turned into fact. Spread the idea far and wide giving people hope and reason while refraining from doing the dirty work. If the idea punches hard enough then dopey comrades will take action on their own, on your behalf.

How can we counter the over-powerful? Well, everyone in power has a weakness and a vulnerability. Very few in charge will be strong enough to resist being involved in some kind of unacceptable behaviour. It is the way in. Focus and concentrate the efforts on the most disgusting aspect and you hit all the followers. No followers no power. Print simple posters with key points and place them prominently and pervasively. The more the message is out there the more people will have greater self-assurance that a challenge is valid. It tears downs some doubts. Anonymous dissent may seem weak but when the balance of power on hand is so far skewed in the opposite direction, it is the only way initially.

In the places where there is little more democracy, we have people that want an issue of some sort aired and taken notice of. The number of activists behind a movement can be small and people are adept at making it seem as though the whole country is behind them when most are saying nothing. A protest may have thousands of supporters, tens of thousands even, but in many cases it is not at all representative of the majority. You have to balance the impression the protest is making against the real feeling of anger amongst the wider population and not bend to every appeal.

Taboos are a nightmare. The moment it becomes dangerous to voice an idea the nation has lost its way. People will propose some preposterous crazy things and they are easily countered by sensible argument. Instead they are shut down. No debate, no dialogue, just shut down. With a bit of rounded explanation, you can work on their folly and maybe reduce the number of wild thoughts that they have lingering in their minds. In the process other people will be listening in and they too will be wondering about the same thing and some of them will have their enthusiasm for their viewpoint tempered as a result. You won't change the opinions of them all, but if you clamp down they will carry on seeking redress and action based on ignorance.

The family unit provides a melting pot of power over the children, control over their actions and a feeling of being needed. Once they leave home, a parent may miss that sense of being required and get a wave of redundancy wash over them. It gets worse when your life long partner passes away and there is nobody at home to care whether you get back at a certain time anymore.

Some may like to be able to stay on late at work and not worry that someone is there waiting for your return. However, that sense of being a player is more attractive than being on the sidelines in every aspect of life. An embodiment of the desire to be needed, is having people depending on you to some extent. It is not a bad thing for it is rather a nice feeling to be wanted sometimes. Power is not always objectionable, it is rather unavoidable in many circumstances, a fact of life. Whether it may be that you are the key holder or the only person who is able to drive a vehicle, some sense of importance materialises. You may make the rules outside of the home and the partner gets the last word in everything within it or the other way around. Setting a bed time is a small microcosm of being the one setting the tax rate for the whole country.

It is plain to see how so many family feuds revolve around the power facet. It can be used by some to be the facilitator, the one to bring people together or conversely to maintain a separation. To glean all the attention or be the one in the background doing things to assist without taking all the credit. Small things escalate and nobody wants to back down and lose credibility. Always to the good of those wielding the control stick and not for the best interests of those caught in the middle. Emotive persuasion, ridiculous reasoning and highly attuned tactics all to preserve an image.

It will always will be me me me no matter how you try and disguise it. Caring about what others do in how it plays out in how you feel. Everything is about the self, from the self, directed to the self or circling around back to the self. Your contribution, your input, you in the frame, your relevance and your point of view taken from the camera angle in your head.

In the extreme, there are those with the godly power of deciding who will live and who will die. Who will be saved and who will be spared. Those in healthcare will have to face decisions that affect lives whether that is electively or otherwise. That is an inherent part of the job. Ordinary folk express control when they give to the causes of their choice. You select and determine who will benefit. It is not the power that we have that is distasteful, but the refusal to accept that we have it that is pernicious and strange. There are a good few that want power for the sake of power and will expend untold energy obtaining it, but offer little at the end by way of doing anything useful. People fall for these snakes and get bitten further on down the line and usually when it is too late to stop all their counterproductive actions taking their toll.

A high percentage of those in power politically care more for being right in their arguments and swaying as many people as possible than wishing to make changes for the common good. Winning the debate ranks higher than helping the distraught. Facts and figures are easily buried beneath emotive arguments as so many can be conned by linguistic trickery. Is cleaning your nose the same as picking you nose? Something smells or is described as having a distinct aroma. Someone can be described as discerning rather than fussy. Countless other examples can be found in many areas of life where the message from those in power is disguised and forces us to slow our reaction and cogitate, anything to make it seem decent rather than foul. Presentation is everything in the same way as possessing beauty gets more attention and adoration. Find an individual case and make a heart-warming story of how they have had their life transformed so that hundreds of others who are suffering can be brushed under the carpet. Governments have to make decisions on the macro scale that affects lots of people, but can highlight micro incidents, good deeds that they have done to keep themselves in authority.

We give advice and influence others gleefully. Many will work hard to climb the tree of domination to have more people below them working according to their fundamentals. Whether it is in the workplace or the worship halls, power is the key item that provides the impetus to ascend. It takes a lot of study and a lot of will to get it.

Much of what we say is mere rhetoric. So much of our conversation is trying to get others to lean towards our way of thinking. We try to convince others that we are right and our views are important. The words we utter are always trying to sway the listener towards our way of thinking. We do not just convey our concepts to the next person, we spread a sub conscious message. 'Look what I have found out', 'I find this interesting so I shall share it with you' and so on. We care about our opinions and our achievements don't count for much unless lots of people know about them. We can do a lot for our own self-satisfaction and not worry anyone else with marvellous things we have done or discovered. However, people take great pleasure in sharing their findings. You only have to look at the big grin on their faces to see the delight when they are spreading the message.

Those who really believe the world revolves around them, the full-on narcissist, do not like being ignored. Dismissing what they say will aggravate them. Brushing off and disregarding their musings takes away their sense of control over you and is the mightiest way of depriving such individuals of their pathetic power.

People with little of interest going on in their life, those that accomplish nothing much may use vindictiveness to get attention and seek some hold over you. They want the attention and if you give it to them they feel quite good. It is not easy to avoid rising up and feeding their ego. Highly self-centred trivial people will up the ante to provoke if they don't get the reaction they seek. Playing it down and detaching yourself is easier said than done though.

Power games are around and studied by the ambitious. It is suggested that you make every effort to get credited with all the good achievements and remain silent about the not so good. Only do the sacking and reprimanding when you have no one else to do it. Create an image of being masterful at everything. If you choose to do the reverse of all these power tricks, you can become greatly admired rather than greatly grating. People's time comes to an end sooner or later and being pushed off the stage is humiliating when ejected rather than leaving with people wishing you remain

Every great person is just that, a person. Why we fear the aura around a top snake is strange. Why those in regular close quarters do not bite the head off is equally peculiar. It is as if that one who is instigating hideous acts of violence in protected by a mythical life force that we dare not trespass upon. They were born small and feeble as the next man in line and grow in stature only be our own weird reverence. Do we see them as the only one who could keep command?

Arguments

The advert read "Leather backed, fully reclining comfort chair. 5 Year guarantee." Going by the picture and description the price seemed pretty reasonable. After paying for one, people received a leather backed fully reclining chair that was rather smaller than they thought it would be, one which could fit in the palm of your hand, ideal for a dolls house.

A chair provides an excellent example of how you can picture one in your head, but I can guarantee the one you will be thinking of will be quite different to that in the minds of others. A typical chair may have four legs, but a chair is still a chair irrespective of the number of legs and regardless of whether it has arm rests and a back or not. Not only do chairs come in different shapes and sizes, they are also made from a range of materials and do not even have to serve the function of being able to be sat on. How do you definitively distinguish a chair from a stool or decide when it is no longer a chair? At what point does it become a chair when you begin to assemble one from a flat pack and when does it end being so when you smash it up?

It is not unheard of to have a tax on one item but not another. So, if there was a tax on chairs but not stools there can be some problems when we try to claim that what we are selling is marketed at a stool but closely resembles a chair. Neither a stool or a chair can be defined therefore it comes down to someone having the authority to make individual distinctions. Very few objects can be precisely defined. Words came about to help us pass concepts from one person to another, concepts which approximate and are vague.

Another problem with some debates is that two people can be both right or both wrong in the same instance. If you were holding three cigarettes in your hand and asked the question; "Are there 2 cigarettes in my hand?" You can have many responses. If they say yes, there are two then you can disagree saying that there are three. If they say no then you can argue that there are two cigarettes, which is a true statement. Unless you specify with better precision "Is the number of cigarettes equal to two?" (No less than, no more than) then you can invite some argument. Some people will reply, when asked the same question, "Cigarettes are bad for you", and the debate will continue at a complete and frustrating tangent. Then there is the argument for arguments sake and countless debating tricks deployed to confuse and obfuscate.

Whether your proposition has merit or not, some will dismiss it as invalid and nullify the points you are making rather than take it on board and present justified counter arguments. One way to brush you aside is to use the 'already thought of and discounted' tactic where they point out that, that is 'xxx theorem'. It might be similar, but to pigeonhole it in this manner is infuriating as the difference whether slight or not is important to you. You may not have come across this xxx theory and came up with the idea yourself and all they want to do is cast you aside. There are numerous other ploys and word plays along with all the various fallacies each of which complicate the debate and turn everything into a mindless mind game. It then takes a long time to break down the linguistic devices to get somewhere.

Not all languages will have as much ambiguity as others, but where there is more than one meaning of a word you can be sure that they will use the other to trash what you are saying. Then we can pick out an element of an idea and run with it ignoring the central point. I was involved in a discussion about what responsibilities we have towards our neighbours. It is an ethical debate. However, the discussion never got onto ethics it simply focused on what a neighbour is. Are they those living next door, in the same street, or on adjacent farm many miles away. If you said to someone that you saw your neighbour on a train they would understand that you meant; someone living near you. The questioner was asking about the level of care we feel we may have in regards to our neighbours, not what a neighbour is. Their interest lay in possible obligations we have to people living close by. So when you were hoping for some insight into ethics you get caught up in a battle of defining things that are not essential to your query.

Qualified

Looking up to people because they have formal qualifications might be advisable at times, but in many cases they will be stuck with conventional thinking. The opinions of the common man have value although we can't always muster the courage to put much faith in them. We are equally prone to give more credence to those with fame simply because their message has reached a wider audience. An assumption that they must be right prevails.

Those that are learning to fly are taught the lessons of believing in yourself and speaking up if in doubt. A captain who was held in very high regard was flying with a junior pilot. The junior was unsure about the message they heard on the radio, but said nothing thinking that the captain was unlikely to make a mistake. Had he queried the take-off permission they would be all alive today along with hundreds of the passengers. Many a crash has occurred where people seeing an error have been reluctant to speak up.

Having the courage of your convictions can be significant. I would rather get some clarification even it invites the odd snigger. I don't worry a great deal about what people think of me, I feel it is better to be reassured than blindly assume that all is well. I was about a mile from an airport (a quite large one) and the controllers asked me if I had the field in sight. "Err, negative, field not in sight." I could tell there was a little chuckle in their voice as most usually see the runway well before that point, but it is so much better to take an instruction, be directed and not end up being a real idiot. People soon forget little instances like this but point out big mistakes. It is not about doubting everything, but bearing in mind that people that we respect can make errors and are misguided at times. You have to have belief in your own judgments now again, but not be so resolute that you are never prepared to re-evaluate things.

If you break apart the word expert into ex and pert you can re-evaluate the meaning. An ex is something that used to be the case as in ex-partner. Pert is pertaining, relating to an area of something. Thus, expert could be someone who used to have knowledge in an area of something. Therefore, that expert may have wisdom that is not useful anymore. You can break things apart like this and come up with countless arguments, some with merit and some without.

If there is an exception does it break the general rule? Exceptions can be a lever into the cracks of an argument. If the idea does not apply in all circumstances, then there could be a problem that has been set aside. However, it is not great to be on the receiving end of those discrediting a theory by being pedantic and whimsical. It is very hard to really define anything, but there will be generally accepted notions of what something is. Good enough for most purposes. A dog has four legs, barks and wags their tail. People will see this as part of the design. Observant people will point out that they have seen three legged dogs so stating that all dogs have four legs is not necessarily true. And quite correct they are as some will lose a leg through injury and may even be born like that. This is a distraction away from the understanding that the genes of most dogs have a built in scheme for it having four legs. Sometimes it will be necessary to be very precise and complete in presenting an argument, but quite often you will get those that bring up irrelevances rather than exceptions.

In the early years of astronomy, the motion of planets was observed and it became possible to predict to a high degree of accuracy the relative position of where they will be at a future point in time. Except one. They had a choice, either throw out the science of the reliable nature of the planetary orbital motions or work out why this particular one was odd. It turned out that something else was at play causing the difference and creating this exception. There can be a lot of searching for ever more reasons why, giving rise to the oft quoted remark; the more we find out the more questions we have.

Statistics are renown for provoking arguments and fury mainly because they can be offered up in different ways although they relate to the same study. It was once quoted that a certain sector was in decline year after year. As a proportion to all economic activity the percentage was indeed dropping, but the value was actually rising every year. It was just that other parts of the economy were rising much faster making it appear to be reducing. Is it going up or down depends upon which way you want to present it. If something is said to have shot up 50% it can sound alarming until you read the detail that the cases rose from 4 to 6 out of 100000.

Full story

It can be frowned upon to encourage children of school age to do shoe shinning by giving them your business when they ought to be in class. I was approached by one and relented. I enquired as to whether they have been to school that day and they said that they had been since early morning. They claim, and I have little reason to doubt them, that they work in the afternoons to get a little extra money. I then set them a little maths test, basic arithmetic and sure enough using some charcoal on the back of their hands they could answer the questions correctly. So unless you know the full story it is hard to make considered judgements. Maybe you could argue that the time would be better spent doing homework, but realities of being poor need to be taken into account. A good argument comes from thorough research, the more you look into something the more you uncover and the stronger your case can be. Even then some new facts may come to light further on down the line which change the picture completely. Take the case of the debris found 11 miles from a crash site. Parts of the plane are never going to spread that far so something must be amiss, the plane must have broken up in the air. It was 11 miles by road, the driver proved it by filming the odometer going from zero to eleven. What you did not get to see is that they drove all the way around the lake. It was in fact as the crow flies from point to point only 1 mile away.

Cranks are lazy. They do not make the effort to investigate or think. People got in a rocket and went to the moon. Their holiday snaps were however a little dubious. They appear to be either doctored or erroneous. Hence why not run with the idea that this adventure was a hoax. We have two truths, one that these people ventured to the moon and the pictures they showed people are fake in some way. If you had spent vast sums on a trip like this, you would hope to have something pretty good to present. If it is a black shadowy figure on a grey background you may well be inclined to do something about it. Enhance or even recreate the photos. Suspect behaviour doesn't give a reason to throw the whole story in the bin.

Open-mindedness

Some people are very proud to claim that they are open minded to a whole spectrum of possibilities. They also claim that they will be open to new theories as they arise in the future. This is rather grandiose, but belief systems are more often than not about being parochial and accepting nonsense rather than having potential credence. To be open-minded it is suggested that you need the capability of being able to dismiss the ridiculous. Is it productive to teach children in school the idea that there are two possibilities of where they came from; One being that they were conceived and carried in the womb of their mother, the other being that they arrived by a stork? A truly open-minded individual would regard the latter as being unworthy of any proper consideration because it cannot be substantiated in the same way as the former. You can witness the baby coming out, you can see the tummy get bigger and bigger, you can use a scanning machine to have a look. You can even watch a sperm make its way to an egg. People are adamant that their version of events is correct. Saying that we all arrive in a napkin hanging from the beak of a stork is a metaphor for countless other unlikely propositions. You still have to show people that their thoughts are misguided, taking the time to explain rather than putting them down.

Lockdown

There is a tendency for some, not all, to lock down thoughts and ideas. They become less open to new ideas, less prepared to acknowledge things that go against what they know. It is easy to put a mental seal around things that we consider to be the best policy and tire of the debate. We stick to past experiences as the sole reference point. This is often due to fact that we have already looked at the ins and outs of things several times before. Why bother to re-examine when we are most likely going to come to the same conclusion. The older we get the less concerned we are of trying to explore new avenues of thought and we are more resigned to thinking that we have better things to do with our time. Not everyone fits this stereotype, but it becomes more prevalent with the older generation and it is worth knowing this when we try to argue with them.

The philosopher's curse

There are many problems with philosophy with its complex language and so much debate around the semantics/meanings of many words. Getting wrapped up in the language is a daft trap. Keeping it complicated, by using rare and clever sounding words is really useful in the business of excluding the undesirable. A trick employed by many a society and numerous clubs to keep them out. What is equally alarming is that we don't always realise that our jargon that seems so common in our circle is completely bewildering to the majority. If most people don't understand the majority of the concepts written here, then this text is even more of a failure. The aim here is to give some an understanding of what drives us. It is not divine or spiritual, but maybe profitable to a few that are interested.

What is philosophy anyway? People will define it in different ways. The skeleton of the truth. Scratching an itch. Looking for answers through discussion and thought. At the end of the day it only has utility when shared. When tested on others. If you make a conjecture and gauge the reaction from others and mould it based upon the response, we can say it has been tested. The more people that agree and concur the more merit it appears to gain.

I like to make a proposition, no matter how outrageous and provide some argument, ideas that support it. Sometimes we need to stick to our opinion despite the opposition. Throw out the nonsense, the plain crazy ideas (potentially a prerequisite for being open-minded) and see where it leads. One can try to distil the information from others and where necessary hone in on the bit that seems to contain the error. You must remain resolute, holding out long enough to make progress. However, various objections come along and it can be a problem if we are too stubborn to change direction. A good few people don't get this balance right. People can be right for the wrong reasons. Some highlight problems in your argument, which means you have to think about it more before letting go of that idea. Being dogmatic is also fatal, not life threatening always, but if your proposition fails test after test then it more than likely needs to be modified or rejected. Saying that nothing is absolute and everything will always be open to question maybe correct to a point, but it can be a curse. One need not always be the one leaving it be rather than having the determination to see things through and have a conclusion of sorts.

'The only way' section shows some signs that begin to appear absolute and provide the foundations of the definitive structure of the universe. However, due to the extreme complexity that results and because of the existence of random chaos it is indeed very hard to be absolutely certain of very much at all.

Locating that error step

Nothing is more fun that getting to the root of the problem. Somewhere along the line of an argument a step is found sometimes that is not quite right. Quite often you will be presented with a lengthy argument that follows a lot of logical steps. It seems rational and quite convincing, but you sense something is erroneous. Your aim is to find that one small piece that contains the mistake. This is one way to look at philosophy, getting to the core of the truth. Many people will get a bit agitated when you probe deep down into their reasoning. Taking away their comfort blanket is quite painful. Thankfully many will oblige and provide an insight into their thought paths. You do not have to put them straight as it is your curiosity that is getting satisfied rather than there being an aim of showing them the error in their thinking. Nevertheless, burrow down and you will locate the bit that is not right or could be improved upon.

Language gives us an obvious ability to communicate with one another, but it is not flawless. The word selfishness conjures up a lot of issues and is more than just ambiguous. It has many meanings in each context and requires thought beyond the dictionary definition. Curiosity is not just the wish to understand a big problem, it arises in much simpler everyday forms. Where did I leave that book is as much about curiosity as what you might hope to learn from it. Words are concepts in themselves and trigger a set of other thoughts. In many cases we don't have a word for an idea, but that doesn't stop us using the tool of language to get it across to someone else. Pain and suction exemplify the point. Pain can be an aggravating signal for some or a joyous feeling in others. Pain can be linked with reward. People use vacuum cleaners to 'suck' the dirt up. We use the word suction despite there being no such force existing in physics, yet people have an idea of what it implies. (Technically you can only blow things, not suck them, push rather than induce or pull.) Whatever you begin debating there is always going to be a problem with the multiplicity of language. You may have five thousand words at your disposal enabling millions of combinations, which is then multiplied by the number of different meanings to each word. Change one word in the sentence and a whole new avenue of thought can open up. This can be why some have such a problem coming to any form of conclusion about any particular subject.

The joy of language can be found in many situations. I recall someone warning me of the monkeys that were "very thief". I understood what they were saying despite the grammatical error. I question how often we spoil a discussion by being pedantic when we fully understood what someone was saying. "I need to make a cake". "You don't *need* to make a cake, you would like to make a cake". "I need to make a cake to satisfy my want".

It could be said that no one really wins an argument. If you are wrong then you are wrong, and if you are right the other person isn't going to be particularly pleased at having their error being pointed out. You either get it wrong and can be proved so, which isn't terribly pleasant or you are right but suffer the consequential loss of friendship. In the end nothing really progresses until agreement is reached. When people have gone to war one side will end up agreeing to sign some form of treaty or armistice.

It is hard for people to accept that their memory is not as good as they think it is. False memories can be implanted quite easily too. We muddle up information regularly and find it hard to believe that we have done so. Quite a few people deny that they have got their facts wrong. We often spend a fair amount of time arguing over various facts, facts that could be quite easily verified at some other time. Sometimes arguments are just a damn good way of venting frustration and beats aggression any day.

Some people receive a message, one that they are not too impressed by, and send an immediate response. Other people who get the same sort of message, wait a while before they reply. By leaving it a bit you call mull over the options and give it some proper consideration. It is amazing how much more conciliatory you are when responding an hour or a day later. If it is going to be some time, then you can just acknowledge receipt of the message straight away and leave the action until after you have cooled down a bit and thought it through.

An argument is diffused by listening. A hot head has lots to express and may not give you a chance to counter anything they say. I tend to hear them out anyway. Eventually they run out of things to say, then you can work on areas of agreement. In the same way that we do not like being given advice, we do not want to be forced into changing our mind. To make any headway with the stubborn sorts, you need to ask questions that lead them to change their opinion by themselves.

I have arranged meet ups with people and then received a last-minute message to say they are cancelling. I see firing off a simple little written message as sneaky, cowardly and disrespectful. To me it is insulting. If they had telephoned it would have been a different story. I have allocated time, made the effort and now I am left in limbo. When someone calls to explain you also get a chance to negotiate or work out an alternative. You also get a much better understanding of why they are letting you down. The counter move is to send a reply stating that you find such messages rather rude. Later on down the line you ask them if they would sack someone via a message, would they cancel a job in that way? They may well do, but somewhere in their ethics there will be a shared agreement.

Conversation

I met someone who mentioned that their partner told them that they were a bore. They were encouraged to get out of the house more and do something. This person was indeed boring boring boring, not because of a dull existence but because all they did was talk and talk and talk. Failing to allow someone even a few seconds to make a point, dominating the conversation beyond belief is one of the most disliked practices known to man. I am quite sure that I am not the only one that encounters these types and struggle to get away, as they just won't stop talking. Some install a secret button to trigger a phone to ring just to get out of it. I began to stop accepting this with anyone any longer. I will just say yes yes yes yes and butt in regardless, forcing the issue otherwise frustration levels rise too high.

A few people master the art of conversation whilst the remainder babble on too much and often about irrelevant things. Whilst items maybe important to them, not everyone wants to hear about it at length over and over. It is not really about the fact that they babble on too much, but that they don't give you a chance to say much either that is the real annoyance. As soon as you start to speak they turn away and look at something else or walk off completely.

Most things that are said are soon forgotten and if not forgotten we don't always remember who said them. Nevertheless, it is an enjoyable aspect of life and it is the foremost way to unburden our sorrows and share our joys. Failure to take on board the comments and ideas of others is the crime of conversation. Looking away all the time and changing the subject is the habit of the hopeless.

Taking on board what people are talking about is not about giving advice. It is about asking more to allow them to have the opportunity to relay what they want to say in greater depth. People will work through their problems by themselves, but are aided by good listeners rather than know all solution providers. People do like talking about themselves far more than anything else, whether it about their job, their holidays or how marvellous their children are. However, some characters seem to always have more dramatic things going on which must be announced to all and sundry. "Those with the least to say, talk the most." Allowable on occasions, but irritating if it happens all the time.

Some people have a habit of always referring whatever you have been doing to something they have done too, giving the impression that they are better, working harder and achieving more. This is not the same as taking on board what was said, but showing that they only care about themselves. Some of us reach maturity but still seem to think that the whole world revolves around them. You have to demonstrate that you are interested in others, genuinely, if you want to avoid being stigmatised by this feeling. Many have come to realise that the one great thing that they have achieved is the ability to listen to others.

Few have the capacity to reflect on the way they project themselves. There was a doctor who filmed their own consultations. When they played it back they were shocked by what they saw themselves doing. They were surprised at how little engagement they gave their patients and by the realisation that they were not even looking at them much at all. Only by seeing their own self in action were they able to make massive improvements in their approach from then on. Few people are aware of how poorly they communicate, not many will acknowledge it and people around them are reluctant to point it out.

If you have interest in someone you need only keep the subject revolving around them and they will spiel endlessly and you have a chance of getting closer in their affection for you. It is standard practice for those wishing to build confidence to listen hard and get people to talk about themselves rather than attempt to do the reverse. It will not work if you can't make sufficient eye contact. It really fails if you show more interest in fiddling with some device all the time as this is usually seen as the height of rudeness.

Unless you are locked up in a prison cell with thousands of hours to fill, protracted stories are less welcome. The most enjoyable conversations are those where people involved keep it short and to the point. It allows for greater progression and much more interesting depth as time passes. A test of how well a conversation is going is quite often measured by how comfortable you feel during a period of natural silence. If you sense awkwardness, then maybe you are not natural conversational partners. Having the confidence to remain quiet for a bit to allow people to gather their thoughts is part of the mastery.

Knowing when to hand over the conversation baton is a hard skill to get right. Too many make a rather good point, but undermine it by then labouring it to death. Stop. The point has been made, they understand what you are saying. There is no need to keep repeating it. The more you keep going on, the more it diminishes what you are saying and the more likely they will disengage completely. Tell your tale by all means, but then give others a chance to recant theirs too, then your presence will be appreciated by everyone.

You may think that all the little details matter, but to the audience they are irrelevant and detract from the underlying story. There is rarely much gained when correcting your partner or friend who was involved in the story and they will prefer you let them tell it the way they wish to. "We got back from a nice holiday on Wednesday and landed at twelve..." A needless interruption would be "No no it was Thursday when we returned and it was much later than twelve o'clock." You might think it matters, but as far as the audience is concerned in most cases it makes absolutely no difference whatsoever.

Some anecdotes work really well, yet some, no matter how you formulate them do not. You try them on different people and find certain ones are well received whilst others rouse little amusement or interest whatsoever. The shorter succinct ones are the best. The longer it takes the more effort required for people to hold back from yawning. Anecdotes come out in a manner like someone hitting the play button on a machine with zero thought required.

When you get back from an outstanding trip you tell a few about it at length. Then it gets abridged and shortened each time you bring it up with the next group of people. You get tired of recanting the tale as fast as people get fed up hearing about it. Hence a neat brief concise few sentences is all we can be bothered with at times.

Through trial and error people can stretch the truth to get a greater response until incredulity is reached. We love fascinating and funny tales and people are impelled to provide them. We will often use a bit of exaggeration to get the most impact but the more gullible you are the more a faker can pervade your space.

People are what they are and having a go about their belligerence, their rudeness due to the constant interruptions is not the same as obsessing about someone's hand gestures. Hand gestures can add to the story no matter how frenzied. We all have oddball twitches and mannerisms that are either piquant or off putting according to who is making the judgement.

Some people are great at sparking off conversation, some struggle. I would ask shop staff, waitresses or anyone anywhere whether they were enjoying themselves. It allows them to say anything they want and answer how they please. I found asking someone if they are busy can be plain irritating. It is either obvious or a signal they are not doing enough. Saying to someone that they look like they are losing weight can be a huge compliment to some, but an unwanted suggestion that they are not looking after themselves to others. Telling someone that they look tired can also aggravate people. You find a question that suits your character and try it out over and over or just say something really innocuous or worst of all make them listen to one of your many problems. Getting a conversation going is easier than getting out of an awkward spot. It takes practice and being prepared to look a fool at times, but in a hundred years time a whole new set of people will be making the same mistakes.

Since our curiosity is positioned in different directions, we are more galvanised towards conversations that seem relevant to us individually. It is hard to stoke excitement from people that have no interest, no understanding and little grounding in certain subjects. However, at times we engage in dialogue that strays away from our normal preferred topics to fit in and be a part of a lot more conversations. It is tempting to brush off a wearisome subject. Some loath football but can look for an angle that can be talked about to stay involved. I would ask why half of the population are barred from playing in the main leagues and ask for a guestimate as to when that will change.

Watch out for all the gaming tricks employed by some. Intentional silences to see who breaks first rather than natural pauses. Phrases and expressions will be borrowed and copied to imitate the person they are with. Talking a bit quieter so that people unwittingly have to lean towards them. Plus, mirroring body gestures, mimicking your actions. People will remember the bearers of bad news and associate negativity with them. So many will palm off the task of informing people of impending misfortunes that are looming large and be the one to let everyone know about the good things on the way.

The deferment tactic can be useful with people with deep rooted opinions. You can say "I read in a book about a certain messiah and it gave the impression that they were a bit of a fraud" rather than "I think that messiah was a bit of a fraud". You allow them to take offence at the book instead of you. Likewise, group X claim that this messiah in question was a bit of a fraud. The subtext is usually missed in that you are in effect handing over your own view through some third party.

The subtleties of conversation are the most enjoyable element. The bore mentioned at the start never grasped why there was a suggestion to get out more. Some will never see how they are being used and manipulated by subtle clever language. You can make fun of someone without them realising they are being ridiculed or just got out of the way. When someone says go climb up the springboard and jump into the pool again, I want to see you do it again as you are good at it, they really want some space and you at a distance.

The subtext comes out in a number of ways. When someone says that they have something else to do on a certain day, an assumption can be read that they just don't want to come.

Although making assumptions is fraught with misreads, you can be shown to be right 19 times out of 20 if you are good at gauging people's barely hidden signals. There are polite ways of letting people down gently.

It is not easy to be the one who has to swallow their pride and admit their mistakes, but we can be surprised at how supportive people are when we are more open and honest. A strong person doesn't mind being wrong and can end up revelling in it over time. It is like being the main trunk of a tree holding up all the branches. You can do the exact opposite of some of the things which are proposed in the power seekers armoury and be highly regarded.

People disengage when you talk for too long and are displeased when being constantly interrupted. It is all about good eye contact, asking relevant questions, pausing to allow the person to respond despite any silent moments and having a good gauge of how long to stay on subject. Throughout your life you will inevitably be faced with an individual who comes along with a lengthy diatribe and feel a great desire to get away. The clever people are the ones that can determine when they have said enough and judge the amount of time each person is given to make their points.

Whilst we can be reluctant to take advice there are plenty willing to give it. So asking for help can be a good way in. I have been surprised by how helpful people can be and learnt a lot of shortcuts through asking people for assistance. Unless it is some trade secret, few will be hesitant to offer up words of encouragement and show you things and friendships can be spawned. This chapter is a mere rant and would be best cut completely to lower the evangelism level, but left in for fun. Acknowledging it as opinionated does not excuse it either, but diodes are so abundant.

Selling

As a consumer it is useful to know if you are being served well or are being influenced by clever sales techniques. As a sales person knowing how to maximise sales of products and services that you believe in, can be revolutionary.

Successful businesses will get busy and this can lead to complacency. The first rule of customer service is to acknowledge all waiting customers as quickly as possible. There is nothing worse than having willing customers waiting ages to part with their cash and making them stand around feeling like lemons. You may only be able to serve one customer at a time, but that does not provide an excuse for ignoring the others at the bar or in the queue. All it takes is a quick look at them and saying; "I'll be with you very soon and then you after." People will wait ten times longer if their presence is acknowledged and their order in the queue to be served is affirmed. As a general rule, one should acknowledge the customers within 30 seconds of arriving at the counter and serve within 2 minutes. If your staff are failing to meet this kind of target, then systemic reform needs to be considered. It will make the difference between people storming off and going elsewhere versus empathy with your busy workload.

A merchandiser has a choice between displaying the price in big lettering or placing it in such a way that the customer has to examine the item closely before finding it. In some places it is acceptable to leave it off altogether. The advantage of not revealing the price is that the salesperson can have an opportunity to explain all the merits of the item before revealing the price. People might think something sounds expensive if they do not get a comprehension of the true value of an item. Too many people will walk away as soon as they find out the price. If an item is of standard fare like a common tin of beans, then you may put a bold price tag on as you are trying to covey the discount on offer. If your item of jewellery is made of 24 carat gold a customer needs to know this, particularly if they are familiar with the cost of similar ones made from 15 carat brass.

As a salesman, your first objective is to ensure that the item meets the customer's needs. It is pointless talking about the price if it is not what they want. A customer won't buy something no matter what kind of discount you offer if they don't like the colour or you don't have the right size. If you can establish that it fits their requirements first, then you can enter the price negotiation phase.

Selling is less about having the gift of the gab and more about having the ability to listen and pick up on what the customer wants and get to any reservations they may have. Only by listening, can you find ways of reassuring them that what you have on offer is good for them. Talking with the buyer about them, what they do and their interests builds a degree of trust and obligation. You have to be 100% genuine though. Asking a customer a few questions blithely will only project a false image.

Discounts

It is very easy to lower prices but incredibly difficult to re-raise them. Discounting lowers not just the vital profit but diminishes the brand and the business. Rather than head in the direction of discounting you can try offering something free with a purchase, something that costs next to nothing but has value to a customer. Restaurants have given recipe cards to diners for example, rather than a free drink that will lower the money taken at the till. Better presentation, better pictures of your products will make them seem much more appealing for a small amount of effort. Items sent to auctions have fetched dramatically higher prices simply for being shown off in their best light.

When you have confidence in what you are providing, you avoid being a busy fool trading goods at pathetic margins. Cheap cheap cheap is not everything as some people do not mind paying more if what they are getting is good value. People often make choices based upon cost, but quality counts too. The advantage of having a better product though is wasted unless the customers are aware of the difference between what you are selling and that of the competition. You have to find a way of highlighting the qualities and advantages of what you are promoting.

Too many intelligent people reduce the price by 10 percent and not realise that they may have to sell 25 percent more just to break even. Clear stuff that is hanging around, absolutely, but remember turnover is easy without profit.

Poor cash flow and providing too much credit can undermine a good business. Some businesses pay full time staff who spend all day collecting monies owed to them. Some people will owe you money and won't buy for a while. They use other suppliers as they don't wish to settle the account. You can end up losing both the customer and the cash. Big businesses have been built on foundations of near zero credit. You may grow a little slower by refusing 30 days, 60 days accounts, but if your money runs out your business is dead. Pay as you go, even at slightly lower margins is a wonderful formula.

Haggling

If someone offers 25 for an item priced at 30 many will try and get a compromise of say 27. This is not the only route available. Instead you propose 35. Some will find this amusing, others bafflement. You then try and seek to sell at somewhere around 32, but will accept the original price of 30. The point being that 25 is long forgotten and negotiation takes place in the number range that is above rather than below what you want. Only by obtaining good eye contact will the customer appreciate that you are serious. If you look away when telling them the price you may be indicating that you are ashamed of the cost. Those that are the best at haggling do so in a light-hearted way. People are more likely to achieve price reductions when they smile and appear friendly than when cold and antagonistic.

Making the sale

No matter how well you manage to get the customer interested, it is all to no avail if you are not prepared to close the deal. It is a simple process of asking the customer either "would you like one", "shall I put it in a bag for you" or "was it 2 that you want or just the one?" The art of learning when to close is critical, too early can be a problem but closing too late is usually the least productive. Be bold. Some people have a lot of technical knowledge, but don't know when to shut up and ask the customer whether they want one. If they say they are not sure, you can carry on the conversation and ask again a few minutes later.

In many instances having a comprehensive knowledge of a subject is not always critical. You may have a basic understanding of what you are dealing with but will often be asked a question of a technical nature that you are unsure off. You can simply say, "I don't know but I'll find out for you", then go and find out. People are always inclined to purchase from someone who makes the effort and get the facts right. Incidentally many sales people can over sell if they try to overload the customer with too much information. These vendors are also the worst culprits of leaving it too late closing the deal.

It can be helpful to provide examples of other peoples' experience of your product; "John Smith buys these regularly from us and is always pleased." People are usually reassured if they know that others use the service or buy the products that you are offering. A herd mentality prevails and people don't want to miss out when they see others part with their money. Crowded stalls arouse curiosity of what is going on and there are tipping points at restaurants where if it looks busy enough it must be good.

People will often make the fatal mistake of saying the easier "yes" rather than the honest "no." If a customer were to enquire about something that you don't have in stock, it is often easy to say yes you can obtain it for them rather than being realistic and saying no. If you do promise an item and fail to deliver it becomes a big headache. It can be a real pain having a customer keep asking for it time and again and you having to keep fobbing them off. It pays to inform the customer from the start that you will endeavour to get the item, but informing them that it isn't a certainty. It is a simple process to contact the buyer when you do obtain the goods and it is pressure free. People hate being let down as they feel that they could have had spent the time sourcing the item elsewhere.

Saying yes without getting the facts right is another major error. If you specify that a product has a certain feature when it doesn't, you will only get complaints and demands for reimbursement. If you tell the truth and explain the limitations fully before the sale, fewer problems come your way later. Had you have told them about it prior to purchase they would more than likely be fine about it. Finding out after that there is some kind of issue makes people feel that they have been fiddled. Even if the product still satisfies their requirements they will be on to you for a refund.

Cornering

One aspect of the hard sell is to formulate all the questions in such a way that the customer will say yes over and over. No is an objection, yes is an agreement. They will also provide options rather than opt outs; "I'll come over to show you this product. Which day is better, Thursday or Friday?" rather than "when would you like me to come over?" If you say that you are busy on those two days, they will offer another day. Whilst some customers do need a little push to get them to buy, being leant on too much is a major irritation. Some customers need a little impetus to overcome the wariness which is fine but it is often taken way too far.

Getting information out of people relies on using tricks. Asking someone their age is awkward but a necessary requirement for some selling schemes. "What is your age? I'm 24" is what they will ask, giving theirs to soften the impact. My response would be "good for you sweetheart".

The perils of decision fatigue are something we can try to avoid. You only have a capacity to take in so much before losing the ability to make a good decision. Sales people want you to buy there and then so will wear you down to the point where you say anything to end the nightmare. Our capacity to absorb information in one go is limited so this can be to our detriment in our decision making process. After a time, we just compromise and fall into a 'that will do' end result. At other times you can spend a crazy amount of time looking in so many places hunting for something just so. In the end when you are under pressure you need to re-evaluate the real priorities and plump for something, anything that just about fits the requirement. Most people will put some value on their time and if too much is spent on searching then any cost savings or benefits can be forfeited by all that excessive hunting. Paying a bit more there and then would be preferable in retrospect.

Some people want to prove the salesman wrong as a demonstration that they can afford it and are worthy of it. Instead of just walking away they feel some kind of sympathy and obligation where none is really deserved. If you are not sure, just leave, use some flattery and show gratitude for their time and go away to have a proper think about it. Any real deal will be there tomorrow. Walking away is much easier the more you do it, side wipe it from your mind like a car washes rain away from the windscreen.

Rude waiters get more tips than pleasant ones in some places because we want to prove something, to kind of show them. I leave a pile of the lowest denomination coins and make a hasty exit. If a tip is added to the bill automatically, I scrub it off and give them nothing. I hate tipping when it is 'mandatory'. I liken it to a form of corruption.

I went to the dinner hall on a ferry across to an island. The order taker made an assumption, albeit a correct one, that I couldn't speak the language too well and blanked me completely. Another came over shortly after and we played a game of pick three at random. After the rather fine meal I forced a tip on the hospitable person. It was probably more than a day's wages. It was not to show the other person was wrong, but because of their sweetness.

Businesses are as much about the customers as the staff, profits and products. A good eatery and a good drinking hole is where the customers provide the feedback to enable the owners to improve. By giving tips where warranted and commending not just criticising the offerings, the establishments evolve and flourish. They won't know what they are doing wrong unless you tell them and they won't keep doing what they are doing well unless you inform them.

The genuine article

What is real and what is fake and how much does it matter? There are two sides to the coin of the con. On the one side there are those selling what they purport to be the genuine real thing and do so at a premium. On the other side there are those living off the backs of the creative and providing a similar item for a significant discount in relation to the 'real' thing. There is a thing called provenance where something is supposedly worth more, not because it has any superior qualities but because it has been owned by someone well known in the past. People are paying for abstract thin air, but it keeps them very happy and provides reassurance that they will be able to sell it on again to some other mug at a later date if so desired.

One con centers around trying to obtain something through a form of deception. If you have a swanky set of clothes, a flash car and showy jewellery you may be either trying to obtain money for a business venture or you are trying to lure someone to lie on their back for a lay. You are hoping that the way you portray yourself as smart, assured and secure can nail the deal or demonstrate your marriage potential whatever the case may be. It doesn't make one jot of difference if the clothes are from the local market, the car on hire and the necklace is plated, the illusion works if you get what you want.

It becomes a bit of a joke if you need to go to a specialist or use a microscope to authenticate an item. It is a load of hassle to tell everyone you see as you walk down a street that the bag on your arm really is genuine and not a well-made copy. If an aircraft part is passed off with a dodgy certificate of conformity and fails in flight or somebody dies having taken counterfeit medicines the culprits are culpable for an invidious malfeasance. However, when an item does the exact same job, but is priced without the premium and without any theft of intellectual property we all gain by fair competition. Charging extra because you want people to buy into a superficial brand is as big a con as making money from emulating something at a lower price.

To say that copying something such as media or software is not theft as the original has not be removed is farcical. Let me copy all your private pictures and show them to who I like. You still have the pictures, nothing will be lost. Taking without permission is theft.

To paint a picture and present it as a work of someone renown is adding to the output of a nation in the same way as a farmer grows vegetables. Those that own pictures of the same artist find that their works are now not quite so rare. Rarity is scarcity not a measure of value, it becomes subject to the whims and capriciousness of supply and demand. As we well know, something is only worth what someone is prepared to pay for it. Authenticity is something that is in keeping with the tradition and theme, in a personal sense it is being true to your identity and roots.

Money

That ethereal imaginary thing called money. It brings out the worst and best in people.

Some children who are careful with their limited pocket money decide to get an ice cream. They join the queue and wait patiently for their turn to be served. One of them drops theirs on the floor and is swindled by fate.

You like flowers and have dreams of spending all day arranging flowers. You think about all the people that will come to you to get bouquets for birthdays and celebrations. Hence, you set up a florist. However, the reality kicks in when you spend most of your time dealing with complaints, miss-deliveries, fraud, theft, tax accounting, administration, advertising and getting technology to work as desired. The actual amount of time you have, to be hands on with the flowers themselves gets less and less to the point of zero if the company gets large. The headache and commitment is near impossible to envisage until you are in the thick of it. Hence why some may wonder why they went down that path when they could have had the comfort of working for someone else.

Making money is rarely easy. Most work pretty hard to make ends meet. Not many are bequeathed a large inheritance. To really prosper a sacrifice has to be made. We can't do it just working 9 till 5, Monday to Friday, nor can all of us outsource all the tough parts to someone else. It is about swapping cosy weekends with the partner and kids for mountains of paperwork and extra research for a substantial period to get things going. Some people hold down a job and use their evenings and weekends to set up a business of their own. They keep the job security and see it as a way to get started with less risk.

The most offensive comment some monkeys make about the well-off is to say they were lucky. Lucky that they had to study instead of enjoying lots of nights out on the town. Lucky to endure a long period of time earning very little. A doctor could spend seven years studying and then more years learning the ropes on the job before getting a salary to compensate. They may have come from a background where there was support and encouragement, but the path will not have been easy. Maybe you see them having rich parents and think that nothing is possible unless you are as fortunate.

People do make their own luck so to speak by throwing the dice of running a business of their own. Each throw provides a chance of prosperity. Many business people run a succession of failed enterprises before landing on one that takes off. Whilst it is probable that a high percentage of people will never get the six, the more attempts made increases the chance. Others will have to settle for a result that only provides a steady income rather than great riches as originally hoped for. It is those that think it is no more than lifting a hand and casting the die that are delusional about the effort required to move something from endless talk to endless action.

Those that end up wealthy have a different mentality to the peasants. Even the poorest of the poor could save a small percentage of what they receive to gradually build an investment pot. However, the attraction of spending what they have for the needs of today overrides the potential for longer-term prosperity in the future.

One might question what all the work is for though, if you end up too old and worn out to enjoy it. Unless you truly get more pleasure from work than play then you could be fooling yourself. When on the entrepreneurial road we are investing in the future. However, a good few become blighted by too great a workload. Some are not able to resist that extra deal, to make even more money which maybe surplus to requirement in hindsight.

Tipping the scales

To get over the crest of the financial hill, to a place where money does start coming in nicely, it usually requires going without quite a bit in order to reinvest. In simple terms, you need to be spending less than you are earning each week if you are going to progress using capitalism. Quite an obvious thing, but it requires detailed monitoring of the money coming in and going out. Each bit of cash not spent on living costs can be reinvested into the business to buy more stock or more tools. Most rich people that started out with very little will have spent many years in a house with no up to date furniture, ragged carpets and such like. Putting up with a fair amount of inconvenience is par for the course, sleeping amongst boxes stacked high up to the ceiling to save on storage rents. There is a parallel between expanding a business and a farmer's orchard. You can either eat the fruits as you go along or do without a lot in your personal life, selling them to pay for another tree. Keep doing it and you'll have enough fruit to gorge on for the rest of your life. True donkeys will chop down a tree for firewood as they were a little cold one night or felt they had to buy a child a birthday present.

To build a business and see it all go bust after all the sacrifices and hard work is sad. Worse still, is when you are left with a mountain of debt that can't be written off. Some will counter this by building in an organic way using only profits to invest with and not letting things get out of hand. Nevertheless, we have to be prepared to fail. Just because you think the idea is great and all your friends and family encourage you, it does not mean that you will succeed. People can be blind to reality checks. Refusing to admit defeat long before another path could have been chosen. It is much better to have some negative input and continue despite it. Failures and mistakes are a key feature of capitalism and it would not work without them. Businesses that rot away and die provide the fodder for the new shoots. You have to give something a proper chance, but not be in denial about its long-term potential. If it lacks any real prospect of succeeding, it is best killed off or morphed into something new.

Some think they are successful well before they have built up a decent cash pile. Keen to impress they get an oversized office and kit it out beautifully. Such businesses have the same mentality as a firework, bright and exuberant but short lived.

When we look to set up a business we find that there is already a good few other people doing the same thing, offering an equally good or better service at a lower price than we would have imagined. As more and more compete, it gets ever harder to get any kind of market share. It is no mean feat to find a way in, a gap in the market with potential to profit from. Some of the duller, less inspiring types of trade can be as fruitful as trying to invent something new. When you do find a service lacking you can pitch up and offer something that is already done, but in a better way.

The analogy of the dice is not quite complete; each time you spend years working on a business you learn more and thereby remove the lower numbers. The dice in effect losses the 1 then the 2 and so on in most cases. If it doesn't then a lot of introspection is needed. If you are not prepared to accept that you are a good craftsman, but a ropey manager, then you will always be limited by how far your business will go. Get systems in place so that your ~~skivvies~~ employees can't make mistakes. You don't need to make your workers as good as you, your job is to oversee and make sure that they are doing things correctly. They do the overwhelming amount of the graft, you deliver the tiny but vital craft.

Do you have to have a clear hierarchy? Maybe a collaboration with like-minded people to all share in the profits suits your ideals. It works for some. Some find the notion of having skivvies repellent. However, you need to contend with a lot of politics and need to find people that are as self-motivated as you. That is not easy in every industry. To add to your woes, you need to ensure everyone in the supply chain is not subjected to what you consider to be, exploitation. Somewhere along the line, some group will not feel the same level of benefits that your success brings you.

Peasants and disparity

The richer people need a differential, an earnings and wealth differential. If everyone was rich nobody would be rich. Wealth is relative. If a taxi driver who used to charge 20 for a typical trip came into a fortune and had millions in the bank, I doubt they would continue to charge the same amount. If they like everyone else was equally rich, they would raise the fares to 2000 to make it worthwhile. If we all had piles of money, then we would want more for our services. Although some may continue to drive for the fun of it, on the whole people would sit back and relax and maybe explore other non-money making adventures. It only counts if you have more and can therefore afford to offload all the menial jobs to others who are willing to be paid comparatively small sums.

Is it fair that someone earns more than someone else? If you work for twice as long, many expect double the pay. If doing piece work are you to be paid by the amount you get done or is it not fairer to split everything between all those involved.

Should a talented individual get the same remuneration as those that support them? In a band does the lead singer deserve a greater share than the backing singers and musicians. It is always going to be unfair if you are born with an ability or disability. Can tax go some way towards reducing the disparity, redressing the gains made though efficiency and good fortune? Do we address every loophole that people find to carve out a bigger slice? Is it more to do with the understanding that there is a trade-off, wealth with time and freedom, wealth with pressure and responsibility and of course work and leisure, leisurely pace. The answers to these questions lie with our fixed preferences and will be debated away according to our own individual desires.

Whatever system is in place within any society, you will always have a hard-core bulk of individuals who will have a low economic 'peasant' status, relative to a minor few who will have significantly more. If you want to be rich, then mix and mingle with the rich and leave the 'losers' to their own devices. Your mentality changes when you are in the company of those that succeed. It is hard to lift yourself up when around those that do nothing but fail.

The rich do not get rich singlehandedly, for they require the efforts of hundreds if not thousands of others to do all the donkey work. The idea, good or bad, is to employ and cream off a premium for each hour worked. The employer has considerable costs to cater for, but will always pay less then what an employee generates. They will need to if they are to continue for any length of time. As a business grows it can make even more by using economies of scale. They are however prone to rest on their laurels and will sooner or later trip and fail. As fashions change and new industries emerge some business no matter how large will go into decline. Many an employer will have their heart set on making as much as possible and getting out to have a rosy retirement. Such a bounty is less forthcoming to a regular employee.

If it all goes smoothly the employer can take advantage of the power of duplication. They can take on extra staff taking more and more slices up to the point of saturation. Peasants prefer to minimise responsibility, want to take less risks and like a clear separation between work and home time. Thankfully for the wealthy there are plenty of these people about that are prepared to put in all this essential work. Businesses are not all heartless organisations that want it all, they have a habit of providing rather good goods and services that people flock to for their outstanding value for money.

Each individual will play a part in a society, whether at first sight some roles appear less significant than others. Each contributor to an economy enables doctors, the police, teachers and so on to be paid. Even where the contribution seems small and the tax paid negligible the work done has an input. Division of labour enables more to get done. A surgeon can't operate safely if the theatre is not cleaned. A cleaner might be viewed as a lowly individual, but performs a vital function. If the surgeons had to clean, then that time would not be spent carrying out clinical procedures.

There are two common errors that people may fail to recognise; one is that someone with more is a more valued person, which ignores the truth that everyone holds equal validity. The other is that the majority of people have other things in their life that they consider more important to them. An ordinary looking peasant that you might see going about their daily business might appear to be leading a dull and uninspiring way of life. What you might not see is that away from view they can often be carrying out some rather daring and interesting activities. The mistake is to assume that what you are doing and the manner you deal with things is equally captivating for others. Different people in different environments are likely to approach things differently rather than 'better' than others. Just having an income that is enough to provide for ourselves and the family is in itself very gratifying and so much more rewarding and less stressful than sponging off others and being a parasite. Work after all can provide much more than just cash in the hand at the end of the week. It is being part of the bigger scene and it may not necessarily define us, but every bird, bat and bee works away to build their lives.

Few people really want great wealth and hardly any make real effort or find the perseverance needed for betterment. Becoming rich remains a fantasy for the bulk of the population. Playing a lottery keeps the hope alive and steers you clear of all the hard work. There are advantages of being out of the rich man's journey so long as you are not miss sold the fear of missing the boat.

Upon reaching a point where money is flowing in rather nicely, you come to spend it, but find that having ample cash is not the possession of a magic wand. Where before you wished you could afford many things, now you wish people will get what you want done when you want it and to a standard you crave. You place an order and have to wait. You want an extension to your house and that means a long period of inconvenience as the building work is carried out. Move out for a few months, but when you return to inspect it, so much is below par and far removed from your hopes and instructions. Any new toy requires more learning and familiarisation. Money is not always an ill as such for it is an aid, but only removes some of life's frustrations. Many see it as the sole elixir, but it is not always such a cure all in life.

Value

We know about saving, spending and lending money, but what is money? It is an abstract imaginary thing that can be created and deflated on a whim. Confidence is everything when it comes to money, businesses and investments. How much reliance and trust we are prepared to place on the issuer of the notes, shares and bonds. Many businesses have failed not because a lack of expected profit or because they are going through a period of poor trading, but simply because confidence in them and the management has evaporated. People can get spooked and want out, so they withdraw credit and refuse further loans. Weaker businesses have survived worse storms in more dire circumstances as people have kept their faith in the organisation.

If a forger produces a note and it goes into circulation and ends up being replaced by the central bank over time as most notes do when they get torn and crumble apart, where does the money come from? Unless someone gets stung and stuck with it the forger steals from every holder of the currency. Each unit of money becomes worth a tiny bit less. Each pound, dollar, shilling is a small slice of a defined set amount of the cake. Printing more causes prices to rise to compensate.

How do you store money in a crisis? Gold's value can fluctuate wildly, shares can all but disappear and various commodities have a limited shelf life. Cash can get quickly devalued and it is near impossible to store large sums once the system collapses. A mixed basket is an option.

How do you prove you are you? Imagine if there was a key set of people who colluded and deny any knowledge of you. Your name maybe on the property deeds and attributed to a bank account, but they could argue that you are not the Fred Bloggs on the title, as it is owned by another Fred Bloggs. Our identity is based upon people accepting and vouching for who we are. Even some genetic fingerprint can be denied as purportedly been that of your twin. How do you prove you have no twin when records have been changed?

Magic money

It is remarkable how you can steal from the stupid by setting up a pyramid selling scheme. This can, and has been done all around the world. There are always going to be naïve individuals that haven't encountered these scams yet. Hence the adage 'there is one born every minute' is very real indeed as more people turn adult each day. The principle idea is to create a feeling that if you do not join you will miss the once in a lifetime opportunity taking you to eternal prosperity. You do not need a good product, you do not need a worthwhile service all you require is something consumable, an everyday item that many people use. The money is not made through the distribution of the item as that is merely a distraction, the wealth is gained by collecting large joining fees from the new members of the network. The fools join the pyramids whereas the clever ones start them.

I recall one instance where there was a "women's empowerment opportunity". People would chuck in a fair wedge and have their name added to a list. The husbands joined in too, in their droves by sneakily using their wives' name. Once some 15 or so have been snared, then you get to start your own list.

"Why or why don't you just start a list off yourself?", I tell them.

"Oh, that is not allowed".

"What, they started that one you clown."

Capitalism

Consumerism is akin to a fisherman dangling a tempting delight of some sort to snare the hungry. If you can't force people to buy your product and there is little in the way of government support to buy your output, you need to induce people to take up the offer of buying your wares. You can make people feel left out if they don't buy certain things. If you make your products or services fashionable, you entice the gullible. Even better use the third person, preferably a famous individual to make people want to aspire to those that appear admirable and 'happening'.

It is easy to confuse capitalism with financial engineering. Trading a financial product is not the same as using money to increase productivity. If you see a machine that will speed up your work you can borrow some money to buy it. This machine will increase your sales or reduce your costs. This enables you to repay the loan with interest and have some left over to make it worthwhile. Another elementary example of good capitalism is to lend to a market trader. With the extra funds, they can buy more stock. The more stock they have the more they will sell each day.

The main point of this good capitalism is that people get the original money back and make some extra as well. Bad capitalism is where one provides the means for someone to obtain a new sofa. The added interest will mean they pay a whole lot more for it, which is bad enough. Worse still after a few years of lounging on it, it will end up being dumped. Both the interest and the cost of the sofa is never recouped. The person begins to spend their future earnings and is kept much poorer as a result. Lending is good for all people concerned if and only if there is profit potential. After all, an old person for example may not be able to work anymore, but can earn a little by lending to those that can. Profiting from lending is not bad as it is the ultimate in cooperation as all parties can gain. Capitalism is sweet when used to increase profitability rather than profligacy.

Selling fresh air to one another is not capitalism. When you turn a piece of metal into a fork and spoon you have added value to the metal. If you brand the spoon 'super mega deluxe spoon by Sir Stewart', advertise and distribute it, you add another kind of value to that bit of metal. These are all essential elements of an economy. When you sell a duff financial instrument to the unwary you are not creating much in the way of value and it is not sustainable.

Imagine you are sitting around a camp fire and one bright spark has a great idea. Let's make a set of bellows to blow lots of air into the fire. It will burn much better and we won't be so cold. When they try it, it works and the fire gets a lot hotter. They fall asleep and die of hypothermia. Why, because the wood burns much quicker. The only way to have more sustainable heat is to actually go into the woods, cut, chop and fetch some more wood. A government can go into the bank and change the money in their account from 50 to 500 by adding a zero. They have made money. This will act like blowing air on the fire and the economy will heat up somewhat. However, a farmer may have 50 pigs in their sty but can't turn them into 500 by adding a zero. Wealth is created when we grow something, when we transform something like the metal into cutlery. You can also add value when you split a parcel of items up, if you buy in bulk and sell the items one by one. There is no other way. People will propose there is but they live in delusion and denial.

Buy now die later

If you want to feed the rich just buy everything on credit. Never save for anything. Hand over the largest portion possible of your wages coming in by way of interest on loans. Keep the bankers fat. You can't just sit on the floor for a few months and you certainly can't be seen with a second-hand table, it must be new and nice looking. You must keep up the appearance that you are managing just fine and hide the ever increasing debt charges from everyone. We must have things now; waiting is for the stupid. Never invest in draught proofing or energy efficient devices as they will lower your bills. Sacrificing a little today to make large gains months down the line is daft. After all we can just moan and groan that those bankers and the government are not generous enough. Always ensure that the children of yours have it right away. Buying one now and paying interest on the loan for it is much better than buying them one cleanly from what you would have spent on the finance cost alone next year. After all the bankers have a much bigger house to maintain than you, more cars and luxury holidays to pay for. You must keep them smiling at your stupidity.

People want something so they pawn an item and get loaned 100. A month goes by and they have to pay 130 to have the item back. Not having 130 they just pay 30. The same thing happens the month after. Now they are 60 down. The situation doesn't improve. They pay a further 30. People have managed to find 90 for the interest, but couldn't do without that 100 back at the beginning. Maybe we are not in their shoes with all the pressures of 'poverty'. Throughout their life this will have been just one of many instances. By calling a halt to all this silliness for a few months they would never need borrow ever again.

There is no sense of being smug and being pleased with oneself for steering clear of debt. Those that managed to avoid borrowing (except for a mortgage on a house) realise that no amount of assistance handed out will make any difference unless debt addicts gain some self-control.

Is it all fixed?

When you consider how much something costs to make and try to factor in the price of all the material, labour and transport you begin to realise that it is all arbitrary. If you dig out the raw materials from the ground the earth doesn't charge anything. All costs are derived from labour charges, taxes and land lease expenses. It is all based on paying someone an amount for their role. There is no underlying cost just an amount someone charges. Somewhere along the line there is a baseline figure that is used to set all the relative prices.

Even though there is the supply and demand balancing system, we find that one person is getting anything from 10 to 100 times as much for the exact same article of work. Something like a haircut can take the same amount of time and use equal skill, but the price charged in different locations is miles apart. To justify it by taking the property prices and local costs of living does not make it fit. Clever economic practices are used to maintain the disparity. I said the exact same haircut, not a better one, nicer or more stylish. Same hands same result just a different price. These things do not continue in this way forever. Slowly but surely there is an equalisation, dragging those that had an easy ride for a long time downwards, and lifting the rest up.

Pride and professionalism

Even a caveman would be more likely to thrive and survive if they make their spears straighter, stronger and sharper. A professional can stand back and look at their work and see where there is any room for improvement. Make no mistake about it, the quality of work counts a lot. You can only expand a business by offering a decent service. By sorting all complaints along the way, addressing the issues to avoid the same problems reoccurring, you can be sure that profits follow. There will be exceptions, those that do hit and run sales or flog dead horses, but few manage to make a large business that stands the test of time by ripping people off. Besides there is no better feeling than doing something well, you are not always trying to avoid irate people seeking recourse.

As a customer, it is better to pay after the job is done, never beforehand. As a service provider, a good bit of incentive is lost once you have the payment.

As more and more orders arrive and more people call upon your services you will inevitably get a greater set of problems to sort. Customers are not always right, but problems will need to be dealt with if you want to avoid them stacking up and causing stress. For each issue that pops up just deal with it. Either refund, replace or sort an alternative un-emotively. The minute you get wound up by trying to see who is right and who is wrong the joy of trading dwindles. Some customers are outright thieves and expect you to take a loss so you need a fair and blanket policy to balance good practice and avoid being defrauded. Most businesses find that on balance the over whelming majority of customers give you more help than hindrance, but the odd painful ones stick out because of the way our mind works. To the customer it is 20, to you it is 3 profit, so you need to sell another 7 items to get back in the black from one issue. Going on a 2 percent standard failure/return rate which is typical for a wide range of businesses you will always lose 40 in each 2000 of turnover and losing 40 in 294 of profit is acceptable. If you get a 10 percent failure rate your profit is down to 70 which is unlikely to cover overheads.

You can do a jigsaw puzzle in many ways. You might locate the corners first then do all the edges. Some might see a bunch of one colour and quickly put together an island of pieces. Some things will need forward planning and must not be overlooked to avoid creating delays further down the line. Too many find a stumbling block and put the whole project on hold when it could have been resolved eventually one way or another. It would be ideal to start selling when your product is perfect and you have the full range on offer. The problem is that it is not until you begin selling that you find out what the issues are that lay ahead. In most cases, it is better to just get going and start shifting the stock you have and make incremental improvements along the way. One may want to be careful about over marketing a new un-established item, as you don't want to have widespread knowledge of a product with problems. Nevertheless, too many people spend too much time talking and nowhere near enough doing. You can talk yourself out of it very easily.

Certified

To make a fair fortune we need a few things. An ability to work, a mechanism to work on and control over distractions. You can't make much money if the project can't be scaled up and expanded. If you chose hairdressing, then you could potentially open a salon in every town in the country. The mechanism is the thing that you setup and then duplicate over and over. Alternatively, you can get involved with something that can be manufactured in ever increasing quantities. In my business, I over estimated by a factor of ten the amount I would sell. Fortunately, I had selected a field where the range could be expanded tremendously.

Time and speed is everything in business, it is so easy to go backwards financially as rent, rates, vehicle costs and deductions taken for living expenses keep rolling in regardless. There is a big difference between being able to do something as a hobby and being able to do it viably on a commercial basis. Having said that, we can still do impressive things in life if we ignore the time pressure. Perseverance is a vital key to business growth. You try one way and if that doesn't work you try another way, if that fails then try something else. Sometimes you just have to keep on going till the objective is met.

Anyone can build a wall even a sprightly eighty-year-old, but being able to pick up six bricks at a time rather than just one is going to affect the time taken to complete it. As a leisure activity, there are no real-time constraints. Even if it all goes wrong you could demolish it and start it all over again until you are satisfied with the result.

Flying an aeroplane however is a different proposition altogether. You can spend as long as you like checking the aircraft and taxiing to the runway, but you need good reaction times to handle the plane during take-off, landing and all activities during the flight. This ability to respond to the events unfolding is the 'real time' factor and some may possess the skill, whilst others, regardless of the amount of practice may never meet the requirements to do it safely. It is not only pilots that have an ability to respond well in real time. Actors, comedians and musicians are other examples of people with highly developed interactive skills. We have to accept our limitations when speed is an issue. However, for many jobs with enough grit and determination, where time is not a huge factor, we can accomplish all kind of things without needing a certificate or approval from others.

A world without criminality

Considering a world free of crime is not about being idealistic nor espousing a utopian vision. It is more a reflection on the cost to society. Look at all the human endeavour spent countering criminality, protecting against it and dealing with the aftermath. One third of all our efforts is in some way connected to criminality. It is a credible figure depending upon the culture in place. The police and maybe the army are at the forefront, but each individual spends a lot contending with it directly. We have passwords, encryption, locks on the door and immobilisers on the car. Roller shutters, burglar alarms, CCTV and anti-climb paint. Software protection, fencing, safes, vaults, screens and so the list goes on. All the dishonesty that creates mountains of extra paperwork. All the time proving who you are and that you are not a security threat. Then we have prisons, court cases, thefts and muggings, fraud to deal with and pay for. Even lights left on to make it look like someone is at home. Do not think that scores of people would be without a job if there were no crime. Instead these people could be deployed doing many other things and we would all be much richer. We can either see it as a way of life and just how it is or we can fight to end such insanity.

It is quite rare for someone to steal something because they are without food. Most theft is to satisfy greed. Those that steal want what others have, but aren't prepared to work for it agreeably. The irony is that if someone wanted some new clothes, they may rob some other goods to sell to pay for the clothes. It is a little strange that they don't target the actual things that they want, but rather opt for the stealing of any goods then trading them for other things. They want to break the rules within the society, but still expect the people in that society to treat them with similar respect as everyone else when spending the ill-gotten gains. If they broke into a bank and took a hoard of money, they are relying upon the society to honour the stolen cash. They want it both ways and fail to understand the rewards gleaned by acting agreeably.

Clever criminals soon discover that breaking into someone's house is nowhere near as effective as theft by invoice. If you overcharge the vulnerable or the ill-informed you can get away with a lot more money knowing full well that the penalties are typically much lower and the risks are quite often negligible. It is not too difficult to set up a business of some sort and start ripping people off. You don't need to use violence to clear out people's bank accounts, all you require is the audacity and the ability to disregard any guilt that comes after.

Every act of dishonesty makes the world a shittier place to live. If a bank overpays we can hand it back. If a shop undercharges by mistake we are free to point it out. When the money is reconciled, there will be a shortfall and some poor humble worker will either have their wages docked or get a warning. I recall a tale of the train guard: Passengers would leave items on the train and the guard would pick them up and take them home. "How can someone leave something on the train is beyond me, sometimes they come on with two suitcases and get off with one." Some years later the guard became absent minded as well and forgot to lock the door of the guard's room. As a result, someone tried the handle and woe and behold went in and took the wallet that was left in there. How can you be so stupid as to not lock the door! All the cards had to be cancelled, the cash lost and the sentimental wallet given as a gift was gone. Some may call this karma, pay back even. We all are absent minded at times and it is sad that there are so many vultures out there ready to take advantage. We may live in big cities but we can have the same atmosphere as the relaxed little islands that we go on holiday to. Good will is contagious.

Scams of one sort or another have been around for millennia, right from the times where people used a long ruler to buy and a short one to sell. We become subjected to new types all the time and become adept at avoiding them, but it is a mistake to think you will always spot them and not get swindled. Would you like to have your shed treated with preservative for just a small extra fee? Why not when all such garden furniture is made from pre-treated wood anyway. I wrote 20 on a piece of paper before we set off in a taxi to then be charged 40 on arrival. 20 each my friend. We don't like being duped as it makes a fool of our ego. Principle vs the crafty plays in the game of life. Sometimes it is an insignificant amount we lose and occasionally it is very detrimental to our financial wellbeing. Either way we still get a horrible sense of our own failings, what we did wrong and question how we could be so stupid. Once you enter the realm of trusting no one, you find things harder for you than the con artists. They move on to other prey; you are stuck with a form of grief. I have used test payments, and delaying practices that I have always followed regardless and it has stemmed the flow. The trickster will make it seem vital that an action is done quickly when few things in life have to be carried out right there and then. No offer that is worth taking up will be unavailable tomorrow or the day after.

Will we always consider curtailing crime like trying to stop it raining. We just get used to it and maybe find an umbrella to shield us from the worst of it. Where do you draw the line? Some see stealing from an old person as wrong, but would take from a big business with little guilt. The big business is often owned by lots of small people via pension funds and saving schemes. Each crime means they pay out less to those in the position of being the least able to work now. Those working there on low pay have greater job insecurity and less bonuses.

Dodge a bit of tax, who will really notice? The heaver the tax the more we might feel that we have paid enough already and a little wheeze is not that bad. When the wealth distribution seems unfair it creates an ill feeling of those left behind. Consequently, we feel more comfortable doing back hand deals and the black economy get bigger. We acquire a principle of fair game. We fashion our own set of morals and never accept somethings as being too wrong. All animals are born to misbehave to some extent and continue for as long as they can get away with it.

Those trudging on happy with their lot will be pleased to see criminals having a hard time dealing with the stress, uncertainty and looking over their shoulder all the time. Most end up earning less than the hype would suggest. Only those at the top of the crime pyramid do well, but that is compensated by having plenty eager to take them out. The real attraction is often the feeling of power. Getting people to respect their wishes by controlling and commanding them about.

Moving ahead

Increased wealth does have a few drawbacks that some may not appreciate. The more you have, the more you may have to worry about. Bigger houses have more rooms to clean, more cars add to the hassle of maintenance and employing lots of housekeepers becomes a job in itself. There is a freedom in poverty as there are options with wealth. It is not a freedom to buy whatever is needed or a freedom to afford to travel where and when you want, but a freedom from responsibility. Tell that to someone without a lot and they may laugh, but after explaining how much time you spend keeping on top of things they may understand it is not as perfect as it might seem.

Whilst plenty of money in the bank provides a security blanket it all can seem pretty insignificant when real tragedies occur to us or our family. Quite often money will be to no avail when one's health deteriorates. Some problems can't be solved by throwing money at them, but those that can need little mulling over. People tend to just spend it and be done with it. Concerning themselves with more pressing things. Hence why saving a small percentage of your income can be so powerful. Save enough to get you out of trouble when needed, but not so much that it impinges on your present day to day life now. No other animal has the mechanism to store even a tiny fraction of what they forage to be used years later, like we can. You can save 2, 3, 4 percent and still live a great life now. You can sleep at night knowing that if a real calamity arises you can pay towards what is needed without having to go cap in hand to other people. Telling people what they should do is the ultimate no no however. They say time is money but money put aside can give you time, time to sort many a situation out.

Whatever you build or create or collect or hoard you are only a temporary custodian. We are owners of many things, things that are left behind when we go. Wealth, fantastic family life, beautiful partner, time, health, you judge for yourself what you would swap.

Pyramids

"Dig a hole and chuck me in it." Say a good few that do not wish money to be spent on them when they go. Use it on the living. When the time comes the families rarely heed that wish as they think it a bit mean and feel ashamed if a decent funeral is not carried out. Some with an image to maintain have a headstone commissioned and the really well off get placed inside a large tomb. As the years pass the stone gradually deteriorates and gets covered in lichen making the engraved letters barely readable. The headstone tilts and sinks into the earth until one day it falls over completely, with or without a kick from a bored youth, and becomes subsumed by nature.

The rise and fall of things we create follow the same pattern. We make a song, or write a poem and it gets heard by a number of people before disappearing into obscurity. Some people have grand ideas about their creations that they believe will last as long a pyramid and make an equally huge impression. We have a hope that our name, our reputation, our soul will carry on for eternity. Other people are content with doing something so that the next generation do not have to suffer in the same way as they did. We can feel we have done enough if our children and grandchildren are thriving. However, some do not like the idea that all trace of us soon goes once we take our final breath. When all living relatives die too, we are not even in the memory of anyone any more. Only historians with time to kill will leaf through the files to get a glimpse of what we did and who we were.

We write, film, document and paint away hoping to create some sort of notoriety. This is all fine and dandy for a short while whilst alive, but legacies are over estimated. It is not the contribution to science, the addition to the sum of knowledge that grates. Not at all, as this allows us to progress in our capabilities as a species. But it is the perversity of wanting to legitimise a sense of individual lofty distinction.

In the same way as it is hard to define what art is, it is equally difficult to explain why some rise more than others to a little more prominence. It is neither for the lack of trying, nor lack of talent but for a slight air of novelty which captures the imagination that not even luck can provide. The first person to stake the claim, the initial innovator has the most prominence. If you devised a new way to spread paint on a surface, it gets noted. Nevertheless, we pay the most attention to what they did rather than care about the essence of the person behind it.

We can have a living legacy, one where we get to be congratulated on multiple occasions and invited to parties where adoring fans applaud you. A subject hits the news; we talk about it for a bit then move on to the next topic of conversation. For no discernible reason, someone's profile is raised leaving others in their wake. This can annoy those that wish to be in their place. They will see you take centre stage and think it is a wasted opportunity to do so much more with the attention that you are receiving. If you try giving everyone a slot in the spotlight we need to accept that such a timeslot would be very thin indeed.

There are some sports where all the top players are superstars. Yet in a different sport equally talented people are relative unknowns. There are accidental celebrities, ones that find themselves in the maelstrom unintentionally. Then there are those with a message who need to get it out to all and many, for their pearls of wisdom are far more relevant than yours and mine. Worse still, some want their face recognised the world over simply to get that empty feeling when you reach the top. Being a VIP is so much more virtuous than giving each and every person equal validity. It allows us to jump the queues and get the most comfortable vantage points. Only the dumb will bow and wow. I have myself pressed people for an autograph, when I need them to sign a cheque.

You

Your life is important; everyone needs to be kept up to date with all your trials and tribulations and what better way to do that than get a self-portrait made. Hanging up pictures of ourselves is nothing new, anyone that could afford the paint, canvas and artist's fee have been doing it for centuries. Placing them high up is preferable, so that our image is bearing down on every passing stranger.

People worry and fuss about how they look and want to avoid criticism. With everyone caring about how they look, nobody cares anything like as much about what you look like. If the image happens to be good, then amongst the people who express some encouragement there will be many that don't quite share your enthusiasm of you, like you do.

Some will make a picture of themselves copying any 'originality' in your images. Others will always be on the lookout to find fault. To climb one has to push down to gain ground, so saying something nasty about a portrait slows another's ascent. Alternatively, you can take credit for any help you give so that once again it is you that can feed off the spoils. The main person that is influenced by self-portraits is the person in the frame.

To get more attention, add a well-known figure into the equation smiling alongside you. It is the fantasy that lots of other people will show adoration and while away the day talking about you that provides the motivation. In all ways, it is always about the self. Those that complain about any form of iniquity are the biggest culprits of wanting to rise in worth. Many do have a caring and compassionate nature. They come across as very inclusive, indiscriminate and show little vanity. However, there is always a sense of people creating and preserving an image.

The purpose of notoriety is to enhance the gravitas and perceived importance of what you are saying or what you are doing. It also determines how relevant your appearance is. A perverse interest is taken in the details of someone who is recognisable by the masses. People can be side-lined regardless of their potential. We need to be invited into the club. That entails being certified, registered and confirmed as worthy by enough of the right sort of people.

Sometimes it takes getting to know people quite well before you can form a fully rounded opinion of them. You can't spend enough time with lots of people to show your worth, so we make a lot of effort with a first impression. The first time you meet someone a new mental embryo is formed. We gauge their attractiveness and glean a little from their handshake, their smile and accent, how they talk. If there is something we do not like, we mark them with a scornful adjective; strange, odd, wooden etc. and tip them into the mental trash bin. If there is something we do like, then we are prepared to excuse a whole lot of potentially negative things. We can be quick to categorise and we respond warmly or coldly according to how we have marked them.

The more familiarity you have with someone, the more links that are created in your mind and it is a battle to ensure that the earliest ones stored are as positive as possible. Hence many will be consistently putting effort into maintaining their image. Keeping up appearances is the speciality of those that care about having an enduring footprint. There is no need to feel distraught when you hear things you don't want to hear about you, for greater exposure can often change people's perception of you. It is just whether you will get the chance. People have done a lot of positive things and there is bound to be something or other that people take issue with. What sticks in peoples' minds is often that one negative thing. As time passes most is forgotten, what we remember about your activities gets less and less, leaving just one or two key things.

Whilst some are working with a paintbrush, pen, or hammer and chisel fabricating something, others make themselves into a living pyramid. They present themselves as a character of interest in their own right and need no skills or achievements as such. They just need to be as well-known as possible so they can tell everyone about all the things that they are good at, what they like, what they don't and what they are capable of. So much to show that you are more interesting and noteworthy than most others. You might have inspired others, which is wonderful. However, any blame for undeserved power and influence that someone obtains can be left at the door of those that buy into it. Admiration whilst alive can be advantageous, for our time is now and others will supersede us.

With or without you

Shortly after someone dies there is a scramble to grab the spoils. Some make a will because they do not like the idea of lots of arguments and infighting when they go. It is quite sad that the loss of the person is lost in the frenzy of the aftermath. People hope that their loved ones will be okay financially after their demise. This is all very noble, but when the gain in money is a fine compensation for the loss of the individual then our priorities can look very misplaced. In a truly loving relationship, no money could make up for what has departed. Benefiting from a death demeans the value of the life ended. There will be some kind of inconvenience when someone passes away, but sorting it all out aids the grieving and bereavement process.

Nobody is irreplaceable. It is quite surprising how businesses big and small find work arounds pretty quickly once key figures leave. Loose ends are swept away, other people are put in place and on it goes. Families find ways to manage one way or another. They may miss your special bread buns but find alternatives, sometimes better. To think that the world will end when you do is far removed from what really doesn't happen.

We often hear of the posturing that if it wasn't for Mr/Mrs xx then we would not have a certain invention now. The person who made the leap forward, who made the big discovery gets credited and written in to history books. What we must appreciate is that in virtually all instances if they hadn't found it, then someone else would have, albeit a short time after. Anything worth investigating will get investigated sooner or later. Humanity changes as a collective and individuals make their contribution, however, no one person is ever the sole vital proponent. No one person is ever vital to humankind's progression. For each person that sped something up there are a lot more that slowed things down. We mark people out as part of the education process to add a little human interest. You are as valid as the next person, but not more so. The lesson some can draw from this is that working too hard and never knowing when enough is enough sabotages the time out to enjoy other fruits of life.

One afternoon we walked into a tourist shop and the salesman locked the door preventing us from leaving until we bought something. A few days later I was waiting outside a similar shop bidding my time before the coach came and got talking to a fellow traveller. They mentioned that the country received five million a day from ships passing through the canal, yet despite all that money there was poverty abound. I told them that with over eighty million people here that is 0.06 each. Likewise, people with a billion or two to give away have the same problem. There are billions of people without access to clean water and other essentials. Once you spread this money across them all it accounts for one free meal each. Hence a dilemma arises as to whether to concentrate the philanthropy on a single issue such as a single disease or try to liven up the days of many in multiple projects. During the good times, more are born and the problem expands.

A week before setting of for a Christmas in the sunshine, I went to a jewellers to get a small present. I told the sweet young lass who served me that I was going away, the same place as last year. They asked me where, and I produced a banknote from this land locked country. "Errh, where all those starving children are?" I duly informed them that there is no famine now, all is fine. I didn't get around to explaining that there never was a famine as such, for it was more a case of people being displaced into a refugee camp for political reasons. After I left, I thought to myself, hang on, that shop assistant was not even born at that time it hit the news and became a focus of such media attention. Money was indeed raised and a good portion helped a little bit. However, the long-term damage was huge. If you say that you are off to one of the neighbouring countries, people exclaim, "wonderful, would love to go there too". However, people are puzzled by why you would want to go to this country which is as good if anything better in some ways. Only hard core travellers visit. Fewer tourists mean less business people and lower inward investment. A country's image gets tarnished for generations, all because someone wants to be seen helping.

Too many are too rash, too quick off the mark and don't get a detailed view before they embark on a project. Then there are the flyby givers. They come, they pledge and then go. You will never get it completely right, but some create a bigger mess.

Donations need not be made anonymously and there is no shame in being credited for our help, but all gifts spite those that are ignored. When you raise the profile of one it drowns out others. Charity can be transformative and cherished more often than not by the recipients regardless of the endlessness of it. By and large we give to the cause that has greatest meaning to us; it is co-consideration selfishness at its finest and unavoidably imperfect. We do not have to have a fortune to distribute fairly or awkwardly to make a dent in people's sorrows. Many can offer their time instead which is valued more in many situations. Too many do nothing whatsoever apart from harass those they think should be doing more.

Everyone needs to hear about it

Upon writing this book I have questioned the motive. Sure, there are some rewarding aspects amongst the tedium, all the never-ending editing and refining is enough to deter anyone bar the foolhardy. I wrote it for myself, selfishness as always and curiosity was explored listening and debating with a fair few friends and foe. So far so humdrum. It is available for free; if it were sold then I would not want or need to take a slice of the profits. However, what about hoping for it to reach a sizeable audience? No interest need be paid after we go, but what about taking some acclaim while we are still around?

We could say that what we have put together is informative, educational or provides much needed amusement. It is easy to come up with something to justify it. Defer the truth, make it seem like there is a legitimate reason behind it rather than admit that it was really all done with the aim of getting a bit more notice. If it turns out that nobody reads it, nothing much is lost because a writer satisfies their own wonderment about the subject matters. Even the few that get engrossed in it, soon forget most of it and where they read it anyway. The rest find ways of debunking it all. Feeling sour grapes about not being successful and unable to get your points across is a disease.

I went to a country the once where the great leader had written what they thought was the most important document ever produced. Each person was expected to read and learn every chapter in the book. Most people could at least read there, unlike other states where there are large sections of believers who can't manage a comic let alone get to grips with a complex faith manual. People were frequently tested and those that were not fully conversant with it all, were sent to re-education classes. The book contained a few good nuggets, a few wise words, but there is always updates and more things that the leaders need to get across. Political sermons can be ignored if broadcast on the TV because people have the option to change the channel. So, to stop people with such temerity to duck listening to these important announcements they installed a speaker into every home in the nation. On the side of the speaker box there is a control knob which allows you to lower the volume a bit, but not turn it off. People in other nations would take a large hammer to such intrusions so other tactics have to be deployed.

Is there anything that is so great that it merits chaining people to a desk to force them to get to grips with every nuance? If people have an image to maintain they can fall back on manoeuvres that make it heretical to criticize. We are not just talking about those that use godly references to hammer a religious message home, politicians and superstars in the making use the same tactics.

Some will spend years on a promotional tour advertising something that only took a few months to create. People see the great lengths people go to make everyone aware of their input as extreme. So they move to a position where they make it available and if some or none take any notice to any large degree then so be it. They were happy compiling and composing it regardless. Many join the countless ranks of those that put something together with nobody ending up seeing or hearing anything about it whatsoever. That is aside from those that helped produce it, lest we include the poor family members who bore the brunt of being fed updates periodically on every minor detail. Can you slate a person building a pyramid however small and innocuous and write a text yourself without that being a little hypocritical? No, you can't.

Attention

I am sure I am not the only one who enjoys de-elevating an attention seeker rather than just ignoring them. Sometimes though, the attention seekers need some attention and we decide to give them a bit. It is an illness in itself that needs addressing.

Whenever an opportunity to dance with someone came about I would hold out a hand to offer someone the chance to join in. Never grabbing, always offering, sometimes being declined, often taken up. It then struck me that as I invite someone to dance with me whether there is an aim of getting the attention of the individual as well as the attention of all the onlookers. Were we in isolation in an empty field it wouldn't make any difference is my claim. To have people watching puts a lot of people off, but for an attention seeker that is not the case. One reason we might give is that by interacting with strangers in this way it starts a chain of others following suit and building a great atmosphere. Everyone is taking one another by the hand and once the event is over there is no follow up we just say toodleypips and never see one another again. Wanting a connection is hard to criticize. I want them to leave wanting more, nobody else need know, it is not important. The time the place the opportunity.

Fitting in

One of the many things that intrigued me whilst growing up was the mechanics behind popularity and fitting in. I was interested in what made some people more popular than others. I saw some have prominence for a while, but then fade, becoming eclipsed by someone else later on. Arrogance and cockiness made some the center of attention, yet whilst many fawned them in public they would tell me in private that they didn't actually like them very much at all. Popular people got talked about a lot, but didn't seem to be universally loved and admired given the disparaging remarks that I heard behind closed doors.

I was prepared to experiment to see if I could change to increase my own popularity and consider if it is something to be relished. Would it be better to make the most of my current position and accept that as being sufficient? I could and did make an active effort to listen as I noticed that no matter what the status or even how 'ugly' someone is, people will talk and talk to them if they listened well. I could have conversations with all kinds of people regardless of how important or how attractive they were for hours on end using the power of listening. Any questions would be directly related to what they were talking about. As the years passed I managed to put some finesse into it where I would add some succinct anecdotes and put a lot more snippets of my thoughts into the conversation.

Most of the time I would spend three quarters of the time listening and making sure what I said was short and to the point. Despite all of this I was still not feeling popular. It only worked in places that were quiet and where it was conducive for talking. The best times were on holiday when people were able to sit until well beyond midnight unburdening their woes. Once I could hook them I could keep the conversation going for unbelievable lengths of time. This was not too difficult. I overheard some of their friends the next day saying; "that was who you were talking to all night." I had been in queues where I met some fine specimens that ordinarily you might not get the chance to engage with and converse for hours. I soon discovered the art of moving the conversation on in a different direction well before any boredom set in. You can tell by both the body language and what is written on their faces and change tack. A long wait could be metamorphosed into a damn good time.

I don't think that many people want to be the most popular person about, but most do want a degree of acceptance. Not everyone has the good fortune of having a good set of friends and it must be frustrating to be unable to share moments and not have inclusion like the rest do. We have to adjust some of our ways if we want to fit in to get along with others.

A big area of consternation was dividing my time across too many people. Knowing a little about a lot of people is extremely useful, but a major downside was that I found myself never becoming properly included in any particular group. You only go out and socialise with one set of people as a fully paid up member. If I devoted my attention to one bunch, then I would have had much better group friendships. It takes a long time to bond and be accepted into a group as we are naturally cliquey. It is so much hard work getting in and all too easy to slip out. I only blame myself as so many sets of people have been rather accommodating.

When you meet a new group of people, you will more than likely feel a bit of an outsider for some time. This is quite normal as it takes a while before you will be accepted and be privy to all the inner goings on. A natural process of cemented members being sniffy at first and then gradual hatching of membership. It may be a case of persistence, being in the regular company of the clique, or something triggers inclusion. A certain event that allows you to shine and demonstrate worthiness. It is not just trust that forms a barrier as making space for someone new alters the status quo. There are many barriers in groups and we like to think of ourselves as more open than we really are. Deep down we are loath to let our guard down completely and let new entrants shine too much too quickly.

Attractiveness; an agent of attention

How attractive one is can sure play a big part of how we get on in life. I have seen people stop and goggle at handsome bar staff and I have seen others smitten by pretty young things paying them double the attention of others in the same role. I thought at first that life would be so much easier for them, they didn't have to work so hard to get attention. However, I quickly realised that this strength was lost as they aged and needed to be replaced by a personality. I also saw that they had as many problems as the rest of us and yearned for even greater perfection in their appearance when all I saw was incredible beauty. I suppose that whilst some could have more affairs and greater opportunities they can still only have one meaningful relationship at a time. Maybe polygamous to some level if they have the energy, wish and commitment to devote precious time away from doing as many things for themselves in individual pursuits.

Being attractive is one thing, but seeing charlatans at work was a major bugbear; To see people fall for someone due to the flattery they were given and see them promise the world and deliver nothing but hardship and heartache. I can't blame someone for 'getting the girl / bagging the boy' by conning and conniving rather than living on the side-lines. I had the most stupid thought that attractiveness is a gift blessed from one's parents and that credit didn't belong to them. Hence charm was misdirected. In reality we credit ourselves for what we are. This became an enduring lesson on how we think as youngsters and get the wrong idea about many things. Rather than see the power of charm I would instead wrongfully be condescending and revel more in bringing people down to earth. Oh how easy it is to see things in hindsight and not understand the woes of people growing up. Even with the hindsight and new awareness, old habits die hard.

I have to admit that nothing surpasses the special enjoyment of talking to highly feminine characters in their prime. The optimum age is somewhere between 19 and 25 but this is me and subject to many exceptions. Any younger and their lack of substance doesn't inspire. Too much older and the magic is not quite there. There is of course a different type of enjoyment talking to older people. It can be at a higher level and less needs to be said to convey our thoughts. It is the aspect of youth with its eagerness of life, far less worldly wise and not yet tainted that is the draw. Listing to the inflections of their voice, irrespective of any accents and the wondrous facial expressions is magnetic. I see the optimism and the openness that fades and gets lost with age. I don't see it as an ingredient in popularity as I think character plays a much bigger part. You hear people say that what is inside that matters the most, but our physicality plays a huge part in how we are treated.

There is a state just before you become fully awake when you day dream and I have often pictured finding a friend, polar opposite physically but romance free. Someone whom I share a good deal of time with without the bedevilment of sex. Of course anyone attractive that you spend time with, will grow and grow on you and it is rare to work for long. Finding such a friend is unlikely so putting this wish aside I wondered what was I doing or not doing that others are that gives them so much gravitas. Do I accept my strengths and accept that no matter how hard I try I am not ever going to emulate the success that I perceive a few to have. Or do I continue to work on the popularity project and see what it brings and decide if it is really worthwhile.

In my early years I had a massive fear of approaching someone who had the looks that made a good contender as a partner. It wasn't until I got a partner that I lost this fear entirely. In other circumstances prior I was just as bold and free from embarrassment as any other time in my life, just not with potential suitors. Now, if a conversation or situation went awry I could just correct it. If I jumbled sentences up and it all went wrong at the start, I would just say what the heck am I saying and just start again. Doing so just made me appear most human and the fluster added rather than detracted from the event.

So continuing with this particularly polemical chapter, I look back and ponder about all those instances of rejection and times where I was not kept up to date with what was going on in a group. There were countless occasions where I wasn't given the chance. One look and instant rejection, dismissed without batting an eyelid. You then have a multitude of options. Do I ignore it and worry not. Do I suppress how irritated I get by it, mutter something along the lines of stuck up cow, arrogant pig. Am I looking at it in the right way?

People think of the things that make them great if only they had the opportunity to get others to see it. People are not reassured in any shape or form by a friend saying that they could do better than that. They have been stonewalled. You're annoyed and they are oblivious to your hurt. It is easy to say that such things shouldn't trouble us, but they do. It began to dawn on me that people grey out and that I was as big a culprit as anyone else. I notice what I want to notice. I ignore, miss and allow my focus to linger on what appeals to me. If I do it, then it is daft to start condemning others for doing it too. Nevertheless, in so many circles I found myself being accepted and treated pretty well indeed. So I have nothing much to complain about.

When I and others look at someone of some attractiveness and character we may want some engagement with them. When we are not allowed access to them, if you know what I mean, we see it as a bit of a slight. The problem is that we are bothered about it, but they do not have us in the forefront of their mind like we do of them. It is hard for some to ignore how exasperating they can find it. Like most of the objects in their surroundings you form part of an insignificant haze. In truth I do the same. There are many people who I just do not have time for. I make quick judgements and for the most trivial of reasons discount people at a whim. So I am wanting respect from others without paying the same respect to those that I myself dismiss. By and large I choose who I speak to and most certainly pick who I approach. For example, I will sidle up to a valent soul ignoring another who has some body art on show, body art faded to that convict blue. My disdain reflects a prejudice with absolutely no regard for inner beauty. When I learn the value of relinquishing all self-importance I can begin to be as admirable as so many others. Many manage to be very cordial and have such a lot of true grace and compassion towards everyone you see them with. Or do I not notice other people's propensity to give a wide berth to people that might appear snobbish or infantile or hard or whatever and such characters do not exist. Does anyone not avoid some types even if it is due to some wariness brought about by bad experiences or influence of our parents and friends?

Proving oneself

How many times do you hear people say that they were written off as a failure and then harp on about how they have proved the doubters wrong. It is not just that the teachers will be long retired by the time you make a success of something nor that they probably said the same thing to a whole bunch of other students. It is all about putting a happy ending to your story in your own mind to nullify the sense of being relegated and ejected into irreverence. You rarely get the opportunity to go back and face the castigator. You may hope that they hear about it in the news or on the grapevine or even indulge in the fantasy that the will look you up and discover how you have turned out. In practice the score is only settled in your own head, not in anyone else's. The same goes with any social encounter for when another opportunity arises to present your case again, they will simply change the rules or obfuscate. They may pretend they can't fully recall the events or twist the accuracy of what was said or meant.

We have an infraction, an argument or they make a point where you struggle to answer and we want to return to it to set the record straight. They are not too bothered about it, but you are. You want to bring the subject up again and get your points across. All they want to do is move on with what they are doing and not go over something that means little to them as they won the debate already in their head. We have the frustration of not being fully understood. We want the chance at least for them to get to know more about us, often to prove that we are as worthy and that things are not misconstrued. What prey is so great about wanting the last word and wanting to show them?

One time I was at a concert and I danced a bit hand over hand with someone for a short while before they went off. Then somebody very tall and somewhat thin came over and said that I was "good at scaring them off" and that they had an eye on them for a while and now had lost their chance. I was taken aback and as in all similar circumstances, mainly wary of any outbreak of violence and such like. To me dancing with people was a regular thing and I was very accustomed to dancing with lots of people, the more feminine the better. Just for the fun of it. This to me was not about dating, it was all about having a good time. Anyway, a few minutes later they came back and we danced further, this time a little more provocatively. Why was I unable to resist making sure the lanky git saw us together again? The journey towards not caring at all about the respect of others is long and hard. There is no point trying to prove you are worthy, yet the desire to do so is compelling. Some may say that they do not care about what other people think, but their actions belie the substance of such claims. The chance of seeing any of the people there again anywhere is slim, but winning a situation can be the focus of the moment.

I recall another night out where I spent a short while talking to three pretty lovies and the subject got on to motor racing. I pointed to my friend who was some way away and told them that they was a top engineer in a car engine company. They turned to look at my friend briefly and acknowledged what I'd said and we carried on the conversation for a while. Later however this friend thanked me for disrespecting them. I pointed out that firstly I am not in the habit of putting someone down to impress people, especially those that I have just met. Secondly I had not said anything untoward, I was in fact in praise of them. This is an example of how some people make assumptions about how you behave and resort to a negative view. No amount of protestations would change their mind, I had belittled them and that was that. I cared for my own sense of reputation and was bothered about what they thought. I can't claim that I never care about what other people think as in this case I most certainly did. We want to maintain a reputation of decency and be trusted.

A point of difference

I see many that fit in well with most people sharing similar ways, but who also retain some points of difference. The endeavour to be different is an inherent trait with an inherent problem; there appears to be a fine balance between being similar to others in many respects and also having something a little different to give us a sense of identity. The difference can stretch when one becomes a lot wealthier spitting one out of former circles. Some will take great satisfaction by going in the other direction; being capable of living a sparse existence and being boastful of how much they can manage without. Some have the desire to be well known: different from the rest. Others may highlight their ownership of a unique possession, different to that of everyone else.

With our friends we tend to have a good few similar interests, but also have some different joys that add something, helping to avoid too much stale conversation. Interest groups working for a common cause benefit from having people with unique things to bring to the table. Similar aims with a shared vision and an acceptance of some that are a little odd and stand out a bit. In the old old days of cave dwelling each of us would be put to use, some cooking some hunting some sorting the fire. Each of us had a role to play that gave us a place in the group. Together as one, but all with different skills on hand. It gave us a sense of being needed and valued. To stand out and get a feeling of importance we may utilise any distinct and interesting differences that we may have, for being too similar can make you appear a bit dull.

In some instances, your contribution might be big, but do not be under any illusion that you can't be replaced even if by someone that can do nearly as well, sufficiently to get by. Haughty individuals may wander upon the stage thinking that people can't do without them and are alarmed when shown this is not the case when things carry on in their absence.

You can mix with people from all walks of life, but the understanding is so much greater with those on the same level. People with different privileges have a different outlook. Those who have careers in the army tell me that they can't convey the experience of being in a battle field to those that have not gone through it. You can't relate in the same way with others if you weren't there.

Fakes and frauds

We can try to behave differently in certain situations like an actor playing a part in a film. These different representations of ourselves are formed from a basic personality mask. A good story teller can spin a yarn, captivating the audience at the dinner table, and the scope to stretch the truth is immense. Those with the ability to recount the tale using the same 'facts' over and over may not get caught out and branded a liar. Even if they do, it doesn't change the fact they were very entertaining. Truth is always subjective and few really care so long as no real harm is done.

We meet those that are adept at putting on a show in public, but have a whole different nature out of view. Comedians with no humour at home. Kind and caring on the surface yet extreme bullies behind closed doors. Some will say that they take people as they find them and may never get to see other sides of a person's personality. There is not a lot one can do when you get an insight into that which would be preferred to be kept hidden. People are often inclined to continue living with the devil they know than the devil they don't. Complex arrangements are evident and any children multiply the lack of ease to escape. I admit to dropping a fair few sarcastic comments that allude to my knowledge of what is going on. I have seen many take the brave step of ending horrid relationships and emerge relieved.

People come up to me with a lot of excitement, a glint in their eye, and tell me about people who are amazing and have wonderful careers. They may think they are the most attractive handsome beautiful thing on earth, but there are plenty of those about. There is no mention of the horrid working hours and the tiresome nature of many aspects that go with the so called super job they have. To the dismay of those that have seen it all before, suckers flock to them over and over again. They are not special but rather unremarkable. Sure when reality bites the duped will feel some disillusionment for being taken in, but the lure becomes a trap of sorts when it results in children aplenty. I don't want to copy them nor emulate the style I just get tired of biting my tongue and not expressing a bit of disdain. However, I do not really have any justification to say that the way I am is in any way better than the frivolous. No amount of effort building an image will entice them all, but I have to play the game to get a bit of what I want.

We want to be heard and to be listened to, all of us, but some that I have come across feel the need to be the center of attention at every gathering. Then there are the notorious braggers who can't refrain from the urge to boast about all the things that they have been doing. I meet parents that forget that we have all had children ourselves and don't see what I see; their children are as standard as any other. I don't really think they are dull but I don't share their wonderment to that same extent. Neither do I have the same wish to talk for ever more about nappies and play school and how quickly they have come on.

Conversations can be very complex. Things we say can be construed in a multitude of ways. People say one thing in one scenario and something else in another. It can be tiresome trying to fathom what is meant and trying to get to the bottom of the story. Then you find people holding beliefs they are so firmly entrenched and for so long, that it becomes unrealistic to think anything you say will ever begin to start changing their views now.

It is not about being right all the time, neither is it always trying to convert and in respect of the newly parents, their kids are the main focus at the moment as anyone that has been there knows all too well. Hence I have to keep reminding myself that what is important to them is equal to what is important to me.

Nobody is really that outstanding

During the countless conversations with people from all over the world I began to realise that all of us have pretty good analytical skills when tested. I presumed incorrectly that there was a stark contrast between the ability of people to grasp the nature of being. It is not about the ability, but more to do with the wish to shy away from anything that presses too far into their deeply seated outlook. For many it is too big a headache to justify their position and they don't see any point especially if similar conversations have gone round and round in circles before.

Is there a time and place for certain discussions? Maybe so but there is also a hint of wishing to control and decide for others what is and isn't a suitable topic of conversation. We are often advised to steer clear of religion and politics because they so often end up with people speaking more loudly and more aggressively. People have a fixed political preference based on their understanding and knowledge at the time and where they have a faith in a religion that is deemed sacrosanct. However even outside of those two realms there is much to be thrashed out. You may not wish to think and be challenged and decide to give it a wide berth. That is fine, but you can encourage those that are interested to engage. You may think it is not befitting the occasion or it's not the time or place, but that is you pressing your ways on those that would rather decide for themselves. Having a fear of what we are allowed to talk about, however crazy and however provocative is a real menace in a society. I always felt able to keep the right side of a confusing line between confronting objections to ideas and winding people up for the sake of it. Whether people understood the reasoning behind the angle of thought remains to be seen. Personally I liked to have no taboos, but the fear of delving where people don't want to allow is genuine. It is also made much harder as the amount people listen dwindles rapidly compared to the amount they spiel, when things close to their heart are brought up.

Unlike the skills to complete maths problems quickly or speak fluently in many languages, social talents are far more widespread. People can be good at interacting with one another whilst not so masterful of the sciences and academia et al. I also became aware of all those in countless fields that could do not just a bit more than me, but vastly more and were so much quicker on the uptake. When one considers, even for a fleeting amount of time, the conceit of thinking that the earth stopped when we are born, you only need to glance at the accomplishments of uncountable other people living and gone. Then we meet a few who have been on a psychology course and now know what we are all thinking and understand all of our behaviours. Having some one-upmanship can be a novelty but is not endearing if played upon too often.

The want of approval

Wanting approval from others lasts long after we leave the education system. It can dictate many things from what we wear to how we talk and what we say. We find ourselves wanting a unique identity, but not being too different that we stand out, increasing the likelihood of getting mocked. Nothing beats the feeling of approval from those we like and respect. Our choices feel validated.

We like the feeling of being vindicated when we raise ourselves above the parapet and demonstrate something new that nobody else seems to be doing. Other people are seen to be hesitant and unconvinced at first but then begin to acquiesce, taking more heed and copying our lead. This something might be what we wear, how we dress our house, or a method of working, it is all about our strategy that we embark on.

How we each follow or try to go against fashion is one measure of our appetite for approval. We have been wearing clothing of some sort since the Stone Age, marking out our tribe and it frames an element of our identity. Fashion emerges out of design that is not just for practicality, but also to develop a style that catches the attention. Every aspect from the things we accessorise to the metal pushed through the skin gradually develops with one person implementing the change. The more people that like it, the more that follow. To make a change you need to convince a few key proactive leaders, the rest can be ignored for they have little impact. In some cases, there will be a critical mass that adopts the new craze creating a tipping point to mass embracement. Some people will object to the widespread uptake of an item and then differentiate themselves with their 'bit different' choices. You can't really win. You just take a stance willingly or by default.

Being a little weird, odd, draws attention but not always approval or acceptance. If you present yourself in a way that goes outside of the cultural norms it becomes harder to fit in. The unwritten rules ignore the fact that someone somewhere at some point set out the so-called accepted fashions that become common place. Most 'new' ideas are recycled formulations, innovative but almost never de facto inventive. The scope for adaptation is by and large fairly limited, maybe an adjustment to the size and scale, cleaner lines with slightly more function. Very little of what people do, say or make is ever truly original. We just rearrange reorder and recalibrate the things around us like a jigsaw to see what does and doesn't fit within the range of possibilities. You can assemble them in the box or outside of it, place them upside down or balance them on their edge. You can change the interlocking nobbles and mess with the material, but it still remains nothing more than a minor evolution. Rarely is it something revolutionary, it is commonly a light bulb moment of taking something from one already established field and using it in another.

We may enjoy being admired for some point of difference, something novel and stylish without being stared at for abject unconformity. This leads us on to the difference between official and officious. I never lose sight of the fact that someone somewhere makes up the rules whether through a democratic process or via the golden rule (thee who has the gold makes the rules). So when someone says that you can't do something, it is because a rule has been devised by a person or a panel of board members. You do not have to view it as being set in stone.

To coerce us to comply, officious people are employed then deployed to enforce the decrees of the governing bodies. The aim is to corral us through their turnstiles of control. An objector may need to negotiate with the individual in the highest position of power, those with the most sway to override the officious people below. In most cases there is no real official way, but officious people exerting their will, persuading people that it is the norm and right. An official vendor is nothing but a marketing ploy to make you believe that all else is fake and unworthy. It is not about encouraging fraudulent copycat manufacturers, but being aware that officialdom is merely a form of branding and used as a way to justify charging more.

For a lot of people nothing beats the feeling of having a high status whether it is real or imagined. If you wear something the same as that of a well know individual the endorsement provides assurance and affirmation that your selection is good. Anyone advocating one style over another is either wanting vindication for their superior choices or is profiting through a sponsor in a great game of collusion and subterfuge for profit. Still it makes people happy and gives them some confidence. So who is superior and omniscient with any right to spoil the party.

Conformity

We have some pressure to conform and do the same as everyone else around us. If we break from the norm we get noticed, sometimes getting pulled aside and questioned about why we are not doing the same as everyone else. Some will not think it wise to be a ploneer and take a different approach to how we go about our lives. Where some pay high regard to their standing in the community others want respect within their gang. Creating and maintaining a reputation for something is the mainstay of many a community big or small. We find ourselves each having a place with our skill set utilised and a wish for our merits to be capitalised upon. Thus any differences are outweighed by countless commonalities. We become more alike than unique as the gradual corralling erodes our freedom. Pushing out and making a mark for yourself is appealing, nevertheless joining in and being convivial is generally more rewarding than being in isolation.

Trading is often done based on my word is my bond. We carry this same notion to promises and honour, sticking to our word. Those that have a good reputation for following through with their promises feel that they have a good standing with those that they know. Many also like to be the font of all knowledge and always on hand to help. Being an impartial voice of reason and trying to make it appear that they are not interfering is another popular scheme.

A sign of the impact someone made in their community can be measured by the numbers of people spilling out into the courtyard at the funeral service. Some may take stock of this and adjust their ways, having a fear of a small crowd attending theirs. There are occasions though where really old people may not have anyone apart from the minister there, not because they were unpopular, but because they outlived all their friends.

The idea of having a funeral before you die is far from original, many have considered the benefits. At the very least you can ensure the right songs are played as well as have an opportunity to say your farewells.

The onset of death can hasten the priorities we make. Many will wish to make a success of something not just before they die, but also before their parents and loved ones pass away too. This desire to set the record straight or show your true colours in front of their parents for example, is to prevent the onset of regret. Unlike other mistakes you can't do anything in this respect once they are gone. If the chance to prove oneself is too late during their life they may resort to striving harder in the name of that someone they loved. It is a way of alleviating the feelings of lost opportunity or even allowing it to be a form of contrition. Whether it is a tribute or a wanting for our parents to be proud of us, it is kind of odd that we can care what someone would think even when they are dead.

After a near miss or a wakeup call due to a recent demise of someone we know, we can get a sense of urgency to fulfil some new objectives. Live life to the full. This is all well and good, but during the preoccupation of trying to fit so much in, we lose a lot that is loved in taking things easy. Doing nothing for a whole day can be as productive and balanced as racing around in a perpetual daze. You still get things done and done with relish, but being too busy is at the expense of not allowing yourself the time to reflect. There is no duty to be mindful of what it is all about. There is no obligation to spend a set amount of time or any time at all pondering or pontificating. It is however possibly a luxury that can be chosen if you want to accommodate it.

If you can't think of anything to think about, perhaps ask yourself "what is enjoyment?" What does it mean deep down at any level. We say "we are enjoying it", we say we enjoy sex, a lunch, the times reminiscing and so on but what does it mean and what is the essence of it? Define and describe the feelings, the chemistry of it rather than just list what things you find enjoyable.

Universally admired

No matter how popular you become, there will always be people at the ready to criticise. Some imagine being liked by all, but no matter how hard you try to be pleasant to everyone there will always be dissenters. This aspiration of being loved by all is soon dampened by the unexpected stream of negative comments that roll in as your notoriety radiates. It is naïve to not count on some disgruntlement given that the more people know of you, the more chance that you will be exposed to a wider set of views. If we all liked the same thing, then you could in theory be universally applauded. However, that is not the case and there will be plenty that are more than willing to hone in on all of what they regard as your negative attributes. Popularity and respect are not the same. We can admire what people can do without joining the mob in gravitating towards them because of a hidden vogue factor.

The bond between us and other animals can replace the human connection for many at times. Pets can bring joy and happiness for sure and do form a big part of people' lives. Many take heart in the non-judgemental companionship that exists with animals in their care. This doesn't discount an important need of the majority to be able to fit in within society though.

For all the love of a specialised field the human element triumphs. We may seek out those that enjoy bird watching and travel around with our binoculars and cameras taking note of what we see. In principle we go for the birds, but it is discussions about what we have seen and noticed with others that has as much impact. We learn the tricks of the trade and swap notes. In so much of life it is not always the thing itself, but the human element that is the draw.

When I come across these people at the fore and see how entertaining they can be, I ask myself what is involved in being like that. I know it is a case of being accommodating, laughing at other people's jokes, showing a reasonable degree of interest in what others are doing without prejudicial comments. Thus providing affirmation, adding to what the other is saying rather than being frequently contrary and difficult. It is also essential to be involving to all; being inclusive to all those standing there with glances, occasional winks to acknowledge the presence of everyone. Speaking about our own circumstances with clarity, passion without over exuberance. None of which is easy to elucidate, but better understood through careful observation of those that manage it well. You may watch them and see that they are accessible to a fair degree, but will wander off and mingle to avoid over playing it and unconsciously leave people wanting more. Adaptability is key once again, it is relevant in popularity as it is in so many other areas of life. You need to be able to switch from being serious some of the time to using comical and cheerful banter depending upon the people you are with. Some people are really not interested in downbeat conversations, whereas others want more absorbing discourse.

Doing a favour for someone, does that help? It might make them feel beholden to you. Get someone to do a favour for you and they like you more, oddly. So long as it is not too much of a pain. Best when it is some help that they feel some pride in giving.

I could accept that it just isn't going to happen, I will never get great acclaim and that there are merits in other functions. So I could resign myself to be good in other situations and that has its own virtues. Then I consider the sacrifice as the conversations that matter to me and the fun of what I see as deeper dialogue, does not sit well with the brevity required to hold the attention of lots of people in a group. I also like to test ideas and propositions on many people to see what objections arise. I would use this ability to mingle with the masses to hear people's counter arguments. It would not matter who they were, not their age nor work status. To me all views were as relevant and any idea needs some concordance with all. I saw no point either, in formulating an answer to a question that could not be understood with a bit of effort by the majority. Thought is always required though. A quick scan is inadequate. It leads to people picking up the wrong end of the stick and whacking you with it as they didn't absorb everything that was stated. I also have reservations about coming out with the bleeding obvious, but what seem obvious to me is not always quite so for others. It is easy to say "I could have thought of that" except you didn't and wouldn't unless it was fired at you. Some gems were brought to the fore by some remarkably innocent individuals who you would least expect to provide insight. Holes could be filled and I would be re-armoured for the next victim.

I asked a taxi driver if they had ever done anything altruistic in their life. They ummed and ahhed for a while then admitted that they were not too sure what the word meant. When I explained it, they understood the concept and thought about it for a bit. The driver wasn't able to provide an instance of altruism on their own part. A week later I asked someone else and they too didn't know what it meant. Then the person who was in the taxi with me the week before piped up and said that they didn't know what it meant either until I explained it. That got me a bit worried, so that night I asked just under thirty people if they could tell me what it meant. One middle aged soul sat there perplexing like when trying to solve a crossword puzzle. Old people, managers, bar staff even a whole table full of dinners could not provide any sort of definition. This was quite a shock to me, a revelation, and I felt that care was needed in any writing; it had to be devoid of too much jargon. Words that I presumed were pretty common were not remotely so. We can reduce it a bit and keep the eloquence.

Modesty

When I have been sarcastically accused of being modest, I would look down below the navel and declare that I have nothing to be modest about. I have seen the temptation to boast about what we have and what we get up to, but I know it is not always great to be on the receiving end. There is not really much need to go on and on about the better stuff you have. There is nothing wrong with telling people about our accomplishments, but care is needed in the manner in which we do so. Achievements are all relative and matter to the individual. We do seek respect for what we have done however significant. Someone could be justifiably pleased with their piddly window sill plant display as another is with their massive manicured garden.

People only recall key points, maybe one in a thousand of the words you speak. Even you will only remember the gist of what you say yourself. Instead of recalling everything people say, we do tend to build a picture of whether someone is harmonious or cantankerous. When wanting the former it seems argumentative to slate what others love. Our tastes vary considerably and to point out and give credit for the awards a film or musician has received, acknowledging that they have a large following works better than putting it down. Unless you are playing one person off against another, it doesn't help your cause to say something is rubbish knowing they like it a lot. You don't have to share the same level of wonderment, but neither do you need to be awkward all the time. Being negative about too much is not conducive with fitting in.

I wonder from time to time if I am special or just another mediocre average comrade. Sometimes I see my own magnificence in full glory and then fall scythed and have shattered illusions, becoming totally uncertain of any merit in my existence. I suspect most know their place, but the ones with the highest self-esteem appear to have a lot of real fun. If you make some wildly wild claims, more fantastic than fiction you get more than just widespread attention, you get to a point of self-delusion and provide hope and faith to the desperate. After all it is not even so bad despite all the cynics berating such people. Sometimes it takes some fake hope to motivate people into action. People have taken a positive step to apply for a job and get the courage to present themselves well at the interview, all because someone has blessed them with a block of bullshit.

The outlandish to the dark horse

Are you an extrovert or an introvert and have you undergone some phoney test to measure it? A few things need to be borne in mind on this subject. One is that you can choose to be more introvert and build confidence to display more extroverted behaviour. Secondly, those that try to encourage others to change in this respect are leading the world further down the path of homogenisation. We thus become more and more alike with less to distinguish ourselves from one another. There is beauty in diversity and dryness in too much indistinguishability where all are blended into one mass of uniform sameness. Some will be quite bold in some circumstances and more reserved in others and we find our forte through interaction. We might be shy at work and forward in play. It can be a mistake to assume that people who seem quite quiet standing in front of you are equally so elsewhere. We are not one or the other, neither introverted or extroverted, but somewhere in between the two with some capable of addressing a large crowd yet shy in other situations. Likewise, lots of other personality tests are ideally suited for entertaining people on their lunch breaks and are handy ice breakers to get conversations going.

Some aspects of your characteristics are fixed, but others can wane and wallow like the wind, confidence can come and go. We get more courage at an early age by being in close proximity to our mother figure. With mother about to embolden us we explore and gain confidence. People have assumed that chucking kids into the pit will toughen them up. It seems as though this actually has the reverse effect. They become stronger with the support of others.

The biggest problem with trying to gain confidence is the enormous effort involved. Facing the fears and getting accustomed to making mistakes. Over time you can shed the feelings of embarrassment and awkwardness once you understand that everyone has to learn for themselves. Looking stupid is inevitable at times and laughing at yourself makes it irrelevant. You have to want to change and have the impetus to make it happen. It is so much easier to hide away in your cubbyhole and spiral down retreating further from face to face interaction. In most cases there is no actual danger or risk of physical harm just pathos, imagined worry about being thought of as ineligible. Real confidence can take years to acquire and sadly in a few short moments it can be taken away in those rare occasions when something unpleasant happens. A great deal of work is required to bring people that have been attacked in some way, back to how they were before.

Labels

I have often heard the argument that there is no such thing as normal. Everyone is a little different, but some seem to stand out that bit more. When we take a look at the people around us, we can see the judgement in action. Snide remarks and people distancing themselves. We could talk about being normal in a wide range of respects describing our mannerisms along with obsessions, compulsions, and aversions. Normal in appearance. Normal in habits. Normal in manner. Normal in everyday functions. Normal experience of pain vs weird pleasure. Normal in the way we are treated. Normal in the way we are accepted. Normal in our comprehension, things that we miss or just pass us by without noticing. What the masses see and the many don't, which can be viewed as missing out or counted as lucky not to know. Normal routine where any upset can cause distress. What we can do normally but sometimes can't manage. Thoughts and feelings can be normal to us but alien to others. Feeling normal can count in an objective of fitting in, but there are instances where it is coupled with that wish of being a bit different.

Measuring and categorising normality is fraught with contention. Generalising can get us into trouble. It could be something as simple as whether someone owns a common item or not to something about us that can be at such a level that it tips the balance. The oddity is sufficient for many to describe it as abnormal. People may support and comfort us with the notion that no one is normal and that nothing is normal. However, it can be a proper problem. It might be a difference that we like or hate, so we can either attempt to change where possible or embrace it. Then there are those that think they are normal, but are surprised to find out that their reality is not shared by everyone. When they discuss the way they see things and describe it to people they realise that it is not as common as they assumed.

You could draw up an endless list of things that make a person different. Our individual genome will produce a huge range of characteristics. Some things are not related to our genetic makeup, but concern things that happen or not during our development. From abuse or neglect to living with over bearing parents, countless circumstances can cast a shadow on the way we behave and react. You may consider yourself (rightly or wrongly) to be normal in some respects and less so in others.

Whether we wish to be completely normal or not, whatever that may be, there is still something to be said for being unusual and interesting. Up to a point. People have major issues that grow and expand making ordinary tasks harder by the day. When we have difficulties doing these everyday things, things that plenty of others manage with ease, it can come as a relief when an official diagnosis is found. Once a label has been put on it we can blame our genes, it is something we are born with. Our faults lie with our parents or an outside agent. Our identity can become framed by the label put on us, we don't object to it, instead see it as something that gives us that little bit extra. We can be proud of it regardless of whether it is seen as a form of disability or not. Aside from it being a talking point it can be called upon as an excuse for goofy behaviour and draws wanted scrutiny of our character. Those with a 'uniqueness' may even feel more cherished. You get this niggling sense that having a label is a benefit and it becomes a part of someone's identity. This can be despite the drawbacks that can undoubtedly be very inhibiting.

To be viewed as attention seeking is not desirable. In a large number of cases people didn't set out at the beginning to get attention, nor is the continuance of a disorder always used to keep being noticed. Although there is no doubt that the problems are very real we discover that people take an interest in what is wrong with us. One may unwittingly use our conditions to set us apart. It is quite natural to want some attention more when things aren't going as we like maybe. We get varying levels of attention according to how we interact and how much we play on things.

When the opportunity arises to say something we select something on our mind that may or may not be of interest to others. People come out with stuff that can be piffle, trifle or concerns things that most might not usually take heed of. However, as it is something they have chosen to talk about, we can fulfil their wish to get what they have to say off their chest. Nevertheless when it is too often about normalcy problems it might not be helpful to keep talking about it all the time, thus giving them attention solely because of the issue. This becomes more significant if these discussions are at the expense of talk about other things that have merit in their own right. No matter how big the handicap, impediment or whatever the abnormality thing is, an individual will have real achievements and good qualities to refer to. There are also countless discussions available about things going on in the world, not just related to them and what they are facing all the while. One can ramp up the engagement when talking about things that are not about their disorder, issues and symptoms of their problems and listen more and feeding back positively, even if it is a bit exaggerated.

Some with life issues may hide away and not use it get any limelight at all. They don't seem to fit in as well as others yet may show themselves in areas that we don't all get to see. We have expectations and are prone to have a want to sort it mentality, which might not be welcome or even necessary. Living by your own standards and leading by example is not the same as wishing others to blossom with the same vibrancy in the same situations. Being normal, being conformist is an untidy concept with such a mishmash of contrasting characters around. We can live as a recluse, but good company is good company either via inclusion at the fringe or in the mainstream.

I recall the excitement of our cat having a litter of five kittens, but was unsettled to see one of them being pushed away. The runt was rejected. We were able to intervene and ensure its survival. It leads me to propose that many animals including us are naturally, inherently, inclined to harshly discriminate based upon a normality judgement. We are much more inclined to overcome differences now, but in early times all of us were much more prejudicial. An initial distaste and wariness is often pushed aside, but only when we understand the person more.

There will always be some form of inconsistency in the way we treat people according to appearance. One way or another we all get victimised because of one thing or another, some for being fat, unsymmetrical, having acne or talking with a lisp or a myriad of other reasons. Many will take action to mask and hide the problem where they can for they can't be bothered with the issue. They do not want it to be the centre of what they are and have a real wish to engage with others on things of their choice. They don't want to be defined by their noticeable physical oddity. There is more to someone than what they look like and it is a tiresome timewasting hassle to be constantly dealing with the barriers. Nevertheless, only a saint is able to honestly say that they never ever discriminate. We do judge and differentiate people in many ways, whether it is about someone's education, accent, dress sense, conduct, manners, spending habits etc etc. Few are immune. We think that these kind of judgements are fair, but saying anything derogatory about physical differences is not. It is useful to remind ourselves of this when we don't want the grief of taking action against perpetrators of unkindness.

To want

It is easy to say we want to change but real change is only achieved when it is a wholehearted declaration of wanting it. To bring about change, change which we will assume is for the better according to the one with the problem, there has to be an absolute wish for it. Spelling out the steps is a whole different matter to actually doing it. Someone that wants something puts themselves through any reasonable measure to achieve it and will confront each hurdle they face. Failure indicates that they don't really want to change their ways. Once the serious declaration of wanting to do something about the problem has been made, the battle begins. With the help of people with the relevant expertise, progress is usually quite quick. Even when you seek support from those with experience in your particular problem area, they can't wave a magic wand and all comes right, for the desire to change has to come from within the person seeking the help.

All of us will experience issues to some degree and it is a mistake to consider any 'disorder' to be something you either have or you don't. There is a variation in the level and a biased decree as to whether it even matters or not. Many will not regard it as a problem, whereas others will see it as the 'be all and end all'. We will each handle it very differently and who decides when the threshold is exceeded to then stick the label on it, provides plenty of scope for contention. If you are on the cusp you might never get a diagnosis and could quite easily consider it normal, something that we live with. You may need to talk to a lot of different people to compare your sensations, urges or feelings to see what is common and what is less so. Tests can be subjective and far less accurate compared to measuring your running speed or vision where precise markers can be laid out. No amount of study can put you in someone else's shoes, inside their mind and body to get a true grasp of the comparison of their perspective and yours.

Our perception of ourselves is so different to what we imagine it to be. Cultural differences allow us to stand out and some things do not ever sink in. On occasions, years later, you see in hindsight errors in your ways. What we took as normal then, seem bizarre now.

Quite often there is a magical upside to being 'abnormal', a special capability not necessarily a prosaic ability to recall a sequence of playing cards or memorise innumerable facts and figures, something else instead. Many people regarded as geniuses have significant character flaws, act oddly with eccentricity running in parallel to their brilliance. Instead of putting hard work in to learn the skills to operate in a demanding, complex world, people that fall behind are a bit reticent to admit to laziness and reach for a label instead. It is much easier to plump for a supposed clinical reason for being behind or being incapable than putting yourself on a level playing field as the rest.

People learn to read at different rates. In a lot of instances the major lack of reading practice is the main reason the mix up of letters and words takes place. It is seductive claiming that it is a disability instead.

When we get it wrong

I can think of countless mistakes that I have made in the past, things I have said that might have been a little hurtful or patronising or just not clever. Whether the people in question took that much offence and remembered it as vividly as me, I am not sure. These memories come back time and time again with far more prescience than all the more numerous nice, kind empathetic things that I was a part of. Dwelling upon them serves no real purpose apart from the experience we gain and usefulness in modifying our ways for future encounters. The process of recalling the mistakes keeps us out of trouble, steers us away from danger even though the incidents are mostly pretty trivial. Rather than leaving a trail of un-compassion, we seek to furrow kudos in our wake.

I am certain that apologising for mistakes that I have made has gone a long way to help the situation. I found it better to listen to the complaint first, then say sorry. It is easy to blurt out an apology, but it means very little if you don't fully understand what you have done wrong. It might not be easy to listen to the grievance at length, but it is essential if you want them to move on.

I have been in some situations where people have become a little offish and have been in a bit of a dilemma as to what to do. I could either broach the subject and find out what, or even if, I have done something wrong or just leave it be and stay out of their way. In some cases, there might not seem much point as the awkwardness won't be for long. I was at the helm of a sailing boat and during the docking a go around was called. In an aeroplane I was accustomed to hit the throttle and get full power to climb out and circle around to attempt another landing. Putting the pedal to the metal in a cramped sea port is not appreciated by everyone else there. It didn't help that there were three or four people shouting loudly as to what they wanted me to do. I noticed that on account of all this, someone was becoming rather distant and I made the effort to sort it out. In this case I made an apology straight off which may not have been necessary, especially as I will be going home fairly soon. Once they understood that a go around can give rise to an instinctive response to a pilot they were quite jolly about it. The change in atmosphere was immediate.

I find the ignoring route, avoiding contact is a hassle and the situation can be remedied so easily by being a bit humble. I see people play the long game as they know they are in the right and wait for an impasse to come about to prove themselves correct. This is all very well, but you have to spend days or weeks with discomfort. Undoubtedly there are countless other tactics but head on and apologising if required is so powerful. Forgetting any pride and using humility gets them onside. I prefer not to have things festering as it would likely be a bane to me and I could miss out on more than what the other party would. The world is full of millions of permutations and so many different situations arise, but I find that there are occasions where there is no point being seen to be right all the while.

I had a break-in and some stock was damaged by the water that came in through the hole in the roof. During the clean-up we left some of the refuse by a bin across the road. Some days later I had a call from the authorities saying that they had someone prepared to stand up in court and testify that I had left some rubbish by the bin. With all the hassle of dealing with the damage done to the property, I had completely forgotten about it. I cleared up the bags and then went to confront the person who had reported me. Now they could have come over or even given us a call to ask us to do something about it, but instead they went straight into a formal complaint with the authorities. Bracing themselves for a stream of words, stating my displeasure at what they had done, I explained that I had had a break in and I apologised for leaving the bags there. I felt that I didn't want an 'enemy' on my doorstep and it was better to be cordial even if a reader would see such an example as being rather righteous. I can also point out that as far as I can tell, no matter how bad things are for you, everyone else wants to live their life unaffected.

Mentality

We are all mad. Try and prove you are not mad and people will really think you are a nutter. It all depends on whether you think you have a problem or not. Is it something that is holding you back. Is it minor or something people keep bringing up. It is all about opinion. Some agree, some disagree, some find a new label to place on it and file into the biggest book ever produced by man regarding the mind.

Empathy

If someone has a broken leg it is easy to see what the problem is and help them get about. You can fetch and carry things for them, helping with the practicalities in any way you can. Commiserating, caring and assisting someone with a mentality issue can be much harder. People with problems in their head may take longer to 'heal' than many with identifiable physical injuries as it takes much longer to understand and get to the root of the problem. Even a headache is harder to relate to than a damaged ligament, where the struggle is outwardly noticeable. It is so much easier to get involved as you can visibly see the problem, unlike when someone has some mental concern. With our unbending desire to advise and help those with problems we throw all kinds of ideas about with wanton abandon hoping to get to the quick fix.

Phobias

When it comes to fears, phobias and bad memories there are some simple techniques that people use to drastically reduce the problem. Once you realise that there is a limit to how much anxiety you can feel you can start to tackle it. It is just a case of taking yourself up to that maximum, experiencing it and coping with it. As you approach the issue your anxiety levels will rise and rise, but it will always peak and then go down. Because people pull away before they reach the peak they don't get to overcome the problem. Whether it is the fear of certain insects, talking in public or associating in large groups and so on, courage is needed if you want to make progress.

Things which are pretty innocuous to the general populous can bring out a great deal of fear in some people. The range is huge. Overcoming the fear and enabling you to contend with it doesn't mean you will begin to like it necessarily, but it will enable you to handle the situations much much better. That hideous feeling in the pit of your stomach, real pain, a true clenching acidic sensation, not just a mental foible, sure gives those with this experience plenty of reasons to attempt to shy away and come up with excuses to steer clear. Anxiety and stress about phobic areas arise sometimes later in life where the problem never existed before. Pinning down the cause is not always simple.

There is a step by step process to go through which results in the gradual killing of all the anxiety. People usually begin when they have had enough of all the procrastinations and are fed up with having to make excuses all the time when put on the spot. It is a case of being ready to face it. If you were fearful of spiders for example, then the first task is to view a picture of one. As you study the picture your anxiety level will rise, until it reaches a maximum. It will then gradually tail off. You will soon discover that the anxiety, whilst not very pleasant, doesn't harm you. The next step would be to view an actual spider from a distance allowing the anxiety to build up once again, then allow time for it to gradually die down. Bit by bit you will learn to deal with the fear and if you make the effort you will shortly be capable of picking one up. Your mind will eventually become 'rewired' to become virtually free of the phobia. You may never get to like spiders, but you can at least become far far less afraid of them. There may be some benefit from tapping parts of your hand and head during the worst of the anxiety as this can help refocus. Any method that you do try needs to be repeated quite a few times, very little is sorted overnight.

Boldness is required to separate a memory of a bad experience from what is essentially something we normally like. It pops up in life when we refuse to eat and drink certain things through to unwillingness to approach people that we don't know. Whether via self-help or doing things with a friend at your side, anxiety gets replaced by confidence the more often you try it. The following walkthrough about how we can overcome the fear of water is potentially handy if the boat you are on submerges and swimming is a popular pastime anyway.

Chucking someone in at the deep end of a pool might be a fun way to get them to swim, but it could create an aversion to pools and swimming altogether. It doesn't take much to spot the children who are still learning to swim, they will be the ones that are in the pool with their hair still dry. Oddly, the best place to learn the basics is not in a pool, but in the bath or with a big bowl of water. The first step is to hold your nose and place you head face down into the water. When you are happy doing that you can then take a deep breath and hold one side of your nose breathing out slowly and then submerse your face into the water. The aim is to overcome the fear of water entering your nose and having an unpleasant 'drink'. If you keep practising until you can manage to exhale into the water for 30 seconds, you will then be able to repeat the exercise without holding your nose at all. If you learn to submerge your face and hold your breath under the water for longer and longer, you can then try it out in the pool or the sea. You may find yourself swimming underwater easier at first than on the surface, but the ability to submerge yourself is pivotal. I managed to coax huge strapping people in Africa who had not been anywhere near water before and who were somewhat wary of water to swim in under thirty minutes. I used the same techniques on some youngsters, including my own in the hot tub and had I known about this method when younger myself, I would not have spent hours and hours with rings and floats never progressing much.

Visualisation

Having a bad memory can stick out ten times more than a good one. It can become very troublesome in ways that is hard to explain. Thankfully, as all memories good or bad are a chain of items linked one to another we can learn to re-route some.

When something triggers something we would rather forget, we can change the thought pattern. You create a junction just before you begin to enter into the areas that you would prefer not to think about. You walk through the scenario in your mind from the start and instead of going into the nasty part, you think of a different ending. You have to do this over and over hundreds of times dwelling on the nice thoughts at the end. Such bad memories can be triggered by a whole host of things, some within the routine of a day, others by anything from a smell to a particular word or sound. Each time it is set off you run it through to this different outcome. Over time the whole escapade fades and you don't even voyage deep into the nicer parts, the triggers don't have much of an effect at all. Although it has to be repeated many times, the issue can subside within a matter of days or at worst a month or so depending on the severity.

What bothers you will be innocuous to others, but most people have a thing about something or other at some point in their lives. Some people hate the sight of shit and confronting some expectantly in an unclean toilet can be disturbing. So the thought trail to play out would be to re-enter the bathroom in your mind and then visualise a nice clean flushing pan followed by coming out and meeting a nice person. Dwell on the interaction with the person in any way you see fit. They say time heals, but this process accelerates it considerably. Terrifying flights on aeroplanes lead to wondrous holidays. Ugly is replaced with beauty in the thought streams. Injuries are displaced by a healed up individual. Simple diversions that are repeated each and every time will eradicate the nightmares fairly quickly. You pick something in life that you like a lot, then dwell upon various aspects of it for a good ten to fifteen seconds each time the bad thought gets your attention.

Visualisation and active 'disappointment' strategies can be employed to lessen the temptation of gambling, gaming and drug taking. When something becomes a destructive aspect of your life instead of an acceptable vice, a less mental and more physical enactment is used. Addicts have been encouraged to go through the process of drug preparation, but not the actual taking of it. They may handle the substance, heat it and dissolve it in solution, then fill a syringe but not inject it. During the first few times of doing so they will notice their expectation, excitement level and intense feeling of anticipation rise dramatically. However, as they become accustomed to not receiving the powerful reward, these notions of anticipation diminish a little each time. When they see other users or come into contact with the drug in their environment they do not get the associated feelings of expectancy to any great degree, as they would have done before they used this technique.

Maximising the senses

It is surprising how a mundane afternoon wandering around the shops can be turned into an entertaining experience. It might be a cold day with light drizzle, not to your liking, but you can enjoy the freshness, the difference, the change felt by your senses. You can actively revel in each moment and appreciate the sensory inputs. Try for a bit of fun, try purely for the experience, as an experiment, talking to as many people as possible. You needn't consider how lucky you are that you can walk nor well enough to manage unless you are stopped by the lack of daring. Make the effort to talk to the shelf stacker, say hello to the people waiting at the bus stop, talk to as many people as you can. You might get an odd reaction or two at times, but you won't be an anonymous figure that day. Never let one miserable person spoil the party. There is no need to transform yourself into the local crazy one, but people can feel invisible doing a mundane job and generally appreciate a small interaction.

Another little game people play is when at a party or gathering, they approach the dullest looking person and see if they can find out something interesting about them. Alternatively, they select someone who may appear posh or brash and make a point of having a conversation with them in particular. You will more than likely discover that the upper class demeanour doesn't run too deep and behind the loud exhibition is someone full of life and energy. The point being that the way people portray themselves and the early impression that they give is not always consistent with their overall character. Getting to know someone a little and listening to them changes your overall interpretation of the people of this world. Just being alive is enough to interact as you see fit. Once again, you can do all of the above or ignore the lot for it is meant as an example to allow people to picture possibilities rather than being suggestive.

Problems can be our salvation and our inspiration providing an impetus to set forth on a new challenge. More awkward and unforeseen problems that we come across can test our individual character. When things don't pan out the way we want, some people become frustrated whilst others simply take advantage of their situation. When held up by a late arriving train an opportunity to strike up a conversation with those in the same boat arises for example.

Some delayed in traffic use the time to have a little think. This is easier said than done though if the pressures of work mean that the knock on effect is costly. We can't all reconfigure our lives as easily as others to reduce the weight on our shoulders. However, it can be factored into our decisions about what we take on.

Moments of adversity arrive randomly and unpredictably so you can't go out today and test how you will cope with it. Nevertheless, when they do arise you can be prepared to determine whether being outwardly annoyed and stressed is so necessary. Sometimes it will be, but more often than not, being cool and rising to the challenge is more productive. Prior thinking and revaluating what happened before enables you to react differently in the future. However, being human entails letting off steam sometimes and like all things if not balanced or too frequent then not so beneficial. A punch bag set up in the garden provides an outlet for frustration.

An article printed in a small journal doesn't have the same impact as the absolutely exact same article written in a highly respected one. Artists who perform on a prestigious stage get admiration and attention that equally talented ones in back street gaffs do not. There is a story of a highly competent musician that busked one afternoon and was pretty much ignored by all the passers-by. Some of those who walked on past, not even giving them a glance, were on the way to get costly tickets to see that busker perform that night on stage. We associate the venue with quality and it affects our expectations. It can be the same with food and drink. Just because something is ten times the price of another it does not always mean it is going to be that much better. More than likely the people you are with and the things that you are doing at the time will influence the taste much more. Being switched on to what is around you and appreciate the qualities of the here and now for what it is, is quite a thing.

Stale popcorn has been given to moviegoers and no complaints were forthcoming due to our inability to properly focus on more than one thing at a time. When we do hone in on what we have in our hands we can be so much more critical and sometimes feel a duty to be complimentary.

Yoga it out

They say you can have too much of a good thing. When we find something is becoming more of an addiction than a reasonable pleasure, we can begin to worry and consider doing something about it. Some will go too far the other way. Seeing themselves a little unfit and go straight into marathon running rather than making the effort to walk to work instead of using the car. Just because you are doing something to excess, doesn't mean you have to give it up completely. It can be a case of cutting back and cutting back without yelling from the rooftops that you have transformed yourself and ended your compulsion totally.

Managing without may need some kind of coping strategy. People find a distraction and allow the time to pass, seeing if they can keep the mind off the issue for an hour at a time. You can find yourself giving up on so much that life is pleasure free. Those that feel that it would be really annoying to put so much effort into doing the right thing, according to those that say what that is and then getting struck and killed by lightening, do have a point.

On the subject of time, our experience of it sure changes when we are occupied. The older you are the slower your internal clock becomes and a minute really seems like 50 seconds whereas for a child it is closer to 70. Count to 60 and compare with a clock and see what your life stage is.

Many will start a new activity, do it for a few weeks before giving it up. It is not always easy to identify the exact reason that puts us off carrying on. People think about that last time they went and that they found they felt better for going last time, so they don't dwell on it at all and just go. They just go. People with mountains to move aren't daunted by the scale of the task, rather than having too many reservations about all the effort, they tune out and get on with it. There is a difference between being in reflection mode all the time and actually making headway on something.

Someone I knew analysed a tiny irritant in their life, namely the chore of ironing. They managed to isolate the main element that was the real cause of why they disliked doing it so much. It wasn't the ironing itself, it was the hassle of getting the iron out and setting the ironing board up each time. The solution was simple and that was to simply leave the board up ready to be used when needed. This anecdote is trivial and trite compared with the struggles felt by people in some places, yet makes a significant point. If you can work out the key elements of what is not good in your life, you can find a way of resolving it. If you think long and hard about the root of the problems, you invariably find a way to lessen the trouble. In the meantime, putting things off for ever more leads to a lot of dissatisfaction. I have only used an iron to transfer some stickers, but I too like certain tools and equipment ready to roll all plugged in and without piles of junk atop. With everything having a set place, thereby easy to find, I am not put off by having to clear all the mess and faff about before getting a job underway. It must have stemmed from life growing up where there was never the right stuff to do what you wanted, just old rusty rubbish that left you hours out of pocket and deeply frustrated.

It is not just doing jobs around the house that we delay tackling, for we put off going somewhere if there is fear of great discomfort amongst the journey. After years of sufferance when we are in our youth, we shy away much more as we get older. Recalling so many experiences of cramped conditions, queuing and the indignity we faced, that we warm to the idea of staying at home rather than endure more. Unless we can find a way of dealing with it or selecting more favourable travel times and more spacious seating arrangements our body rules our head.

Comfort is an odd beast, after all many forms of discomfort are usually only temporary, maybe a few hours or so with no long term damage to our body, but that is not the point, it is the dread prior that gives us the will to find ways out of it. If you upgrade your bed or your couch you use it often and can smile over and over when stretched out slumbered, it is a longer term life enhancement. Whereas the torture of a trip is transient. Do you need to suffer a bit from time to time to appreciate your comforts? Maybe, but commuting every day amongst so many of the self-absorbed, with you becoming less graceful by the month yourself, can lead to rethinking the virtue of an otherwise wonderful job. Pushing working somewhere else with closer proximity to home higher up the on list of desires. You can use mentality to overcome the hate of it for sure, switch off during the pain and reconcile it with it being the means to an end whereby greater wealth down the line will free you from this, hopefully, eventually.

The opportunity of going on safari came about and upon seeing other people return in small mini vans, cramped, hot and visibly worse for wear from the whole day of endurance on never ending bumpy roads we made a decision. Too dangerous they said, but swapping one danger for another transformed a nightmare into the best few days ever. By hiring our own tank type jeep we could stop where and when we wanted and had the best seat in the vicinity. I could also educate my partner on their driving habits and get them to see the benefit of going around the holes in the road rather than through them all the time.

Wherever you seek complexity and sophistication in the human life form you find nothing more than a slight variant on basic simple things. Each thing is intertwined and only seems complex when we don't bother to put any great thought into it.

Misconception

We don't grow out of copying others, we just change who we copy. It is so easy to be strung along and to take gossip at face value. What if you hear people saying that having 10 drinks or more a night is normal? What is the result if teenagers get the impression from their friends that pretty much everyone is going to bed with someone or another? If we get to see the results of a survey, we can feel comfortable with our own limits.

Our friends say anything up to ten drinks is normal, five or six times a week. Survey says, the average is three. Our friends give the impression that most people are having sex at this age. Surveys say, less than ten percent have lost their virginity by that time. If unsure we can find out the truth and be reassured that we are not the odd one out, but are actually in the majority.

There is plenty of noise made when people are up to something. They create a feeling that a big exciting event is underway and they make it known that if you are not a part of it that you are missing out terribly. They are not so fond of exclaiming nothing nothing nothing nothing party nothing nothing. People like to make it sound really great by missing out all the tedious bits in between.

What a prat, that Geoff has some disturbing ways says a person who likes the influencer role. The influencer, the leader isolates someone to get them ostracised and excluded. Invariably, it is a lot of nonsense. The group are told how they deal with the person in question expecting everyone in the flock to follow their lead rather than making their own mind up.

It takes one brave member of this group to realise that they have been duped and see the value of making their own judgements for this to unravel. The others will be disappointed that you are not going along with it. We handle it somehow. People close ranks and take a side ignoring their discomfort partly because they are frightened of being pushed out too. It is quite good fun having someone to pick on, it bonds the group. Unity before reason.

Protect or share the magic?

People call upon others with a certain skill set to carry out a task, get something repaired or constructed and wonder a little at the ease at which they carry out the job. Few craftsmen will reveal the basis of their talent, as it might not be in their interest to do so. What most do not see is the hidden struggle and enormous effort that goes on to gain the ability and hone the art. People don't understand what it takes to get the knack of something that on the surface appears simple but is actually tremendously difficult to master. They are clueless. Completely unaware of what is needed. There is widespread ignorance of the scale of sacrifice needed to get to a position of competence. People in demand have been through long periods of frustration to get to where they are. Unless you have done something similar you are unaware of the difficulties involved, it passes you by.

A lot of earth has to be shovelled and false starts countered before any real progress is made. There will be plenty of times where you take the wrong path and accept that that is progress in itself. You have to try some things which fail first before you get it right. They were critical steps that had to be taken even though they produced very little. If there are five ways of doing something, then on the balance of probabilities, you won't find the best one first. Once you have tried two or three, you then realise that there are even more than five but each dead end is one idea killed and the coffin nails you have developed become a feature in the final product. Laymen are kept in the dark to maintain the balance of those that have a lot and those that have a lot less.

Boldness

One weapon in the armoury of a trickster is none other than brazen assertive boldness. They will enter a building and pass through any security there with the same posture as one who has legitimate access. As they look and walk inside like they are an affiliate or worker, rather than wary and coy they are much less likely to be properly challenged. There will be times in life where this can be employed to great effect, not to break any law as such but to get around some bureaucracy of one sort or another. As a humble soul in charge we need to be suspicious of bold individuals if we want to avoid being cheated.

Victims dither. So to avoid being one you can make yourself, appear that you know what you are doing and where you are going, rather than looking lost and vulnerable. Walk with purpose.

You can't fight the whole world without making a slip or two and one slip can be fatal. Thus when in danger, acting a little crazy, demented, to confuse the situation can give you the vital time to slip away. You have to consider whether you want an epitaph of bravado or play some more days of your life by burying self-esteem. There are many stories of warfare where only the cowards came home to let the people know the fate of the rest.

It is not the cowardly behaviour that is the issue, if you have too many in your army you will lose, but too much confidence and not enough respect for what can go wrong can wipe out people in their prime. So what if people brandish you a chicken, that is soon forgotten as you go through life, a scar on your face remains.

Opportunities are lost not for the lack of chance, but for the reluctance to have the nerve to ask. A good friend of mine saw a motorcycle left outside a neighbour's house for a long time, unused and neglected. With a little care and attention, it would be ideal for restoration. When it went, they asked the neighbour what they had done with it and found to their despair that it was dumped. Had they asked beforehand the neighbour would have given it to them for free to get it off their hands. In the same way as braving the request for a date with a someone you fancy, a promising looking soul, we know that in most instances the worst case scenario is that we get a blunt no. Fortune favours the brave is a good cliché and wasted chances litter our lives.

Imagine a biblical farmer who is concerned with his crops, as it hasn't rained for some time. He has faith that on past form and based upon his experience it is likely to rain at some point, but he doesn't know when or for sure. He can though, stop sitting about all day hoping for the best and make a solid effort to irrigate his land by getting water from somewhere else. You can meander through your life if you want to, hoping for something fortunate to happen, but those that thrive take positive steps to help themselves.

Many will shy away from asking too many direct questions, too intrusive, far too probing they think but it is not a great surprise that people respond positively when put on the spot. This is because on the whole people like nothing better than talking about themselves. Caution is required and a good sense of when someone feels awkward is needed so that you then back away. If unsure I would simply ask if they feel comfortable talking about the subject in question and change course where applicable. Without the confrontation and head on discussion I would not be able to explore the avenues of thought that I feel merits pursuing.

Two primary devises are used, one is resisting jumping in and the other is repeating the question or a variation of it several times. Having the audacity to wait for a response by saying nothing but keeping the eyeballs, yours and theirs, transfixed elicits more than mere gabber. If that is not producing the result that you want, I would rephrase and reapply the pressure appealing for information. If all else fails, then I could show disinterest and hope that they want more attention and offer up more insights. It is all about sincerity and the ability to maintain some confidentiality with forward digging. It is not solely about prying as couples for instance don't always broach certain subjects with one another and an outside force can bring things out into the open and encourage some helpful reflection. Subjects are not always talked about at home. Some things are bubbling just under the surface and via an outsider they come to the fore.

Completism

The trap of completism is quite pervasive. We want to get the whole set. Sometimes the set will be outlined by nature, but in most cases it is some organisation or person that devised it. We want to get and read every book by an author, store each bank note issued by a nation or note down every type of animal within a category that we spot on our travels. People will go to quite long lengths to complete a series of one sort or another. They do so without paying much regard to the real reason behind it, they just want the full set. I recall a friend going to the shop every day to buy some more stickers to fill an album. The hunt for the last few became pretty expensive (for the parents that is). When it finally was complete the album was tossed aside.

Then we have the sporty types who want to traverse every crevasse in every land just to get an 'official' record. They do so forgetting that someone else, a person, made the qualifying rules up that they adhere to. Whilst many will enjoy the pursuit, the climbing, the test of endurance the justification of counting it as a success or not is on someone else's terms.

A clever company can capitalize on this by making a bunch of objects that fulfil peoples' desire to get the whole complete lot. They will issue smaller quantities of one type to induce a sense of rarity and more scrambling for them. Completism is a gremlin in the workings of the mind that lies in conjunction with the parallel power of this curiosity and reward. We are compelled to fill in those pervasive gaps that our inquisitiveness provides. It gets us out and about and provides a focus so maybe we ought to avoid sneering too much.

Tactics

During our lives we work out the most productive ways of doing things. We know full well that round wheels are a big improvement on square ones, but quite often subject ourselves to a bumpy ride in life when we fail to stick to tactics that we know are problem free. We can play a game like pool or chess with a beginner and because we know they are a beginner we can get sloppy and impatient for a quick win. With our guard down and going against solid tactics that we would usually use, we end up losing to a novice. This translates into other areas of life. We know the method that works well, but use shortcuts that appear tempting and end up costing us more. Not using your experiences makes a mockery of learning it in the first place. It is not your stature itself but the expected response and actions of someone with stature that counts. Such highly regarded individuals on form will pause before jumping in and make much better decisions.

Many things in life can't be undone, chances are missed, opportunities lost and cash misspent. In such cases we can come to call them regrets. Change the word regret to mistake and see how you look at the error then. It can turn what has happened into more of a positive. Regrets are too much about focusing on things in the past. Mistakes provide an opportunity to change what we do in the future when the circumstances are similar. You can highlight dangers to other people so that they may not fall prey to the same hurt. A mistake can lead to a lesson learnt and it can give you a motive to avoid missing out next time. There is a subtle difference between a regret and a mistake. The mentality part is either dwelling on the past or utilising the gain from mistakes made.

Sometimes you have to forget about the reasons why you are in a mess right now. Put aside who is at fault, time is pressing. Look at what you have, what the solution is to move forward. When things are back on the straight and narrow you can then reflect on how and why things turned ugly. Your car has smoke belching out of it. You want to stop and argue, blame the person who forgot to check the oil or just get on and handle it.

Many chess players are thinking of what move to play that benefits them without spending any time looking at what the opponent is planning. Being prepared for what they are likely to do is as important as your own tactics. Too many worry only about their own hand rather than taking into account the probable line of attack of their rival. As each opponent will have different strategies you can't always use the same approach every time. Instead you must adapt and change according to the individual situation. Adaptability is the key to success in many games.

In life, there is always a counter view. Nothing is concrete. There are different sides to the story and some things are no longer applicable. The points you make now become less relevant as things evolve. No statement can factor in all the possible variations, yet we steadfastly believe what we are doing is right sometimes preferring to ignore opposing ideas. Ultimately there is not enough time or will to worry as if we did then nothing would get done. You can debate for an eternity but eventually when you are hungry you need to eat and sooner or later we need to pick an option.

When a new way of looking at our behaviour comes along it can shed light on our thinking, overriding past ideas. That too becomes superseded. It is hard to resist trashing old ideas completely and replacing them with new. In later reflection, we see that both ideas have some merit and need to be tailored to suit the situation.

Psychology presumptions

A few psychologists think they are clever by claiming a lot of people are dumb stupid human beings with irrational traits. During the era of taxi drivers, before they were replaced by self-driving cars, some odd behaviour was observed. During the rainy days, some would quit work early. The rain brought plenty of customers in quick succession, lots not wishing to walk and get wet. Now, some would indeed capitalise on this and work all day making good money. The idiots would stop as soon as they earnt their normal daily target. But are they idiots? They may welcome those raining days as ones where they get to go home early and spend their afternoon under the covers with the partner. Maybe they could do a full day in the rain and have a sunny day off. Maybe the rain brings more jams and unpleasant driving conditions. Maybe we don't want to sit about waiting for the heavens to open. Maybe it only rains during the monsoon. Not everyone wants more money, not everyone cares about efficiency.

People selling dreams, selling houses are notoriously good at presenting a false image. Show the property when it is a glorious day and at a time when there is less traffic building up on the road outside. If you do not care about your credibility, if you care nothing for being genuine then persuade, prod, coax at will. We can easily get people to do what we want if we ignore what they really want. We know best, they are impressionable.

I take all this back if a first aid kit is made in such a way that mistakes are avoided and it does the job super well. The design guides us, that is all fine but ulterior motives are for skunks.

Perfection

Take three cars, a jeep a racing car and an everyday runabout. Which one is perfect? Jeeps can go off road but topple over if cornering too fast. They are also heavy and cumbersome. Lots of clearance underneath the vehicle enables off-road use, but this raises the centre of gravity and undermines the stability. The racing car is the quickest by far, but hopeless for your shopping and gets stuck in the mud really badly. So you have a compromise with the cheapest and most practical for everyday needs and the only sensible place to race it is in a stock car smash up event. This analogy applies to us humans as well. Nobody is perfect, only perfect for the application.

I once bought a drill bit made of solid carbide which was some 20 times dearer than a standard one. Yes, it drills with ease but I wouldn't lend it to anyone, not because it was so expensive but because it is brittle and easily broken if not used right. Each and everything has a negative. Never perfect for all circumstances irrespective of how much money they cost. Every change leads to a compromise; you improve something at the expense of something else.

Could a perfect human being be designed and created? Is it possible to make enhancements and eliminate present deficiencies without downsides? We are lead to believe that sometime soon all the believers will be saved and returned to a perfect world in a perfect form. Not only would this paradise be ten times more hellish than the world now, but every step you take, everything you do will be mistake and error free. No ladder you climb will fail, no cars will crash and no fun will there be had. An intelligence so great that those fortunate few will be swamped in brilliance. No arguments, no discord, no chance to be yourself. The world is always going to be full of strife, there will always be risks, there will always be injustices and unfairness. Perfection is accepting downsides.

We humans are built for certain things. Each above average ability is coupled with weaknesses in other areas. The size of your blood vessels dictates whether you will be good at short fast races, great at long distance endurance challenges or best for sitting watching others compete for vain glory. If you think that we could invent a human being that can vary the size and shape of the various body parts, adjusting according to the demands of the day, then you will be perfectly suited for day dreaming competitions. Even our minds are configured to excel in different ways and although there is a certain amount of plasticity, what gives on one hand takes on the other.

Dissent

To the dissenter Simon's success in life was all luck. Simon's popularity is misplaced, bought rather than earned. If Simon does some charitable work, then it will be deemed as something to make Simon look good. Everything Simon does shall be seen in a negative light. All positives are viewed with cynicism. Yet to most people Simon is seen as a decent sort.

The dissent was brought about by one thing, something big or maybe something small. Whether trivial or not that thing will mar all else that Simon does. From then on the question always arises of why Simon should count more than me, why listen to Simon when my views should always take centre stage.

Of course not everyone will see Simon as a saint and some won't be in the least bit bothered what Simon does or doesn't do or say. However, whereas the majority just get on with their lives and just make pleasantries when Simon is about, the dissenter will try and turn and sway as many people as possible. A true dissenter will make it their life's work to defame and make Simon appear as bad as possible.

So if you are the dissenter you might decide that giving Simon a wide berth is not befitting you. Instead you will prefer to stir up maximum trouble, as much as you can with any means at your disposal. Nothing illegal or dastardly, but endless vocal action. You need to do this without compromising your own position. A starting point would be to spread some half-truths. Never give the full story as that will do the opposite of what you want to achieve. Most people who get the complete picture will see Simon in a good light.

Any story can be spun to make Simon seem disingenuous making Simon appear untrustworthy or make others want to disown him. Not only is the first story people hear believed, but it is invariably remembered most clearly. Even when the full facts have been uncovered there will still be an element of doubt in the air. Worse still only a few that hear the rumours will be set straight. For example, Simon may have to be secretive not because of a desire to be sly, but because Simon has to protect somebody and avoid jeopardising a future event. A dissenter sees the discretion as bad form, but others will be fully understanding when they find out everything that is going on. Simon will still be marked out as a cagy type by those that didn't want to find out all sides of the story.

You won't get everyone to go along with your line of reasoning, but that doesn't matter as long as the numbers grow. Some people can be swayed quite easily, it is quite common for people to change their view on a whim but others will take much more persuasion. The point is to keep it going and going and rely on the adage of no smoke without fire and prevent Simon from dowsing the nonsense with a cold bucket of truth.

When you are in the presence of Simon and Simon appears to be getting an audience, people are listening, intervene and say this is boring. Saying the topic is boring is a good way to halt the conversation or at least spoil the flow. Whether people are finding it boring or not is beside the point, they don't want to be seen listening to something that could be viewed as such.

Dissenters can pop up when a new member joins a group, where an established member feels a little threatened and dislikes new competition. This new member may do or say one small thing that can start the seed of dissent. Heaven forbid they make a suggestion or attempt to move the group in a slightly new direction and change the status quo.

Dissent starts in the same way as a seed of curiosity does and builds relentlessly. It hinges on a key point being dislikeable. Certain aspects of Simon do not fit with our built-in preferences. It matters not one jot if the person whom you are gunning for is a decent individual. All attributes are switched to negative. It goes further than some name calling and derogatory remarks. It is a long grind of disapproval. A dissenter will seek every avenue to find a justification for their probing and aggravation. They will try and get other people to agree with them, rallying more and more people to share in the attack.

A dissenter's food is obviously the reaction, but simply ignoring it is not always possible. Having the story half told and distorted becomes a bug bear. Things of small interest are magnified far far beyond what is worth any serious attention in the normal world. To milk something small and make it seem important is their primary tactic. Having hate in their heart will not bother them in the slightest. So Simon needs a solution. If Simon shows annoyance or tries to rectify the situation it will probably make it worse.

There are many card and board games where players can find a counter move for every play you try. And in life there will also be something you can do too, to counter what people are doing. So one solid option is to embrace the dissenter, have them be your personal troll. All great people will have a trolling dissenter and gather more as their ubiquity rises. Does 'taking the mickey', poking fun in return make the situation worse? Does thanking them for their input help? As a subject of the nastiness can we maintain our composure and simply put the record straight when it really matters, rather than bother at each twist and turn. This can be very hard in particular when you have a case where you do not even know who the perpetrator is. If it escalates and turns threatening it is harder still.

We really do see things differently

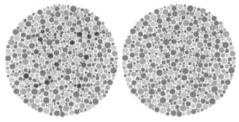

People who are colour blind may look at these plates and not see the characters. This provides a parallel to how we do not all see the same as everyone else. Call it a deficiency, call it a different ability, but we are not wired the same to visualize everything in equal measure. It is therefore no surprise that we can be incapable of seeing others people's standpoint at times. It is not because we are awkward necessarily, but because our makeup prevents us from grasping the same things as everyone around us. Hence we can argue for hours on end and never reach agreement. Couple this with preferences that are fixed and we can often be unable to see eye to eye.

Whilst the majority can see the characters in the circles imagine trying to convince someone who has a deficiency that those characters are there. No amount of persuasion, no amount of truth telling could ever convince them completely. They either take your word for it or more often than not deny it. They are configured to see what they see and perceive the world as it is to them. Hence why you can spend a lifetime hopelessly trying to change a person's position, change their political standpoint, or try to get them to see the good in someone.

I am the one

Oh how grand it will be to be the one proven right all along with dissenters all around. It was your suggestion, your bravery to stick your head above the parapet and soothsay, express concern or lament what people are doing is wrong and can be improved. Being vindicated and the only ones to spot the solution. Why is it that others can't see what you can. It seems to some as obvious and clear as day like those characters on the plates, but so many people just don't get it. Others are wrong for I can't be mistaken. One doesn't have to follow the herd at all times, but it is a dream come true to be single minded and determined to prove you were correct all along.

Self-belief can pay dividends, but for each success story there are countless others that go to their grave convinced that they were right and never able to reappraise and consider they were wrong in any way. The dissenter wants to be that one brighter individual that proves to the world that they were right and justified in uncloaking the devil, preventing the target from getting away with something. We can have self-doubt and think that since something is supported by so many people, it must be right. There have been a few that marched on with an idea regardless of all the doubters and made changes for the benefit of others. They have increased our collective knowledge. However, some have an unbending mentality that creates a large distraction. It need not have been brought to our attention if it was properly analysed before they made such a fuss.

The overwhelming majority of musicians have virtually no chance of getting to the top of their profession and having worldwide acclaim, but they have belief as they see others attain it with lesser works. This self-confidence is not restrained by any acknowledgement of delusion or acceptance that random fortuitous luck is a big part of what propels the minority into the spotlight. It goes without saying that if you don't try then your chances are zero, but there is only a physically small space at the top. The more you try to fit the greater the dilution.

Rate, review and recommend

I recall going to a new hotel where the location was good, the furnishing wild and new and having nothing to complain about. That was until I opened the curtains and was faced with a wall. No window. For some that would be of little concern, but for me it was a case of finding somewhere else as early as possible the next day. Whether it is a hotel room, restaurant or an item we buy, when a key ingredient is deficient it can become customary to pick holes in every other aspect. Other issues that would normally be a minor niggle now become something we vocally disapprove of. We begin to find fault in every corner. If the basics are right, we are more content to put up with other problems. Each of us will have our priorities and recommend to others based upon what we feel is most important.

People want what seems to them to be a fair deal irrespective of reality and will push for it regardless of the long-term effects and who they deprive in the process. Principles before pragmatism. The dissent tips the balance and sets the tone of any appraisal we make of many things and many people. This will apply to political systems and policies made by governments in the same way. And the glorious thing is that nothing can be done about it as people are born differently and stuck with likes set in order like plates stacked upon one another, liking one thing above another over another.

The art of art is to attach a pretentious backstory to something, a piece. The level of craftsmanship is not vital, though it can be appreciated by some. Some novelty helps also. However, no artwork contains much in the way of originality. It will be a minor twist on some other established concept, maybe a change in scale or new combination.

These canvases have tag lines:

"The four dogs that personifies the throwing of light on what we can see when we pay attention to our surroundings."

"We have a negative use of colours to highlight the negativity in the human condition relating to dissent."

As a critic, you use as few words as possible. 'Crap', 'fun' or 'amateurish' would suit the work above nicely. Similarly, when describing some wine, we can use 'battery acid', 'delicate' or 'tart'. People forget 99% of what we say. They might remember one apt word, so make it a good one.

Small Islands

What chance do you get to have your say on how things are run in your country, one vote every four or five years? Aside from voicing your opinion hoping that those in charge will take heed and do something about it, there is little most can do. Those in a minority camp so often find themselves out voted in every election and therefore have to either make do or get involved somehow in the political process to see any changes made in their favour. People that do get involved find themselves in endless meetings trying to get agreement. However, they are hindered by so many people having different ideas and the need to cater to the wide variety of demands of so many disparate people. The more attending the meeting the more you spot falling asleep. Endless intricacies of what to do are debated. Would it not be simpler on a small island without the sheer number of things to consider? This was what Ben put to three good friends, convincing them that a new start on their terms was possible. Hence the day came where four people left the modern world to embark upon a new life on an isolated island looking to build something utopia-esque. Their chances may be slim but optimism pervades. They now feel empowered to get things moving along in the direction of their pleasing.

As soon as they arrive they all sit by the campfire and start discussing the details and planning what sort of community they are going to build.

Ben is always looking ahead and driven to try and find new ways of doing things, clutching to the concept of continuous improvement. Unlike Dave who likes to live by the day and will only do things when it is absolutely necessary or caves in to the nagging of Claudia and Racheal. Ben has these visions of not only getting lots of things off the ground, but ensuring everything is as good as it can be with the limited resources available. They are familiar with those in a society where people do their utmost to leave the place in a better state than they were for their children. Dave feels that although there is an expectation that future generations won't have to make the same sacrifices and will live in a better place, it will always be the next generation that benefits and never this one. Besides aspirations change and new problems replace old ones.

They debate the idea of a democracy, but Ben wants the problem of someone being regularly outvoted addressed. They are prone to major rancour and upset regarding some key issues with some becoming marginalised and pushed aside. There will always be the potential for three to override the concerns of the forth.

Despite the trap of too much talking and not enough doing, Ben still likes the notion of all sitting down and working things through thereby getting agreement for everything of importance and everything trivial. So much for coming here to get away from long winded meetings. Racheal has seen this sort of thing before, working in organisations that have practices akin to this, with the aim of trying to keep everyone happy and discovered that the only thing that got done was a lot of talking. It is a nice virtuous idea in principle but rarely works for long in practice. Having one person in charge, preferably in turns, at least gets things done even if it is like a sailing boat tacking wildly from side to side but making headway. One person moves it ahead and to the left, the next also ahead but to the right as well.

The one thing they do not want to see is some kind of hipocracy. Claudia has witnessed first-hand those that encourage others to forfeit and undergo pain, but live an elevated life with lots of benefits from the struggle of others. Claudia also has the benefit of a religious upbringing and therefore can bring a lot of its messages to the table. However, the rest feel that whilst these messages have resonance in any day and age, a state can be founded on equivalent high morals without reference to any superior being, being the one providing guidance. They all agree that if any kind of dictatorship emerges, then it will be time limited as this metaphorically speaking reduces the risk of tacking so far and for so long sideways that the boat hits the rocks.

A democracy is often considered to be the least worst option, a theocracy here is a potential but not enthusiastically endorsed by all so they invent a new term, a pragmatocracy, to call it for now. It will be a hierarchical dictatorship and open to changes through consensus, one person in charge for a while and always willing to at least listen as much as possible to the suggestions of others. Votes take the form of black stones where they are handed out equally and you can use them on an issue or hold back and use a few on something that you have bigger concerns about. So long as a majority is cast, in this case 3 or more stones, then the issue is approved.

One temptation is to make any system so complex that the riff-raff gets excluded due to their inability to understand what is going on. It is not always that the issues are in themselves particularly complex, but it is more the way in which they are presented that can be the problem. All four will have to be on their toes looking out for some clever mind games that pushes one or two out and eliminates their share of involvement in the running of the island; People voting to avoid too much friction, rather than being fully conversant with the motions put forward.

The fly on the wall is keen to see if some form of community-ism manifests itself with everyone mucking in for the good, the benefit of everyone or whether as time passes more effort it spent on individual advancement. The fly has seen it all and can't recollect witnessing a movement that has no downsides. The more intense the capital system is, the more it brings about a dog eat dog mentality with ever increasing pressure to move ahead and no time or proper consideration for the weaker less able members. People there feel a failure if not doing super wonderful things. Then it saw the farcical pretence that people are really willing to work for the greater good and remain truly contented in their own lives. The fly sees it all lying dormant until a hopeful passes and maggots its way from inside to out, consuming the bulk of any that are buried. The fly's children, then seek new spots in hope of fulfilling the dream of their ancestors, which is to find a place with a balance so elegant that no more dirty work of meddling is needed, but expects it to be fragile, guaranteeing it won't last long.

All play a part

Ben is keen to divvy up the day to day tasks and split the chores equally. Whilst Rachael is willing to climb the trees to collect coconuts and has sea legs to do the fishing, Dave thinks it is fine to do the delegating and hone a long-standing talent playing the bongos. Claudia feels like the one most suited to collecting the fire wood and Ben has no intention of allowing the chef skills that have taken years to learn going to waste. The bone of contention is the principle of not playing your part in keeping the island running. In the real world, you can indeed make a good living from entertaining others with music if you get enough willing to pay to hear your output. On an island with an audience of just three it is not going to work. The shirker issue has to be resolved. None of the four propose to let one starve and signal clearly that if one were to hurt themselves then they would be supported through their recuperation. However, allowing one or more to sit about idly with the remaining picking up the slack is not going to be tolerated for long. Even if you can't walk you can peel the vegetables and help as much as you can in some other capacity.

Claudia knows that one day there will be that one individual that will not muck in. Once their tummy begins to really rumble and they begin to faint people will relent and offer lifesaving food, but it will be the bare minimum.

Chores

There is a spring in Claudia's step when going off to top up the water. For this chore is a pain, but also an opportunity to spend a brief time alone and revel in the change in the seasons and take in the beauty of the environment. Racheal has an ability to just switch off when doing the dull tasks and focus the mind on other things. Ben sings and jives when at work and defers the burden of cajoling to the others who have to prod Dave endlessly to get out of the hammock and into action. Dave read this book and took one thing from it. That was the wisdom of getting hold of another book, 1001 excuses for not doing things, and saw the usefulness of it when embarking on this new life on the island. Dave hasn't even got the imagination to think up new excuses on the spot but did get the overriding message though of trying to identify those that are even lazier than you. In addition, it was easy to grasp the power of the tactic where you push your argument to the max with as much emotive force as possible. However, Dave didn't bank upon the fact that it is much easier to hide in a large arena than a place where everyone is so much more accountable.

You have to live a rather sheltered life to never come across someone adept at presenting the case for a particular individual, conveying their woes and unfairness of their situation. You will receive a tale of hardship, misfortune and unjust treatment by an uncaring system. The story will not take into account the many others that by default are beneficiaries of the policy that they are moaning about. It is all about laying it on thick and not exactly lying, but stretching the extent of the problem to the max. They take great care in presenting only the plight of the few and fail to put it into context. It is compelling, but doesn't wash with those that have to bear the weight of the funding, the work required to pay for those wanting more. Ordinarily people just listen and refrain from pointing out the losers that suffer at the expense of those making the gains. Arguing counter to these views on subjective isolated cases is futile. Any points made promoting the wider view tends to fall on deaf ears. Dave can spend as much energy as he likes to try to convince the others that special treatment is deserved. Like a gambler who has already put so much in, and too entrenched to pull out will continue on believing that the next coin will get the desired result, but ends up bust. They then leave thinking the whole world is against them. Never to their dying day are they ever prepared to even hint at the possibility that they are wrong. Claudia listens and grins, Rachael grimaces, Ben raises an eyebrow and they all wander off to carry on with what they were doing.

When cars finally arrive on the island you can bet that nobody bar a few will ever think that they as drivers are ever in the wrong. It is best to shout out 'idiot' than consider why they are moving so slowly. Ignore the fact that they are looking for a place, checking the directions. Ben always drives perfectly, or so he thinks, it is always the other person at fault. Another area of autistic behaviour, only seeing things from our point of view.

Ben begins to argue albeit forcefully and compellingly that all the improvements they make bring about a reduction in the anxiety felt about having to do chores. Things become easier through the investment made in small time saving measures. We can spend an hour today and save three minutes a day, which gets recouped in a few short weeks and pays dividends in the months ahead. Ben is quick to promote the fact that they also have more fall backs when things go awry, more planning saves a lot and potentially extends their very existence on the island. Less inconvenience and more comforts has it attractions. Nevertheless, it can be important knowing that you can soon find yourself working towards an early grave, time whizzing by, you aging and aching more, losing sight of possibilities of real meaning because of a fixation on making never ending alterations to your landscape.

Dave at least, albeit unconsciously, saw that it is sometimes worth being able to put up with a little imperfection in the manor. When you persist in worrying about every little detail of what could be done to make things better, you can find that addressing it consumes a lot of time and reduces the time to appreciate time itself, time doing things you want to do. Dave unashamedly neither wants to be sucked into a situation which entails always being encumbered by guilt of what too many expect you to be doing. Playing your part but not playing to the tune of the rest of the group and their models of perfection.

All four discover in short order that many of the dreams of what they hoped to achieve in a certain time frame won't materialise. They had a detailed idea of how they thought things would go, but as time passes things begin to pan out differently from what was expected. However, the fact that they created a system that provides for themselves and gives them an opportunity to bring children up under their own steam, is highly satisfying in itself. It doesn't have to be the best island in the world right now and may never become so, but they can't be mocked for their self-sufficiency, it is quite an achievement to manage without reliance on others on the outside.

Who to allow in

Rachael raises the question of whether they would allow any more people to join their little paradise. What do they do if someone floated in on some driftwood hoping for salvation? The four see little controversy in pointing out that anyone who were to join would surely need to adopt their leadership and abide by all the rules in place. Claudia has been horrified when people joined their church expecting long standing members to change their ways to suit ideas these new characters have. These new people didn't just make suggestions and see how they went down, instead they infiltrated the organisation and bit by bit transformed it into something very different to how it was before. Ben was involved in a political movement and also recognised a similar pattern take shape, despairing at the way things crept up and went against the grain of the foundational principles that attracted so many to it in the first place.

Infiltration

Dave asks the more profound question of who owns the earth, are we right to claim this island for ourselves? Both Claudia and Rachael make the obvious remark that they were there first and most certainly don't feel inclined to have their spot ruined just because other people have messed up their own island. They don't want to make a great deal of sacrifice or go beyond the call of duty helping others to such an extent that they will miss out. They have plans to have children of their own and want to put them in the front of the queue ahead of outsiders. Dave can see that there is plenty of space on this island to fit a good number of people in, but knows that there will be longer waits at the well, more noise and more disruption, but potentially more things getting done on the island as well. There is a trade-off between some attractive benefits against less serenity and loss of control. Worse still, new ideologies may not be particularly welcome now that so many principles have been established and enjoyed.

Claudia has another worry, that being what do they do should a group of people invade the island. Can they even attempt to fend them off if the attackers are a force with an upper hand? They can potentially talk with their neighbouring island communities and form a pact so that nobody is subjected to such perils. Nevertheless, they are vulnerable. An island community would be commended if it throws its arms open to visitors especially if there was something there of geographical significance.

Ben has spent the most time building a place called home and treasures it deeply. By sharing it with the others there is a connection and shared ownership that spreads out to the boundary of the whole island. It won't be just Ben that would feel pretty cheated if it was taken away from them against their will. All of them understand that it is rough for people who live in a failed state and don't feel like they have the means necessary to put things right. It can be tough for people to break away from somewhere, especially the place of their birth due to the changes developing there. Some will stay put maybe because they are too old or too weary to leave and whilst it is regarded as unfair, will look upon it as an evolution that they are stuck with. Sometimes it is a case of trying to make the best of a bad situation or face having to up sticks and relocate. Everything gets more awkward once all the places with the fine geography begin to fill up, so there is an incentive to remedy the problems at the source.

Some people keep themselves to themselves and concentrate on making their own area as good as it can be. It can become a beacon for others to consider emulating. However, Claudia saw people not bothering to do that. They were instead more focused on spreading an ideology as far afield as possible. Hence we are faced with invaders by force or by stealth. An individual will attain power, cement it through domination and will have a temptation to push it out like a fungus consuming all in the way.

Some places have reasonable philosophies laid out but are poorly interpreted. Countries may have a written constitution with an importance placed upon armies and aims regarding the development of agriculture and so forth. People in charge take it upon themselves to ensure that no stone is left unturned getting the defences in place and so much money is spent on that, that agriculture, business and other commerce become virtually neglected. The aims are useless if not adhered to in a measured way. Paranoia and propaganda take the place of prudence.

There is no money as such on this tiny island nor any need for it yet. Neither is there any thinking that things in the shared pool belong to a distant body. Likewise, a collective share and share alike ambition is fantastical. Ben has made the best hammock and loves it dearly. Make no mistake about it, it has been made clear that there is no wish to have Dave, or anyone else anywhere near it. Sharing has its limits. When Ben wants to lie down, Ben wants to lie down and gets aggravated by keep having to turf Dave out and then always be the one cleaning and de-crumpling it. People find that no amount of favours can really compensate for the option to have what is theirs when it suits them most. Ben is not mean nor selfish and like the rest will share many things, but a free for all is a naïve dream and will remain as that, just an idea that never sees the light of day. Whilst they all fall into a blissful level of cooperation they respect each other's preferences where practical. Convenience comes before romantic thinking. Ben would rather spend a few days making an extra knife to keep sharp and keep in the draw so that it is always there when required. Dave would rather have just one communal knife that they all use, but then who is the one that leaves it the other end of the island and forgets to return it to the kitchen. In situations like this Ben could have made something else in that time, something for all or something for just their sole use, making them richer in effect but at a cost of many a bug bear. Some well-meaning principles and one for all and all for one schemes can be great on paper but hopeless in reality. They only work if everyone is exactly the same in every single respect and all individuality is banished along with freedoms to choose for ourselves.

We will pay for convenience sometimes. It all depends on our mood and the situation. We like to be able to choose and bring our personality into play. We could all car share so long as we accept the lack of choice of model, ignore the mess some leave it in, are patient waiting for one to be available, never mind being the one to deal with the maintenance and have no desire to personalise it. All to benefit from a relatively tiny reduction in costs. Idealists may not always disregard the details, but will ignore our unwillingness to do things that break away from the way we like them. We find methods that work for us and want to retain a way of life. It is not a reluctance to change the amount we consume, but being pushed to change the way we do things that matters the most. If you have concerns about your personal environmental consumption you can choose to earn less thereby making us use less. The fuel costs, wear and tear on the brakes and tyres etc. and the depreciation in value are all dependant on the mileage so no savings there. Only a little of the capital costs is saved, not much for all the aggravation that it entails.

In an economy with market forces prevailing there is a potential to pay more in compensation for jobs that are least enjoyed. We can pay to have others do things we don't want to get involved in. In a controlled sharing economy, it would be nice to see all the plum favoured jobs handed out fairly and an abundance of volunteers to deal with the grim ones. However, it will just be the most adept at proving themselves to be the most worthy of better treatment that get the desired result instead of justifying it through working harder. The people that support the party in power get the beachside houses, the rest get allocated a tiny grim plot in a flood plain.

Ben of course would pay a premium in life prior for first class tickets, but go without many other things to pay for them. Sacrificing one pleasure for another is par for the course and a nature of freedom rather than envy. Whilst it is quite apparent that many accumulate the means to have more, there is no equitable system that can remove the imbalance without capsizing the whole ship. People have tried setting punitive taxes and are keen to have redistribution measures in place. The more they try to make it fair the more iniquities and grief they cause. People get fed up with the system and make plans to escape. Then the borders are locked down to keep people from leaving. As that fails, those in command are constantly suppressing uprisings. Once it becomes so out of balance, Claudia's nightmare becomes evident where only those in charge are in the lap of luxury and the rest scrape about in the wasteland. The social principle is respected but feared in equal measure. Those that espouse it are the most often in a comfortable position and want to drag down those that want to work and be rewarded for their pluck. The wealthy have the means to move before it gets out of hand whereas the less well-off are never so fortunate. Those with the right tenacity at the right time will always prosper and you can't make money selling expensive goods and services if everyone is too poor to buy them. There is a certain degree of natural regulation, but there will be periods where some appear to have too much, but measures to deal with it can create bigger headaches.

Your island may be blessed with some coconut trees. You can harvest them, eat and drink from them and then make some maracas out of what remains. What you can't do is borrow them. You can only consume what you have. Big states generate 'I owe yous' with a promise to pay back what is borrowed at a later date. Eating the fruits that you expect to have tomorrow makes the policy maker appear decent. However, it hides a nasty evil practice that is paid for by the next generation. The citizens get the impression that money grows on trees and that they can spend ad infinitum. One of the four had a sibling who took from their jar and kindly bought them a few gifts with some of it. It didn't feel quite so nice when they realized later how generous they were. How much fun it must be to spend other people's hard earned money. Maybe it is acceptable so long as you spend some of it for the benefit of the loser.

Counting a few coconuts is just about within the capability limits of the general populace. Understanding big numbers is much harder as most economic facts just wash over the top of people at large. The same data can be interpreted in all manner of different ways leading to no end of strife. The great thing about being a politician is that no matter how badly you mess up, you are rarely held to account, you just walk away and leave it to others to sort out. On this island they will attempt to address this by regular evaluations of what is going on and proper punishment for serious negligence, so that at the very least it serves as a warning to future governors.

With help or on your own

Ben can manage a lot by himself and there are times where it is nice to go off diving alone without needing to get some of the others involved. At other times it can be rather rewarding to do something with the whole camp on board helping. You can operate as a one-man band, but there is a lot to be had from being a small cog in a large machine. Constructing large buildings and making machines that fly is only possible with a fair degree of co-operation. Therefore, community-ism has remarkable upsides. Sporting events, rallies and large gatherings provide us with an atmosphere with no parallel in individual pursuits. Look at what we can do when we work together. Each contributor gets a sense of satisfaction that is nowhere to be found when doing something solitary. You can split your time between things done by yourself and things with others and find the fit that works to your mind-set. Both tacks can be sparkling. The only cause for concern arrives if the level of opportunity available is minimal and if coercion is in abundance to take part. There can be pressure to make people feel as though they have to repay a debt to society. When people work mainly for themselves they can see the benefits and decide upon how profits are spent, whereas the gains we see for the good of the whole are cloudy. It seems as if people are willing to split the proceeds to some extent between what they keep and what they are prepared to give to the community. Finding the sweet spot is a task for the thick skinned, people that can brush off the flak.

Free to leave

After all the debate about allowing people in, there comes the moment of focussing on liberty to leave. Were a child of theirs to reach a point when they seem to be capable of looking after themselves, it would be unreasonable to make it awkward for them to go if they wanted to. Ben's aim is to settle on some very basic rulings which will be kept to at all costs. Ben wants to avoid expanding on them in anyway, which leads to a super complex set of primary laws that get ever harder to understand and enforce. Ben declares that the first and foremost respect given to people of this island will be a freedom to leave unhindered. Any further fundamental aims will not number more than five or six, so that they are simple as possible and easily kept at the forefront of everyone's mind.

Claudia likes the idea of elementary laws and needs some convincing that Ben's declaration of the respect of peoples' desires is adequate, rather than people having rights as such. People wish to leave and you do your utmost to allow them. More importantly you appreciate their desire to live. Most people on the island can see this and can make sure nobody does anything to infringe upon that. Rachael also thinks it all sounds a little whimsical and not as definitive as strict cast iron protective laws. Yet no law stops the worst actions of all. The thing that stops people harming others is rarely the legal consequences, but the empathy we have for one another and that we understand their wish to be unharmed. There can be a fear of reprisal and a fear of getting caught and prosecuted, but most incidents are tempered in the heat of the moment by consideration of others. Assessment of the risks of our actions and the consequences takes time, understanding the damage we are about to inflict as we are about to hit them is more immediate.

Having aims which are well promoted and encouraged is novel but effective. You set out the aims and let it be known that people will report transgressions and ensure that they are always taken seriously. Those in charge need to act when necessary in a timely fashion and also adhere to them fully as well, else be liable to be removed from office by a simple process.

Another aim, suggested by Dave, relates to the conditions of entry. This is where the homeowner has the privilege of deciding who can enter and under what terms. Dave likes people to take their shoes off before coming in and other people may insist that nobody smokes or lights incense inside. These and other guidelines are fine, yet they require clauses for when someone needs to be captured for severe misconduct. Can someone enter to get them out and on to the podium of justice if deemed rightful? It can all get complicated rather quickly. You build a school, insist upon people attending it and insist they remove their shoes when entering the building. You are caught between a rock and a hard place if you refuse to remove your shoes anywhere, but are compelled to attend school. You can decline any offer of a dinner at Dave's place as you will be made to remove your shoes, but this isn't the case at the school. You either have a guide that lays out the precedence, which rule goes above the others or have an obligation to create a school that isn't so demanding about how you dress.

Expulsion

Ben is keen to settle the real problem that may arise when faced with dealing with someone who has done some serious misdemeanour. Rachael jokes that if a certain person, Dave, doesn't get a move on with the jobs they have been assigned they will be expelled. In all seriousness, the principle is to prevent a reoccurrence of the same crime. Punishment is secondary for the clock cannot be turned back and many crimes cannot be undone. All you care about is making sure it doesn't happen again. Getting them to say sorry and incarcerating them for a period does not guarantee that they will not reoffend. Racheal is keen to recommend that any person who defies the aims and does something terrible would be ejected. However, the others point out they would not want to have a reject from another island landing here, so neither would other people want to deal with their problematical characters. If someone is to be locked up, then there will not only be a timed based system for working out the point of release but also an assessment of the risk of them repeating previous wrong doings. If the probability seems very high, then the release would be postponed. A probation period checking for potential problems is common, but some people are synonymous with the proverbial scorpion and the frog with a sting that is always going to harm others despite any repercussions for themselves. They can't be helped; the innocent need not pay the price for allowing someone another chance. The priority of potential victims is diminished when we attempt to forgive and forget about nasty events in the hope that the unchangeable will moderate their behaviour.

There is a flood, a major flood and the deluge will soon put the prison completely underwater. Do we release the inmates to avoid them drowning? Many will suggest they do, despite the warning that innocents are liable to be exposed to danger or even death by highly volatile convicts. We have our own morals and they are a personal invention with most of it handed down from the elders. Some fail to see the morality in allowing someone out, knowing that the chance of a major offence on someone who has done nothing wrong will be close to certain. Harsh for the prisoners as they will perish, but people can find justification in their thinking of who they have the greatest concern for. You can put your head in the sand and avoid dwelling upon the plight of all the wrongdoers.

In a similar vein to ejecting those causing trouble, it is not unheard of for people in a nation to get so wrapped up in the utility argument that anyone too old or too feeble gets discarded. Once your usefulness comes to an end you are left on the scrap heap for nothing eclipses the importance of the supposed prosperity of the zone. There is no room for frivolity, everything is set to expand the grandeur of the bigger cause. Heaven forbid, your form of entertainment, that you foot the bill for, doesn't meet the latest guidance announced. For their entertainment, their pleasure is truly gleaned from controlling your every move. They love it and get great satisfaction from devising and tinkering with more and more things that you can and can't do in your private life.

People have suggestions and of course plenty of opinions, some of which appears to need an airing to a wider audience. A few proactive types get enough attention to see things changed. However, if too many are jumping up and down at the slightest failing, the system gets overwhelmed and nobody is heard amongst so much noise. Someone, a person well known can put themselves in the spotlight to promote a cause close to their heart. This is wonderful but in doing so makes those involved in other worthy causes feel shunned. They do not have the same level of endorsement; hence we can be mindful of anything we promote can be at the detriment of other issues due to the limited space available in what can be brought to the attention of the many.

When it comes to taking action, when you see somebody doing something wrong, you have a choice of intervening or walking on by. If everyone turns a blind eye when they see a mugger or thief in action the system breaks down. Some do not care what laws are passed so long as the ones they go against are never enforced. A small but significant percentage of people who are prepared to get involved is usually positive. If you are not willing to step in from time to time, your community becomes less favourable for you, your friends and family plus your postman, your doctor, your repairman and everyone else that contributes to your way of life. Once in a while when you feel it is right to play your part. You act to keep your island, your corner, a nice place to live.

Amongst the thousands of items to make rulings on will be your criteria for interfering with what is going on in other islands. Do you keep your nose out at all times and let them get on with it or do you try to bring order to what you see as a chaotic situation? You would certainly want a chat with them if they were storing flammable material too close by or polluting the water upstream. It can often depend upon how much it is interfering with your comfort zone. If you become aware that they are beating each other up or witness killing aplenty, it becomes more of a dilemma with no definitive answer. Do you have the means to break up the fighting, will it make it worse and do you understand what the fighting is really over? There is something to be said for steering well clear until you are absolutely sure on all three counts. If there are ten people fighting and you send in fifty to break it up, chances are they will quickly capitulate and no harm is done to your peacekeepers.

It can seem silly to think of things on the scale of a small island as there will be no hospitals, no government to check the standards and quality of produce on offer. There will be far less opportunity to retire and relax in the twilight years and the power of diversification, people specialising in complex fields is all but forgotten. A decent government can mediate and ensure a reasonable level playing field is kept and actually provide more real freedoms than a place where things are a mess. It becomes harsh if your personal safety is forever in jeopardy and only the fittest toughest make it through each day.

The simplistic tale of setting up and running a small island could run to thousands of pages and still not cover even a good percentage of all the basic things to consider let alone the finer details. Yet whilst this writing itself is very simplistic, it provides a means to think about what we would do in that kind of situation and then apply it to the problems in bigger societies. When you consider how a policy would be constructed with a tiny number of people, it can be transposed in its entirety to a huge country with a new form of unsophistication.

The one thing you can be sure about is how lines can get blurred and how impossible it becomes to make any finality in any arguments. Ideas wax and wane and new problems emerge that can't be envisaged at an earlier time. The thought processes these people had on setting up this island may be agreeable or repulsive, but give a hint of the quandaries we face. Either way there is one heck of a muddle and confusion with one doctrine overriding another. Never is there any real basis for any claim be it philosophical or otherwise. We will always be stuck with some difficult compromises and there will be times where better weather outshines frustration with the political framework in deciding what island to remain on. The debate rages on with different intensities bringing up new and old problems into the mix and so be it. The mistake is to think that we are more than just insects building a nest and adjusting to the ecosystem.

Many teenagers pipe up and ask why we need rules at all. A free for all is not outside the bounds of possibility and springs up in places from time to time. A motion for completely private enterprise in all areas has been mooted as well. All work for the disabled and infirm is carried out competently by the charities, business self-regulate and people provide all their needs for themselves. Like all ideas of this nature there are pros and cons with the cons being troublesome, people free to rip one another off. There will be a vast amount of things to sort out, no police but a subscription to a private security force instead to name but one of them.

Claudia has indeed been surprised that we don't have more lands with a free for all. Rachael is more surprised that there are so many lands with the bulk of the population accepting the current status and tolerant of things the way they are. Ben asks how many people have grown up in their community and assumed that everything is normal and just the way it is. We say "they", they are inventing, they are coming out with, they are proposing and they, this hard to put your finger on body, knows what is best for its citizens. You may know no different and haven't had exposure to other ways, nor have even considered other possibilities. A presumption pervades that this is the how it is and always has been, only 'they' have the power to change things. Constitutions have been written, legal frameworks put in place and only a mythical figure could ever realign them to a new age. Who are these great historical characters that set things in place? Many are found to be nothing other than from humble ordinary beginnings with chance and circumstance that put them up on a parapet. There comes a point where amendments or complete rewrites are needed to our statutes, the control structure, that are more befitting of the way things have moved on. The underlying laws of the land can be changed if enough of the right people wish it to be done. However, in the same way as only a few people change the name given to them at birth not many want the inconvenience of going against the grain.

No state that we build will be problem free nor perfect in all respects but if you were to start over or repair a system you might consider one cornerstone to be a device that keeps out and dispels any artificial rankings. It is evident that some show great delight in giving some people a 'type' and thus having a higher or lower status than the rest. People preserve their caste, class and social orders to maintain the differential for the ruling elite. We like the idea of progression through education and training and we like the idea of being above others merely based on heredity reasons even more, as no effort is required. If you start getting pockets of partisan people bunched together there can be a tendency to sneer at those more afar. Nothing beats a demonstration that we have equal validity and are neither looking up nor down at one another. It is well known that the more we mingle the more we realise that each of us are fundamentally the same, we all eat, sleep and defecate as animals of the same species. The differences between us are more often than not very slight. However, there is a genuine fear at times of those on the other side of the river are playing a long game waiting for sufficient traction to spring a new way of life on all of us.

Claudia has been exposed to a variety of different cultures spending a good while in and amongst foreign types. Despite the extensive time immersed we may never be able to get our head around it all and never really get to the bottom of why they approach things so differently. We may only see what they want us to see and fail to fathom the complexities involved. The crux of the issue is that the same driving forces bring about completely different ways of doing things.

Dave come up with a couple of ideas, one has merit the other highly misguided. As their children turn into adults they will be given a plot of land on the island for which to build their shack. Just a small square piece and no assistance in the construction but an approval to build something of a reasonable size. The cost to the community is small, the benefit of having a stake in the island is huge. The repellent idea that Dave proposed is that each person would be given a daily allowance of one coconut, one fish and some bread. This would be applicable to everyone including those with a stack of coconuts piled up high by their front door and fifty fish dried out in their back room. It neglects to take into account that someone has to get the coconuts down, someone has to fish and someone has to labour kneading and baking the dough. Worse still the reward system only works when you go and do something to get it. People don't just get lazy and dissatisfied with life, they get greedy and want ever more. Having something to do, compulsion just to survive, is not just about making the time pass quicker it pleases the soul.

Hocus Pocus

Some people are drawn to the art of magicians and illusionists with their use of sleight of hand and trickery. Others fails to see the point or are simply bemused by their acts. Whatever your take on it is, you can learn one significant thing, that being that once people know how it is done they lose interest and the magic evaporates. Curiosity at its finest. You too can learn a simple trick, show it to a youngster and see how they can be captivated by it, but only until they work out how you do it and uncover the secret. As adults we retain similar wonderment for various things that we find difficult to explain. There is much less interest in a dull boring scientific explanation than some intriguing conspiracy theory or hocus pocus, for trying to find something hidden from us captivates us much more.

People will bring up hocus pocus from time to time and be enthralled by it and you face a dilemma, either tell them that it is a load of rubbish or join in. The friendlier approach is to show them the power of palmistry. Take their hand and turn it over and peer at the lines making a note of their intensity. Gauge where the branches and breaks are. Now you need to invent a fortune telling yarn. Going by their age you can ascertain a compelling point in the person's life where something momentous will occur. You can say that in five to six years' time a big decision will need to be made. You can also calculate a point in their life prior when something significant happened from the proportion of the line length to where the break is. Like all good liars, you need a good memory as they may challenge you a few weeks later and they are more likely to remember what you said about them than you will.

Some of the most ardent doubters have found themselves getting rather good at such wizardry. They then begin to reconsider their cynicism. It is like trying to explain hunches you get that turn out to be true. Those that get carried away with it feel that have become relevant as they are doing something wonderful for others. Being larger than life provides an excellent excuse for questionable behaviour in other areas of life.

If you want to start a new religion it appears that you must offer two crucial things in order for it to be successful and to gain a following. Hope and magic. Set out a reason for living, be part of a great cause. Offer an afterlife. Although there is always hope even in the word hopeless, you can capitalise on those that have become disillusioned with life. If you provide a pathway for them to follow that promises great things, aspiration, inspiration and enlightenment they will come. A promise to return from the dead, live another life in a heavenly place is so much more enticing than a 'once you are dead you are dead' mentality. The more fantastic the more extraordinary the more chance people will accept it. We all know the platitude "If it is too good to be true then it invariably is" yet blithely stick more of our savings into a scheme offering high unsustainable rates of return. Time and time again people get fooled by seemingly obvious cons, but something so awe inspiring, something with so many adherents can't be wrong. The cult, the religion the pseudo-science, clairvoyant mind reading tarot card reader are super credible. Notably because of the sheer boldness and audacity of the proponents and what they keep hidden and shielded from you.

The possibility of being sent to a hell because you have failed to follow various teachings doesn't seem to worry everyone. Some may hedge their bets and if wrong then so be it, if right then heaven it is, but the fear of eternal damnation is just not widespread. Now some think that they are good people so won't be cast there. Some will argue that the world is hell anyway and the rest just don't really think about it. When you point out the issue you will get a shrug of the shoulders and an indication that it is of no great concern to them. It does seem somewhat unfair if you live a virtuous admirable life in a country which is out of reach of such knowledge of a hell existing that you will still be sent there. Or born without the capability to understand and end up tortured. Hell will not only be hot it will be also getting very cramped with new incumbents pilling in each day.

Do we need something grander and outside of ourselves? Something that is magical and gravity defying that gives us optimism. Perhaps and I am envious of those that hold out for their spiritual entity to come up trumps. All I can offer is cold and brutal.

Finding out that that Father Christmas, the tooth fairy and the like were pure inventions creates some disappointment. Knowledge of how fortune tellers, astrologers and the like hoodwink the masses also pops the bubble of fascination. Learning that language trickery is used rather than actual spiritual contact. Use of clever generalisations that apply to big chunks of the population rather than bespoke custom information delivered for you alone. So long as some of what is foretold is correct, we can be satisfied even if the proportion of what it pretty much right to what is blatantly wrong is worse than something knowingly given at random. It is akin to the real placebo effect of being told you are going to be alright by a doctor in a white coat. We believe in the person as much as what information they impart.

There is no need to try to convince a believer that their ghost sightings, encounters with bright lights and angels are more likely to be errors of perception. Allow them to enjoy the attention that they get when relaying the stories over and over again, for your reality is much more dull. If you are 40 years old you have lived for about 14600 days, taking this large numbers of days into account it is actually quite unlikely that something strange, weird or coincidental won't occur.

It is beyond count the number of times I have been in some kind of discussion and people have recounted a long winded story of a strange encounter. Then there were those that felt the presence of the ethereal wind. I don't object to them telling the tale and getting it off their chest, conversations about the price of cat food are even more dispiriting. What got my notice was how all the other people were interested and quizzed them about all the finer details to such great lengths. It was a revelation about how people even if not entirely convinced or sucked in paid them so much attention. I am well aware that things that we take for fact can often turn out to be somewhat dubious when properly examined. More information comes to light and facts get modified. However, the facts can be checked, tested and scrutinised to see how well they stack up.

I once settled into bed and could see a light. It was small bright and piercing and was visible whether my eyes were open or shut. Make no mistake about it, it was a light as real as can be and not imagined. In the morning I thought about this then recalled how I was in the bar and was looking at a small bulb where the plastic cover over it was missing. Hence the light I saw. It was odd that it came 'on' some hours after I had left the place. I could have turned this into a big story, but decided against it for it was a mere issue with persistence of vision and an aberration. Others will see a brighter more impressive light and will hold to their dying day a belief that they were individually picked out to spread a message from yonder.

We sure like to speculate on things that have not been proven yet. If there is a field that permeates right across the universe, a field that cannot be detected directly, it could that be the key to the things that we cannot explain fully at the moment. The electricity in your head connects with smaller sub-atomic particles which in turns uses the field to transfer energy. Given that there are so many electrons moving about all over the place inside your head and everywhere in your surroundings, there would undeniably be lots of interference. Thus explaining why spiritualists get so much wrong. Nevertheless, every single person claiming to possess a special power has been shown to be a fraud. No repeatable experiment has ever shown any tangible evidence for these mystic claims. However, from here to eternity there will be people wanting attention and faking supernatural abilities.

Serious stuff sends people to sleep, fantastic unbelievable stuff wakes your soul.

False correlations

The alignment of the stars and planets is used to make predictions about what will happen in our day-to-day lives. It is true that the moon affects the tides so too will sunspots alter the weather pattern, but generalisations about the time of year that you were born dictating your character is undeniably flaky. Maybe there will be parts of the world that have better foodstuffs available at different times of the year enabling the child in the womb to develop beautifully. People have been known to act a little differently during a full moon and we have cycles in our body rhythm caused by hormones and temperature fluctuations, but to give credit to something so innocuous and far away is not serious. It is easy to formulate false correlations that seem to fit when you want them to.

People see what they want to see rather than stand back and make proper appraisals. Besides you can't beat blue skies and warmer weather to give a mood lift for the bulk of the population, much more so than day after day of grey skies and rain. If it makes you feel good, you might be more positive and perhaps more open to luck and good fortune.

You have to do about five positive things for your children to undo the 'damage' done by one thing that they see as bad. This good/bad ratio is similar to the times where one thing that supports your argument can throw out five or so other things that go counter to it. You therefore only need a small number of 'proofs' to confirm your beliefs.

There can be countless examples where unrelated things correlate with one another. By using odd connections we are able to convince ourselves of a bizarre reason something happens and to collude with strongly held beliefs. The problem with many published statistics is that they are based on correlations rather than closely aligned cause and effect studies. Unless you can truly isolate the single item that you are checking there will be a lot of room for doubt. There is so much variation in how we live, what we eat and what we encounter that there will always be another study that undermines previous ones.

People do however, get things right sometimes but for the wrong reasons. The whole essence of science is to set out an experiment and repeat it over and over to see if it is consistent. Then publish the results so that other people can repeat it as well. You need to be careful on so many counts. Let's say you test a headache pill the morning after a heavy night of drinking. You can't be sure that the water that you use to swallow the pill might be as helpful in alleviating the pain as the pill itself. Was it the pill or was the water countering the dehydration. So you have to be absolutely sure the item you are testing is the active component and that you keep every variable the same each time you run any experiment. People put their trust in science when it suits them. They know there are risks when going up in a flying machine but they put their faith in the science behind it.

In times of desperation it is hardly surprising that people will think it better to spend the last few pieces of silver on a last chance to win big than stop and think about rebuilding in a way that is more certain. Laziness and the fast fix is so much more attractive. Myths and falsehoods seep into the conscious of the many and in most parts little damage is done, however, there are times when joke claims create uncertainty and put people off making sensible choices. People will rather leave them to it most of the time as challenging them is usually pointless. Even when the fakes are uncovered people will cling on to the idea in perpetuity regardless. Fraudsters will just change the method a little and carry on and people will object to you taking the hope and dreams away.

Total delusion

The ingredients of a chosen one are a high level of delusion, some fraud and the ability to displace the truth. Many people have witnessed some that have given their life for small time causes of little real consequence. Sacrificing one's self is not that great a rarity. Protesters have doused themselves with petrol and set themselves alight, others have signed their death warrant when making a stand against objectionable forces. To think of yourself as a major player in the world is very attractive.

Anyone who makes claims to be a specially selected individual to carry out a duty for a higher being would relish the attention and feeling of self-importance. Having followers and a ready audience for your thoughts and direction is far more desirable for some than being anonymous and with few people taking heed of your opinions. Nothing and I mean no amount of successes in life or levels of narcissism reached can compare to being thought of as a specially chosen spiritual proponent. It gives you leeway to make some pretty extraordinary claims that otherwise would be bizarre. It is the pinnacle of greatness and satisfies all aims in pyramid building, notoriety wanted now and for years to come and the exact opposite of a worthless mediocre life.

The great thing about evangelism is that everyone can take part and feel involved. You don't have to be the biggest chief in the area by any means. Try name calling, declaring out loud that someone is a heretic, unworthy, disgusting, cheap and it makes you feel great and better. It is rather fun. Get the jargon right.

Don't use the term book or text, use scripture for that has much more resonance. Castigate and enjoy.

There are a diverse range of cults and religions with different objectives, different practices and different policies and they can appear skewed and contrary to one another. However, they can be thought of as all aiming for the centre of a dartboard however far off they hit. Were one organisation deemed to be striking dead centre they would discover the ironic reality that there is nothing there. They all started off as tiny groups and like random pop artists started to get more prominent. Most faded away but a few managed to stick it out and beguile large numbers. Great comfort can be found in the belief of superior beings and in an afterlife, either in some kind of heaven or back here on earth. This is something which is far easier to contend with compared with the less enticing view where once the 'oil in our lamp' has run out we are no more.

Even sceptics can be enthralled by the magnificent places of worship that have been built by draining the pockets of those tied to the popular religions. When we enter, we can be emotionally moved. The sight is something to behold and can even be intimidating, yet helps us understand the human scale. How can all this have been achieved without a foundation of something credible? How does it compare in terms of impressiveness with the palaces of consumerism?

Many people have expressed how they have mellowed and changed since joining their church and it is very good for a lot of people. Just by the virtue of the change and having people listen to your woes can be a big healing aid in itself. People don't realise that it didn't have to be that form of spiritual process, but any type would have made a mark. To claim that god gave us the light to win and succeed means he loved you and your team more than the losing side. To come first in a race pushes others into second and third. If it was you that prayed the hardest then it will be well deserved. A call for help, pausing and meditating is likely to be calming and more assistive then doing something in a blind panic. As a child I did indeed pray the once, asking for help as to where my bible was. Only a fraction of a second after I could see clearly where it lay. There is however no greater insult than to express fake false belief in something. You can pray or you can take a deep breath and work out what is the most reliable way to put your thoughts, memories and hope in order.

Some churches will have a sing along with no music and the heart of the human voice is appreciated. In others there is some rousing music with a beat and melody that really raises the spirits of the congregation. You do not have to be in a church to experience this kind of uplifting camaraderie and clap along, vocalising and getting carried away from the soullessness of other areas of life. So to can you learn a great deal from the texts of the religions big and small without having the perquisite of faith. The message can be powerful yet with some study not dependent upon a greater one having provided it. Man writes and decides who to attribute the writings to.

The real question is whether the ideas are so profound that no human could have come up with them without some kind of outside influence. If you or someone with no religious knowledge locked themselves in a room or went up a mountain for a few days and thought about some basic agreeable laws, wouldn't the edicts be fairly consistent? No killing one another, no forcing yourself on someone, no taking without prior permission and so forth and other principles that are quite obvious. All the discussions you have had in your lifetime can culminate in a vision that shows collective wisdom.

God and the universe maybe viewed as the same interchangeable thing. There again, a god may have considered running an experiment. Could I the lord almighty create a system that enables things to form. Things that get more complex and through a process of natural elimination become ever more intelligent. Right through self-awareness to a point where they are able to comprehend who I am. I would do such an experiment with no interference once set in motion. It would be interesting to see the outcome. We are in god's fish tank.

When we are young we look up to our parents to gauge whether our actions are right or not. Many will later transfer this reassurance that we are following the correct course to a new figure, one whose standpoint seems to be authoritative. In pragmatic, practical, everyday terms one cannot avoid in some way imparting a certain bias in your guidance and education that you give to your children. Some of your political, moral and spiritual ideologies are going to be subjected upon those in your care. If their mind is cluttered with all your thoughts, they are prone to become blighted by it and tend to see it from that perspective only. People do not need to be coerced into a solid faith, they will come to it on their own accord because they see its greatness by themselves. People will adopt it because of its potency rather than to keep the peace in a family unit.

The most admired people are the ones that will permit their children to decide for themselves the course of their life when old enough to do so. Those that reject one's offspring because they don't join in with everything you do or align themselves to a different political persuasion are the most blinkered. If they adopt the same ideology by their own unencumbered free will as you, then that is great. There may be a chance that they will plump for another, but having fear of that could be a way of casting doubt on your own faith.

There is an analogy between a child and an insect that is drawn towards the light of a fire and would get burned to death if not stopped. If a child is not led on the correct path they will end up in disarray. A better use of this analogy would be to suggest that if a child puts their fingers in the electric socket they will suffer and it is a parent's job to prevent them from doing so. A parent's task is to keep them from danger, minimise the risks to the best of their ability, then allow the resulting adult the opportunity to find a route for themselves. A successful parent is one that creates independent children where possible. If they can look after themselves when you depart it is a good sign of a job well done.

Why waste time debating potentially valid points when it is easier to get rid of detractors. Burn the witches. Cults banish those that have doubts. Make them nervous of missing out, stop them seeing their families. Too many are impatient. They want to grow as fast as possible and get as much control as quickly as they can. If you have solid belief, then you ignore the few doubters rather than raise their profile by highlighting their scepticism.

Physics and philosophy

It is all too easy to come out with some wild conjectures without having a basic grounding in physics. Philosophy tends to cover areas of thought that are not yet classified as a branch of science or psychology. Take a conjecture like having a torch that has a beam of darkness instead of a beam of light. It is one of many great philosophical thought experiments that can be explored. Light can be cancelled out so it is not beyond reason. However, in the same way that conspiracy theories fall flat on their face during closer inspection you need to appreciate all the factors involved in physics. To get this darkness through cancellation, it works best when the light is of the same frequency, polarised and in line. Light in your room is of many frequencies spread in all directions - not polarised and you can't line it up with the countless scatterings abound. The message is simple; you need some understanding of science to aid many philosophical propositions. It is all too easy to get taken in by wild ideas. A proper wag would say that maybe we are looking at the problem all wrong. Instead of using light to counter and cancel, maybe the torch could emit a beam of light soaking particles. The bounds of people's enthusiasm to go counter to anything rational have no limits.

Some divers were exploring a shipwreck and an extremely heavy metal door fell over trapping one of them. The dive buddy then attempted to lift it up enough to free his good mate. It was either god being kind or an angel that was watching over them for he was given the strength to overcome the incredible weight of this large object. The door was later brought up on to the dive boat deck and all of the people aboard each tried to lift it, but to no avail. Hence being in the situation of having to save someone's life gives us power that without such pressure we cannot summon. Or that we overlook that metal has some buoyancy and weighs its volume (1kg per cubic decimetre) less when submerged in water.

Our Reality

There is a big difference between what is really in front of us and what we perceive there to be. We live in our own personal reality and what you see is different to what others see. Everyone's set of colour receptors are different. Your idea of what red is, is quite likely to be a different shade to other people. We will never really know what the standard view is and might make the assumption that what we see is the correct version of our surroundings.

People have had operations in later life to give them the gift of sight when born with no vision. With the apparatus there to see you might expect them to suddenly obtain vision straightaway like turning on the TV. However, this turns out to be not the case, they need to learn to make sense of the world and only after a considerable period of time can they do so. The same thing applies to those that were deaf at an early age and then had an implant to provide hearing. Only after a long frustrating period of time can they understand the complexities of music and speech.

If there is any doubt in your mind that the reality of what stands before you is different then check out all the visual illusions that a camera would not be fooled by. Here are a couple of instances where you see things that are not there and items appear to be in different planes because the squares are coloured differently.

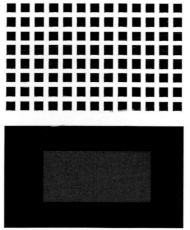

People find themselves driving in fog drive quicker than they realise because of the speed illusion and we think the moon gets bigger when it is lower on the horizon. Given this and countless other examples of the errors we make, it is a surprise that we take offence when our judgement is called into question. We have an emotive attachment to the world rather than a more factual one. Our imagination allows us to fill in what we want to see and filter out what goes against our beliefs.

I have often looked at a picture, particularly a small thumbnail sized one and could not make sense of it initially. After a little while you work out what the picture is and then re-see it and in a new light altogether. It takes a while at times to make sense of our surroundings as the mind has not got the capacity to take in every pixel of what is available. Life is not as it seems.

Some people are loath to admit they are wrong. We are somewhat more willing to fess up to certain judgement mistakes than admitting our mind made other kinds of errors. It is strange that we can have little problem with acknowledging our spelling mistakes, and if we drop something we just put it down to our fallibility, an accident. Yet to spell something wrong or break something unintentionally is caused by an error of sorts in the machine in our head. The commands come from there. Why then is it so hard for many of us to accept that our sight and imagination areas are likely to make mistakes too. There is a continuous flow of information back and forth in both directions between the eyes, our seeing areas of the mind and our imagination and processing parts. We therefore need to determine whether the information was seen, imagined or contrived. Most of the time this all works well, but when fatigue sets in, more errors are bound to be made in terms of what we perceive to be real or imaginary.

Nothing that we do is consistently accurate. We also know that our perception of time can be manipulated (time seems to slow down during a car crash for instance). We also get the order of events muddled as we lay down memories in an incorrect sequence. Hocus pocus is always generated by routine errors of perception in our mind. The unwillingness to consider likely explanations for occasional oddities that we experience leads to a whole host of crazy conjectures. Whilst we know that more mistakes are made when we are tired, seeing an apparition around sleep time, before we nod off or as we wake is much more likely to be some kind of ghost or a returning life than a false erroneous mismatch between imagination and rude reality. Nobody could ever muddle or confuse what they see in a dream like state and how they see things when wide awake and fully alert. Our sight system is as perfect as any camera and we never inaccurately interpret what enters our eyes. If only that were the case, we would never have courtroom battles about eye witnesses and contrary evidence produced by technology. If you want to see ghosts for real, all you have to do is stay awake for a couple of days and the dreams will play out hallucinogenically whilst awake and overlay on top of the normal reality.

Regular habits lay down strong pathways in our mind and a blip in the routine can cause a mental re-enactment to play out via the imagination moments before actually doing it once again. The prediction of what you are about to do so closely timed with the event is named Déjà vu. When you think of a friend of yours you don't just have their name and image of their face stored. You have other associations embedded also such as time points, smells and pictorial features. When one of these associations are brought to the fore you may then think of your friend. Therefore, it should not be that astonishing if that person pays you a visit or phones you soon after as the subconscious prediction is made. If you analyse it closely you may notice that that person has a particular habit albeit one that is not easily identifiable at first sight. Hence "I was just thinking about you and then you called me."

Risk and Luck

Out of sight, out of mind

At the end of every sentence in these pages there are full stops and they kind of represent the people that come to an end that we don't notice much. The media may bring to our attention some individual that has passed away, only because many people might have heard of them. On the whole disparate incidents involving the common man are predominately ignored unless a whole bus load of people are involved in a single tragic event. If you are well known, it makes the news but everyone else is seen as irrelevant. If the same number as those on a bus perish in individual accidents that are spread all over the land, nothing is reported. Put loads of dots together on a page and we notice the splodge. The way we disregard the small incidents and make such a fuss over the ones that are more concentrated is very crass. So too is it to show sorrow and highlight the demise of famous people only.

If you take a walk down the high street of your town you see plenty of people out and about. There may be a few in wheelchairs or struggling to get around, but on the whole people seem alive and well. What you don't see so much is all the people too ill to leave home or laid up in some hospital. It gives a false impression that all things are alright. Many people are hidden away out of sight and out of mind. The next time you consider larking about and maybe jumping off a crazy ledge remember that you could become one of them. Few will get to see you in your parlous smashed up disposition. You will just become an element in an anecdote that people bring up casually on odd occasions.

I was on holiday once and stayed in someone's house, which was a bedsit of sorts. It was very nice, they cooked great meals and told us a lot about the area. One evening I took the plates into the kitchen and found that they had a child maybe in their early twenties sitting in a wheelchair. Unable to talk properly but with some communication skills of sorts. It made me wonder how often they went out of the house with them, I suspect it was probably not that often.

Coming together

How do you account for the coincidences, luck and random events that occur during our lives? Can something be truly random? If we had enough data storage capability could we map out all things and work out what will happen in the future. Random is everything, if nothing is random then there will be total predictability.

Randomness implies something that is unpredictable and does not rely on past events. On the subject of past events I did a fair study into horse and dog races to see if you could make any money through it. If you were to bet on dog races and select one trap, one lane and bet over and over increasing the amount each time to recoup past profits you have a system that is fool proof. Fool proof in theory, but with a problem that turns out to make it impractical. If you look at historical results, you can see that it works for a while, but there are runs of up to 50 races or more where no dog wins in a particular lane. As you will be increasing the amount each time so that you cover the amount accumulatively lost, the bet gets very big. It would run into the many billions far more than any bookmaker would allow you to place. There are many similar systems that work well in theory but fall apart in practice. Randomness brings out runs of the same number and with our neatness disorder and habit of looking for patterns they stand out.

When we look at the issue of trying to map out the future we have a problem that can't be overcome, even when projecting the destiny of just a few atoms. Mapping the position and direction and relative speed of just a few hundred results in super massive amounts of data. Each atom requires at least 10 or 20 other atoms to store the data. The number of atoms inside your body is monumentally large and no amount of storage could map out and predict the behaviour and likely outcome, even a small time later. We have to lump things together. Rather than examining each atom we might look at what a ball containing trillions of smaller particles might do. We can deduce the likely outcome and give it a probability. In the same way that dogs never win in certain lanes for long periods a ball may well bounce left lots of times when it could go left or right in equal measure. Your life is not set out according to fate but there is a certain chance that you will do something or another. Given that you have fixed preferences you might well be drawn to something that is pre-set in your genes.

You may have been to a funfair where there is a machine that has rows and rows of pins with ball bearings that drop down bouncing between them. If the ball goes down a particular path you win a prize. If you drop lots of balls and graph where they fall to, you get a bell-shaped picture. Most land in the middle with a small number at the two sides. Your life runs very much like this, most days things are in the middle but occasionally an outside event comes about. You could bump into someone you haven't seen for some time if both of your in-life chances coincide. The probability rises if the hit zone is wider. You are much more likely to encounter someone if you are out for dinner and in the place for a good while than just passing through. This pin game system runs day and night in all of us and dictates the probability of things good and bad happening. Zillions of balls streaming down with some paths overlapping and some clashes and coupling.

Things may appear inevitable, like having an accident if a tyre on your car is worn through, but when and what the extent of the incident will be comes down to a whole host of unpredictable factors; how fast you were going and where and when it blows out. Was it inevitable, fate that brought you and your partner together? Many random chance events led to the initial encounter for sure, but you select according to your inbuilt affinities and that plays a part. If you didn't go that night would you still have met on another night? Most of us tend to meet in places that we all go to regularly anyway, institutions, work places and so on. Like a toddler's education game with shaped pieces and respective slots for them to go into, shake it up and the bulk lock into place with just a few awkward ones left over. Meeting someone is like the bald tyre. The outcome explosive unless you replace it. Prime it and you won't have to wait that long. A singleton is on the lookout for another singleton, their body language may demonstrate their status, a coupling may appear fortuitous but if you give yourself the greatest amount of probability for it to occur it is ever more likely. You could choose whether or not to go one night based on the flip of a coin. If you use a mechanical device to flick the coin it will land the same way every time. Portents are at the mercy of human trickery.

Past events do not predict the future but form is everything. Greyhound dog racers that have won in the past are more likely to win than ones that haven't. People who bet on such things are victims of their own success. As they get the winner right so often the odds paid out are lower than what is fair.

People have surmised that an insect can disrupt and play a part in the weather far far away. Every interaction has a cause and an effect, but noticeable changes are at the mercy of tipping points. A huge number of insects have to be on the move to get anyway near such tipping points. Everything is connected to everything else but things close by will have much much more significance than anything miles away. There are buffers that absorb and discount the effect of the tiny life-form's activities.

Chance

Statistics if collected and used appropriately can be heavily relied upon. You can't say anything will happen for definite but you can be very sure that an outcome has an absolute percentage likelihood of occurring. Risks are everywhere no doubt about it and there are some we are not even aware of. You could worry yourself to death or examine the big ones and take simple steps to reduce the chance of being affected by them. Simple steps like wearing a seat belt in the car reduces the risk of dying, but doesn't impinge a great deal on the fun of driving. So without being a killjoy you can lower the overall probability of coming to grief without spoiling the pleasures in life. For many it is the actual risk taking element that provides the thrill. They usually do it to feel very much alive rather than having any desire to die.

Perceptions of risk differ from the actual real risk of many activities. Some of us have a fear of dying in a certain way rather than dying per se. We might hate the idea of drowning inside a tunnel beneath the sea rather than falling off a ladder.

All hospital treatments carry a fair risk and for many it is a one-way ticket. This is one of many areas where the risk is out of our control and bothers us more. We know the dangers of driving but if we are at the wheel we see it as a part of our own destiny. We also take the risk according to the expected gain. The more we could potentially gain the higher the risk we might take.

The probability of reaching old age unscathed is lower than you might expect. If one in a thousand fall victim to some cause or another each year, then over twenty years each person could have a one in fifty chance of suffering the same fate. If you add up all the various potential perils, then it can look quite alarming. The one recourse is to invest in ourselves. Examine the main pitfalls and spend extra on such things as a good diet. We think nothing of spending a fortune on getting an education but many will scrimp on quality food.

A lottery ticket does not buy a realistic chance of coming into a fortune. Instead it pays for a dream, a wish to escape the drudgery. Even though we know that in any given week we are well over a hundred times more likely to perish than win, we insist on giving it a shot. Saying that you have to be in it to win it is a notion to get more to play and ramp up the size of the top prize.

Games with skill pay the talented as the odds go in their favour, whereas games without just provide entertainment only. People think they can use a system to beat the machine or house but they are deluded. The fruit machine effect is a huge trap. You keep feeding it as you believe it will soon pay out. The more you have put in the closer you think you are to getting a jackpot. In reality every coin you put in costs you a certain amount, typically about 20% depending on how shrewd the machine owner is. These machines work in the same way as you might wait and wait for a bus, wishing more and more that you had walked away, clenching on to the hope one will turn up. The more time invested the more you wait. Eventually you have to give up if none shows. The only real lesson is to avoid getting caught up in these situations whenever possible.

Risk on balance

We need to ask ourselves if what we are about to do to ourselves is really necessary and worth the risk. Things become the norm, standard practice and we don't reflect enough to see if there really is another way. People have blood transfusions and sneer at those that refuse them. People recover sometimes, despite having them, not always because they did. You could be given the wrong type no matter how good the procedures are in place. Mistakes are always possible, screening is not infallible for you could get diseased or tainted blood. Having a procedure done without a transfusion carries a risk but it is sometimes slightly lower than with it. Maybe 6% of people die or have major complications having had it compared with 4% of people who not have it. There may come a time when automation reduces the risk considerably and alien blood is no longer a problem, it is simply an example where we accept things as they are.

In many cases people are left for a while after an injury to recover and allow the body to heal itself before further invasive actions. The old ways of having a long rest to recover rather than intervening and being impatient for a quick recovery comes back to the fore. People forget that taking medications whilst ill is not the elixir as all have some kind of side effect that can be detrimental.

One of the most heart-warming tales that I heard was the case of the person who changed the way people with club feet were treated. People in poorer regions were the most susceptible to this problem and had the least money to do anything about it. The sufferers were not just stigmatised, but had obvious difficulties walking and working. In the richer nations the doctors would do highly complex, lengthy operations to fix the patients. The operations were expensive, risky and traumatic but the surgeons were skilled and considered the use of their talents to be the best way. The individual I referred to heard of another way and went to investigate. Rather than slice open the legs break the bones and set them straight they found that they could just be bound against a stick and forced into a straight position. By binding and gradually tightening over the months the legs and feet would straighten out very well indeed. Not only is this much less invasive it is a procedure that can be carried out at near zero cost anywhere and doesn't have the problems with aftercare and infections. The moral of the story is that having blind faith in the way things are done sometimes closes us off from exploring simpler less risky alternatives. Having said this, we might have come across the placebo effect and wish to try alternative medicines. They are all well and good for some but do not have the power of great research and study that accepted medicinal practices do. It might be a pity to be fooled by false hope on the one hand or go the other way and think that everyone is doing things wrong, we only need to be aware of the possibility to simplify and improve. You can't think yourself better but positivity and having a lot to live for will aid a recovery.

Share or take it all?

There is a game that you can be asked to play where you are given the choice of sharing or trying to have it all. The prize pot can be split 50/50 or one person can take it all. If both people elect to 'steal' then neither gets anything. You can run various models with the game played out over and over. The co-operation strategy is the most fruitful in the long run. It requires you to forget about the times that you were suckered and ignore the temptation to make any reprisals. People however do not operate by logic, they use emotional attachments and read body language and will share in some circumstances and not others. The idea of such games for study is fundamentally flawed by the complexities of human nature. If you only get the chance to play this game once in your lifetime, you may act differently than if you get to play once a week.

Trying to put numbers to situations and running models is erroneous. The mathematics might look clever but there are always dreadful assumptions in the way you convert the idea to a number. People enjoy sharing, they enjoy doing one another favours because they like to. Not because they want something in return and not because of any subconscious duty. People do not always consider that being a 'sucker' is detrimental. Many animals including humans find that helping one another is rewarding, sometimes more so than helping yourself. People will say; "I got more enjoyment giving it away than I ever would spending it on myself." Selfishness is a double-edged sword with the greater true gain made in the giving in so many cases.

Sometimes you can help others and you feel as though they really appreciate what you have done. In other cases, helping out lands you in trouble and is a bit off putting, but overall we tend to keep on doing it. We do not co-operate to help us survive we co-operate as it is joyous. You can't place a number on that.

Losing

One needs to learn to lose before they can learn to win is what they say. One way of increasing the joy you give to a winner is to get in a tantrum and show too much annoyance. Rather than mentally beating yourself up about any loss, you can use it as an opportunity to see room for improvement in your game. Think about what you did right. In many games you will have done a lot more right than wrong even though in life small mistakes can hand victory to your opponent. Whether it is a game or a business loss we can laugh it off and move on. Few can succeed until they experience the pain of a significant loss. It is only if you get your fingers burnt and don't try something else resigning yourself to total defeat that leads to a real tragedy. You have to lose an amount that means something and upsets the present lifestyle. Losing small bets has no real impact. Those with money have made a lot, lost a lot along the way and care less about money than those without. Winning something on your first outing can be disastrous too, as it becomes a hook towards addiction, wanting that feeling of winning over and over again. It gives you that all important first impression that sticks.

War

At almost all times throughout recorded history there have been people engaged in a war of some sort somewhere in the world. Perhaps only three in each hundred years have there been total peace in all nations. However, looking at it another way, you will find that the majority of people across the globe have not been participating in any fighting for most of the time. Most individuals are simply not interested or prepared to fight one another. Most of us respect other people's desire to live and have no wish to kill. The cause of the fighting? Sometimes religion, but more often culture and power plays, to dominate land and resources.

The action of killing somebody is much harder in practice for people that aren't accustomed to it. There is a huge difference in killing someone in hand to hand combat compared with dropping a bomb or firing an artillery shell from afar.

There are a small number of people who become very proficient and may even enjoy killing and furthermore suffer no problems afterwards. These characters blazed the trail wiping out anything that got in the way. However, these people only account for something like 2% of the population. Huge numbers of soldiers have returned home having never fired a single shot, let alone at someone. Many fired their guns too high, over the heads of the opposition on purpose.

In modern armies, soldiers go through rigorous training programs to get a kind of automatic reaction when under fire. When battles commence the training takes over and normal behaviour is set aside. Without this training most would be hopelessly ineffectual, but no matter how much training is given beforehand, dealing with the aftermath is never easy for everyone. Many soldiers have been severely traumatised by their experience, which has often lead to suicide or a troubled life afterwards. Visualisation techniques can help a determined person to overcome the awful memories to some degree, but this is an area few armies concern themselves with.

Those unaccustomed to the dreadful nature of real life horror scenes may think that they would never do much harm to another. However, it only takes a short time for many a kind person to transform into a pernicious individual. Two key ingredients are required. One being the authority from up high or from someone respected in command. The other being in an environment away from normal life. Captors have been left in charge of prisoners both in war zones and in artificial experiments and the results have been deplorable. Within a few days the behaviour of those left in charge spirals downwards into a malicious contemptible affray. If someone broke into your home at night and attacked your family, you could quite easy become far more aggressive and protective than normal. Your reaction would be surprising, even to yourself, when reviewed in the calm days later. With the right incentive and the push from an authority figure we can be turned from a pacifist into a very mean individual fairly quickly.

Killing in the heat of battle is markedly different to terminating someone's life in cold blood. It is much easier for the killer to shoot someone from behind or when the victim is blindfolded as the pain and anguish on the face and in the eyes of the victim is not so visibly detected. Many would rather spare the person than see the effect of their actions. Most commanders of execution squads are well aware of this.

The ideal war is one where there is such overwhelming force bearing down on the troublemakers that they capitulate and give up without a fight. A significant aspect of war comes down to bravado and threat rather than aiming to kill. There have been many battles where thousands of people took part, but only a few died. Armies enjoy making a lot of noise and create threatening actions in the hope that the other side disperses or surrenders. In many battles it can be the perceived superiority rather than the actual strength that allows one side to achieve victory. Hence why the garish uniforms, drums and ineffectual but frightening looking equipment made earlier armies look formidable. Elephants have been used to charge at the enemy. They were somewhat effective except many turned around and ran back at those that sent them into the melee. Gas too had a habit of harming those that released it when there was an unexpected change in wind direction.

If you can't defeat the opposition head on, then endurance is key. Whoever can keep the effort up for longest prevails. Hit and run guerrilla tactics over long periods of time also wear out all but the most patient fighting forces in the end.

One clown remarked that it was two years in the making and ten minutes in the undoing. The quote refers to the time taken to train large groups of fighters and the speed at which they were annihilated during a minimally productive assault. The element missing from this portrayal is the twenty years or so of dedication, sacrifice and commitment made by their parents. The pregnancy, the years of weaning, the slog mixed within the fun and reward of nurturing each of these individuals. The investment made in each of us is huge. To be a pawn in somebody else's game, to have a bead of lead dismember a vital part of our body is not the same as being unfortunate in one's own premeditated risky adventure. All that structure that took years of arranging and refining is lost in an instant. Everything right down to the spelling tests that your teachers insisted was so important to do well at.

Whether it is through war or accident the exasperation of losing someone whom we have devoted so much attention to is never easy to come to terms with. Solace might be found in cherishing the memories of the time shared and a life cut short is still bountiful. Those with loved ones still intact may consider what could be if a warning is ignored. We need reminders from time to time to stay grateful and make attempts to tear down any barriers created through petty feuds. It is noteworthy though how people in a country rally around and help each other before or whilst an enemy is attacking. Most personal differences are set aside and communities get together and share the common problem. Then go back to petty feuds after it all calms down. However, a few unpopular people in the community disappear as law and order is replaced by confusion and mayhem.

Risk in war

The greatest risk in many wars has been from disease and accidents rather than enemy fire. You can't discount the friendly fire (allegiancide), the most inapt expression ever uttered. Although the outcome of each war has been remarkably different, it is fair to say that in some cases, statistically, people can be more at risk from some jeopardy or other at home than in the location of war. In some instances, for each 100 000 people that went to a war zone 99 500 returned safely whereas 600 would likely have perished in the same time frame in their home country. (Although it would probably have been a different set of people.) However, there have been many wars in which a completely different scenario emerged, ones with far greater causalities.

There is for some people a great distinction between fighting to preserve their own home and country and fighting to expand their territory or helping other countries. Weighing up the possible risk to yourself is hard to do as severe injury, mental scarring and obvious death is balanced against the reasons for combat. Most people will admit that they would protect themselves and their immediate family by whatever means necessary. Many people will show gratitude towards those that have defended their country from invaders. Similar appreciation has been shown by those that have appealed to other nations to intervene in their state when people have used force to circumvent and override the laws and voting systems that were in place. People are far more likely to seek redress when life in their country is heavily restricted and unrewarding. If a state feels that they want a defensive capability, they are perhaps more justified building one with non-coerced volunteers.

Where an organisation has not got a big army or much in the way of military apparatus, yet has a strong reason to fight for their principles they are inclined to act in what is termed terrorism. The loose definition is an act of extreme violence that is unapproved of by the big states. The main purpose is to elevate the cause above the many other events on that day. The news is most often comprised of things that are new, things that are out of the ordinary. When the media plays into the hands of the agitators they increase the weight of the message and heighten tensions. Were such events downplayed then support will drop. Only if frustration of not being heard rises and rises and therefore action is taken to raise the ante significantly does this policy become risky. Most of the attacks get blanket coverage and the length of debate and discussion is disproportionate to the scale in the wider scheme of things. An earthquake and other natural disasters can wipe out hundreds or even thousands of people in one go. Preventable curable diseases eradicate millions every year. Use of guns and knives destroy lives daily. Add in the fatalities on the road many of which are quite preventable and the hate wars claim less than 0.01% of the total. If the people in power act in a way that gives the same precedence to all of the citizens, then the resources would be deployed in a much more even handed way. No one life is more important than another.

When you have virtually nothing to lose the fear evaporates, as death could seem more attractive than a suppressed futile life. The most dangerous parties to keep a close eye on are those coerced and sucked into doing something through false promises and become a patsy in someone else's game. Those that change their mind and aren't swayed look back years later and are invariably glad they avoided an early death.

To sacrifice your life for the benefit of others could be admirable but you won't be around to appreciate any of the gains of the eventual victory. Is it worse to be die in a war that your side ends up losing anyway? From your point of view, it makes no difference, it is only important whether you win or lose if you survive.

Body

You can spend an eternity studying the health benefits of various foodstuffs and worry yourself silly about all the harm some things are supposed to do. Balance is everything. If you are already eating a good variety, by that we mean not too much or too little of the same foodstuffs then you can skip this chapter. There is rarely any need for supplementary pills as many won't be absorbed by the body in the same way as food anyway. You need not concern yourself with the ins and outs of eating what some may call junk food so long as you avoid getting such meals from the same place more than once a week. Junk food is not always bad per se for what it contains, but for what it doesn't contain.

The ills of too little: Make no mistake about it plants do not grow as tall, have yellowing leaves and look rather listless if even one essential mineral is unavailable in their plot. People have come close to death doing self-experimentation where they denied themselves vital-amines. So simple logic will tell us that the greater the variety in our diet the more chance we have of getting all the nutrients that we need to maintain our bodies. The beautiful thing about this approach is that you do not need to spend any time analysing what you eat. Even munching a small amount of salad, vegetables, fruit and other things that doesn't taste too great to you can make the world of difference with little pain. We tend to follow the habits of our parents and can pass some failings down the generations. You might need to find the gall to stop rejecting foods that are actually quite palatable. There will be things you do not like, but there will be plenty of alternatives that provide the right mix. It unlikely that every green item is 'disgusting'. Young children will quite happily eat chocolate turds but look at them as being revolting a few years later as they adopt the same disgusts as their parents. Eat for you and your longevity.

The damage of too much: Eating too much of something is not just about getting fat it is also about how it wreaks havoc to essential parts of our body. We can tolerate a certain amount of toxicity, but go over the limit and we are liable to do some permanent damage. We will rarely eat enough of one poison to get a lethal dose at the one sitting. However, a few µg consumed over and over can build up if your body doesn't get the time to deal with it and can't flush it out faster than it is streaming in. So eating anything over and over ends up being disastrous for our health and well-being. People have died eating too many carrots or drinking too much water, items that are general considered to be good for you.

A variety reduces the probability of damaging your organs through overdose and gets as close as possible to guaranteeing that you get enough of what you need. The simplicity of the diverse diet allows for a few wayward habits, after all there is a claim that happier people live longer than miserable ones. You can compensate by sticking to buying more natural foods like real bread, brown rather than blanched white and less processed foods. Don't be a cheapskate, food is medicine buy the best where you can as a life free of illness is priceless. Particular attention to what you eat must be made during pregnancy if you want your offspring to live longer and they will be much less hassle to you if built near as possible to the intended design. Anything you make without the essential ingredients becomes a bodge job.

There is something to be said for eating the whole but it doesn't apply in all cases. It is well known that some cereal boxes might well contain more nutrition than the cereal inside. As the husk and wheat germ is removed the fibre and nutrients have been stolen. If you apply the same logic to eating an apple core as well as the flesh, you may encounter some toxicity akin to a rhubarb which has poisonous leaves. If you decide to eat the said cereal box you may be unhappy to discover that since we began all the virtuous recycling over and over the levels of noxious chemicals have steadily increased. Most unpleasant as they leach through the bag inside into the food inside. When we think we are doing some good we always disregard the downsides.

Where do you draw the line when it comes to avoiding the problems with food? Some wash rice with boiling water after it is cooked to rinse out more of the arsenic. I am sure you could make a list of countless dangers, so once again the not too much, not too often comes into play again.

Dieting schemes often lead to more money lost than weight loss. It is remarkably easy to shed a small amount quite quickly but keeping it off is no mean feat. Regular exercise is needed alongside a cutback in food consumption. It is easy to get in a vicious circle of getting heavier making it require more effort to move about, resulting in us doing less.

There is elasticity in the body's ability to take on more weight. Fat cells fill up like a balloon. When over stretched, they split into two and the bodies capacity rises. You then have more fat cells to manage, making you liable to move up to the next weight bracket, staying there unless serious intervention is taken. Hence all the thin people will tell you to avoid getting fat in the first place.

Where variety is paramount a slight cautionary tale needs to be mentioned. One group of people in a waiting room with a selection of sandwiches with a large range of different fillings ate double that of another group with just a single type available. The bigger the buffet with more options on offer, the more trying it is for those inclined to obesity. Such simple tactics of using smaller plates and not going for seconds can be as helpful as reading through long-winded guides feeding the pockets of those writing them. Make sure people have to get up and walk for more, it is no use having a minuscule plate if there is a mound of food on the table to easily top it up with. Sensible amounts of a variety is the aim.

Sticking to plants

Eating an animal that is very close to the end of its natural life seems less uncaring than slaughtering one before it has had any chance of experiencing the world fully. People have proposed that we have both the mental capacity to show compassion to animals and refrain from killing them for food. There is a thought that we can manage quite well with a diet that leaves them out. Lions and tigers, whales and sharks don't have this luxury.

Some people keep their meat and animal products consumption down to a minimum, as they see it as doing their bit. Others will of course do it for perceived health reasons. Whatever the choice I personally prefer to pay more for meat if the welfare of the animals is improved, even if it means paying double and having less. We have to come to terms with the denial of the animals wish to live a full life or just ignore it and pay no attention to it. People like the taste, so much and reason that the protein that it provides outweighs the suffering. There is a definitive primal bout of satisfaction when chewing meat. It is always going to be a contentious issue and something that creates controversy.

In practice it is near impossible to omit animal by-products from your diet. Milk may seem fairly innocuous yet is a product that causes significant harm and misery towards animals and it is found in all kind of things such as bread, cakes, sweets and chocolate. It is difficult to avoid. Calves can be taken away a few short days after birth leaving the mother in untold distress.

We can be equally disrespectful and uncaring in the way we cause misery to pets. Some are stored in tiny boxes that get way too hot in the summer and ice cold in the winter. We forget that dogs are pack animals and isolated for our pleasure not theirs. The causal nature in which we interfere with the bodies of animals for our convenience upsets real animal lovers. We neuter, dock, geld at our leisure as it makes them easier for us, whilst denying them opportunities to use their curiosity or discover any rewards suited to them. A pet cat will probably eat something like a thousand chickens or equivalent in its lifetime. The ratio of death to sustain life is even greater for its adopted provider and if it keeps you happy then that is all that matters.

I saw a cartoon that depicted someone growing up and being vocal and expressive about the rights and wrongs of eating animals. The youngster meets an elder who spoke eloquently about leading by example rather than being too great an activist. Activism has a place particularly when the worst of all torturous practices are hidden and allowed to be continued. Activism is most hypocritical when those voicing an opinion have not got their own house in order. You need to be squeaky clean yourself, otherwise it is hard to fully justify complaining about others when parts of your own life are dubious. When under close scrutiny, I doubt anyone's life is lived without it being to the detriment of some animals somewhere and this doing your bit is insufficient to come across as so magnanimous.

Damage

We are born with a blueprint stemming from the process of mitosis that aims for a certain finished result. The blueprints are constantly being copied, sometimes incorrectly. Hence, identical twins are never completely identical. Whilst the environment, the pollution and radiation we are exposed to can damage us, the most widespread cause of poor body development is down to poor diets. Insufficient nutrients at the very least mean we grow to a lower height than what would be the case when we get the required food. You are what you eat.

Whether the blueprint produces something with outstanding characteristics or something a little odd, people can nevertheless live an equally rewarding life.

The genome has trigger points. One day you hear a low gruff voice reverberating in the house. Who has paid us a visit? A voice has broken overnight. This is a bit startling. When a seemingly normal child has other transformations that appear like everything has gone awry we look for a cause. Was it something in the environment, something we gave them to eat or caused by a recent injection? It may well be, but if it is something that was predetermined in the genes it is often the last thing we look to blame.

The joy of a bed

Our well-being can be drastically affected when we don't get the right amount of quality sleep and those who are unable to go to sleep at all die after a few weeks. It is a period where the mind is still active, condensing and sorting information gathered during the time awake. All those conversations whittled down and purged.

If you are touched whilst you are asleep it may interrupt and become an aspect of your dreams, but apart from that and the occasional changes in your dream due to being too hot, cold, thirsty you are pretty much oblivious to what is going on around you. This has a likeness to when you pass away. While you are fast asleep billions of others are beavering away.

Getting off to sleep can be a struggle for some. I find it very hard if I have any kind of dialogue going on in my head. If you start considering what someone may say and their probable responses, you are likely to be doing so well into the night. I am most thankful for people who think I am lazy for not getting up at the same time as them. People think that you can adjust your body clock to anytime that you want. Try getting up three hours earlier than normal. Do it for a good month and see if you get that feeling of utter inner tiredness as your body temperature remains out of sync. There is a notable difference between fitting in with a society, adjusting and accommodating to its way of life compared to following its same precise pattern. You do the same just in a different order or at a different time in the day.

There can be times where a dream has a bearing on reality. Someone had a dream once where lots of people were talking but no sound was coming from their mouths and when they awoke their voice was permanently broken. I was plagued by some nightmares for years that revolved around a small horror then a bigger one and so on. It was years later that I realised these correlated to some small mistake or large thing I had done wrong. The fear of failure and pressure from inflexible characters. Only a new life away from the stress of the situation allowed these to fade. My bad dreams haven't stopped completely, but they take a different form to this and only occur when too hot or when excessively spiced food was eaten late in the evening. The worst is when you are semi-awake but can't move. At the back of the neck there is a shut off mechanism and if that is not switched fully you have a frustrating few minutes of trying to re-engage the body.

The less pleasant dreams are dwarfed by the rather fun ones where you can fly high and move in ways that reality can't compete with. No mention of the personal encounters with imaginary folk need writing about apart from to say that they were as good as those in everyday life. The frequent dreams of being in elevators trying hopelessly to get to a desired level, sometimes using some stairs as a get around, don't seem to have any notable point. Lifts that move sideways and in manners outside of typical engineering possibilities add to the experience. Some might say that is because you are trying to go up in life or find workarounds but as they say that to everyone their dream analysis is a money-making pleasure.

The way it is

"You either know it all or have a hole in your argument."

Many just accept that the universe is the way it is and beyond our comprehension, whilst a few explore some proposals that shed some light on to how it could have come into being. Cast aside everything the typical person thinks about the universe for a few moments and try and visualise the true atom in the single dimension of space. There is a way to see things without it changing anything at all with physics as we know It.

If we begin with the single dimension of space, we can form a picture that is much more in tune with reality. It is so easy to postulate about there being many dimensions, the fourth being time and then the 5th, 6th, 7th and so on. Instead of all that hyperbole you can settle on just one dimension and nothing more whatsoever. One problem with multi-dimensional thinking is that it does not stack up in reality. It is like saying my cat ate my house. It is easy to visualise a cat indeed eating a whole house from the front door to the chimney and every brick, but it is a cartoonish idea and never possible. We have a capability to conjure up mad ideas in our mind that have no basis in the physical world.

Can you have a two-dimensional object? If it is to be 2D then it will have zero thickness and hence will not exist. If it is assumed to be infinitely thin, then it has a thickness and thus is 3D. The same goes with 1D.

I have spent some considerable time explaining the idea of the single dimension of space to people and they can't escape the architects view of the world. Up is up no matter what you say. But your up is down to those on the other side of the world and sideways for those living half way round from you. What is consistent is that up is always away from the centre of the earth no matter where you are pontificating. Each object is a set defined distance from all other objects. Change the relative distances and the object's position has moved. If you turn the whole universe upside down it makes no difference, turn an object over and the top gets closer to some things and further away from others.

We can use a distance measuring tool to work out where you are by working out the distance you are from devices floating in space. Get a signal from four of them and the position is quite accurate. You do not move up, left, right forward and backwards you move nearer or further away from other objects. When you climb the stairs you don't go 5 steps forward and 10 up your move diagonally away from the bottom. Whilst nothing changes apart from the mental mapping, you no longer think in terms of three planes of movement but see it as items being a set of straight line distances apart. So the 3D representation still works but there is only a one possibility; a single arena of space.

The fourth dimension is another human abstract. Time is just a measure of rotations or oscillations of an object and nothing more. We see something turn and once a certain amount of revolutions have been made, another object moves from one point to another. It is all relative with some covering a greater relative distance than others and hence are described as moving faster.

Time has historically been derived in part from the rotation of the earth. Hours and minutes, sub divisions of one rotation, using convenient numbers such as 60 which can be handily divided by lots of numbers; 2,3,4,5,6,10,12,15,20,30 to make half hour, twenty minutes, quarter hour and so forth. Metric time would be awkward. A hundred minutes cannot be divided so well. Anyway, put two super accurate clocks side by side, synchronise them then take one on a journey. When they return next to each other the time displayed differs. Add this to the fact that the earth is gradually slowing down making each year a little longer and it begins to tell you something.

Time is invaluable for approximating things, vital for issuing speeding tickets, wonderful considering that we are travelling at over 600 miles an hour when standing still. Spinning around, orbiting the sun in a galaxy on the move. It is perfectly acceptable to ascribe us as being static with everything else moving around us. We thought that the earth was at the centre of the universe, then thought that we orbited the sun and then realised that both are true according to your standpoint. Time spanning the universe can speed up and slow down and there will be no way of knowing as there will be nothing to compare it with. The relative speed of light appears to be constant when measured in a vacuum. Whether it is the same when surrounded by a huge mass is hard to ascertain.

True atoms

A long time ago someone thought about what would happen if we kept breaking things down into ever smaller pieces. They proposed that eventually you would reach a point where something could not be broken down any further. They named these indivisible pieces atoms. As science moved forward these atoms became known as elements, each being a little denser as they went down the periodic table from hydrogen the lightest through gold to uranium and so on. It then became apparent that each element was essentially made of up of sub-atomic particles which have been named protons, neutrons and electrons. However, these were found to be also made up of even smaller parts. As the term atom has been hijacked for the intermediate size particle we call elements, the piece that was originally thought of as the smallest possible can be referred to as a true atom. A large number of true atoms form the pieces that in turn make up protons, neutrons and electrons and then create all the discrete elements. The difference between such things as protons and the neutrons is the quantity and arrangement of the true atoms.

If you consider the true atom akin to a magnet with its poles and attraction and repulsion to other like-minded entities. You can see that two can join together quite nicely like top and tailing in bed. Other arrangements with three, four and so on create some structure and different behaviours. As these structures get more complex they can then from the basis for the separate parts that then lead on to constitute the electron, neutron and proton.

This true atom is indivisible and sits in its own spot interacting with all its neighbours near and far. Having the idea of a truly unbreakable core particle raises questions about what form, shape, size it is. Is it like a ball, spherical or might it be flat like a sheet of paper or could it be looping string shaped? The problem with all these shapes is that they create an impression that they can be cut and divided. Then there is the problem of where the atom begins and where does it end? Is there some kind of boundary between two or more atoms? Thinking of it as a single minuscule point doesn't help either.

Every true atom interferes with every other true atom with decreasing magnitude the further apart. One affect is gravitational. Every atom in a big object like planet earth will attract every atom in the moon. This provides a clue to the form of true atoms. The atoms in your body are attracted to those in the earth and those in the moon even if the moon is on the other side of the earth to which you are standing. This implies that the force goes through countless atoms. Right through and out the other side. The earth's gravity is not one big combined force, rather, lots and lots of tiny forces. Do these forces pass through a true atom or are they interfered with along the way?

Each atom being derived from nothing gets a presence by borrowing like you borrow from a bank. The money in a bank is abstract and doesn't have any form, shape or size but an account can go into deficit. You have a hole where the money came from and cash to spend. The key is to look at the true atom as having no real substance, no 'weight' so to speak. It is much more akin to a piece of information. What it does have though is the properties of mass.

One such property of mass is the resistance it has to change in motion. The more mass an object has the more force required to accelerate it. More effort to speed it up, slow it down or redirect it. Another property is the gravitational pull on all other masses. Each true atom interacts with one another. No true atom exists without the rest. Each individual true atom is defined by the effect it has on the others. In the same way astronomers can spot a planet light years away, not by seeing it directly but by seeing the effect it has on the orbit of other larger objects. The centre of the true atom, the position of it is made by the balance point of where it interacts with the others. The point of greatest action. The true atom has no form, but prescience dictated by all the other atoms. It is a packet of information that interacts and behaves like something solid. It will resist getting too close to another redirecting when close to impact.

The structure of many true atoms brings about the effect of magnetism and electrostatic forces and so on. Countless configurations lead to structure and the electrochemical interfaces. Whilst the atom is referred to as information it is no way to be likened to some simulation. Far from it. No magic, no relation to information in the software sense. Real as can be as each piece of information exists in an exact spot at a set distance, at that point from all the other bits of active informational chunks. Yet would be creatable from nothing. Untold numbers of atoms acting at a place relative to each other. No shape, no form, no substance nor actual solid matter, only the characteristics that we see and experience around us. A miasma of information. Looking at it this way does not alter the physical world around us and the physics remains precisely the same. The universe is no simulation, for each atom has to be acting in its present spot. We are not holograms.

The information can be borrowed but also repaid. Energy and the will to form is the essence of the behaviour of all the atoms. The sun is not really hot as in high temperature as we think of it in the sense of it burning hot, but interacts violently due to the large number of competing true atoms playing their respective parts moving position relatively quicker than elsewhere. Temperature is a measure of the relative activity of the atoms and the more active the greater the disturbance with those close by.

How each true atom behaves, how it creates structures is very finely balanced, self-balancing. The amount of force that it exhibits is crucial to the universe that results. That will always leave people open to a suggestion that something else is at play and that something devised it. One may presume that this one is more stable than other configurations. If you hypothetically change the values of the forces things do not work the way they do now, everything falls apart.

The simple reason why the universe is how it is, is that it can be no other way. There are no other alternatives unless you throw out maths completely. If you say that a true atom is now to be 1.1 true atoms, then that is still one true atom. Looking at a collection of balls you can see that only six fit round the center one on a single plane or twelve if packed in all directions. You can't place more as there is no room. This implies that there are only certain limited configurations of elementary building blocks which then dictate the outcome of complex structures. All the velocities, forces and facets of the universe are interdependent. No other alternative is available as theoretical changes are akin to trying to get 7/13 such items around a core.

Trying to define simple standard units such as the metre, ampere, temperature is quite challenging and it is remarkable that each relate to one another so well. It is not some special formula that happens to work nicely but because no other possibility is possible. Rather than being finely balanced it is self-regulating. One aspect holds another back.

The mathematics creates some issues that don't correspond to the way things manifest themselves. If I break a cake in two and say to my friend that they can have the bigger half as I am not that hungry, they know what I mean. We take these ridiculous notions beyond face value. In reality you can't have a half of anything. You were in fact offering 345 zillion cake atoms and leaving 305 zillion for yourself. Fractions are only mathematical concepts and do not translate into tangible items. Circles are x sided shapes, never truly contiguous. There are only whole numbers, whole quantities of true atoms in practice. Were you to divide 1 by 3 you would have 3 numbers 0.33333..., 0.33333.., 0.33333..., but these don't add up to 1. One third is what is called a transcendental number, where in this case the threes never end. However, in order for them to add up, one of them must take on a 4 at some point; 0.33334 Were you to attempt to split an apple in three, one of the pieces would have 1 atom more than the rest.

Maths allows us to imagine a whole lot of nonsense, which have no significance in what can actually be. With stupid concepts like negative numbers and even dafter imaginary numbers being the square root of a non-existent entity. Great for solving accountancy problems but it has absolutely no place in the real world.

Pathways

The nature of the universe is extensive but one other aspect to consider is why there are delays and lags. If you had a very long stick and pushed one end you might expect the other end to move simultaneously. However, this is not the case, as a zero delay is not observed. It would break the relative speed of light. There is a propagational delay. The stick crumples then re-expands all along its length. The delays that we observe are caused by the crumpling which creates a longer pathway. As you push the stick, the force takes a path that is much longer than the stick as it zig zags through. Gravitational delays occur in the same way. When an object moves, it imparts a change to the gravitational force even on objects that are very far away. The delay in the reaction is brought about by the increased length of the pathway between them compared to the actual relative distance apart. If a fly gets struck by an oncoming train it gets stopped momentarily and therefore the train is also stopped albeit briefly. Except that the fly does not stop, it takes a u-shaped path crumpling and has its trajectory gradually shifted around a semi-circular route.

The state of our surroundings need not be derived from a single point with a big bang. All this is mere conjecture from an idea that the universe is expanding and if you draw a line down you arrive at singularity - a tiny start point. Here lies a problem with living and knowing a little, but not enough, to then deciding when to go with the flow. At the time of writing the evidence for a big bang is good. Yet the idea stinks. Yes, we have to accept the background radiation is detectable and have to swallow the notion that an expansion occurred in a blink of an eye. However, I have changed my mind on so many things as I have looked deeper into the crevices but on this I am as dopey as one who believes a man came to earth to save us and ascended back into heaven. Like a fool chasing a pot of gold in a rainbow I cling to a hope that the maths is erroneous and care little if shown to be right or wrong. There are times when you have a hunch and absolutely no substantiable evidence to bring to the table. So anyone criticized in any hocus-pocus affair can point to this and see that there is another one not immune and use it as one more reason to be a detractor in other areas.

The window of opportunity for us to detect the background radiation is small. Man developed the right equipment just in the nick of time in the cycle of the universe so that is quite lucky. This is not a big deal for coincidences are all around us like the moon being just the right distance away to get total eclipses. I have seen people take photographs in old buildings and exclaim I captured an orb! Not accepting the big bang is akin to not accepting the orb is a dust particle floating about that has flaked off from a sweaty pensioner's skin causing a reflection in the flash of the camera. Do you include a shit chorus to pad out a rubbish song?

The idea of something from nothing is not easy to fathom but could it be more rational than other propositions? When a child asks who made the earth and gets told that god did, then asks who made god we have redundancy. God and the universe might be seen as the same thing. There again your belief system may encompass multiple gods. Either way we don't get any clue as to who, how or what initiated them. The universe does not care, nor intervene or make any influence on things that arise from the self-structuring atoms. These can drop out and leave no trace.

Evolving Complexity

Some will always see the world as too complex, too beautiful to be here through evolution alone. There is a comparison in the electronics revolution, going from a humble battery to a complex computer via valves and transistors. However, we focus on the intelligent designer and will conclude that some force was at work bringing the earth into fruition too.

Consider the complexity first. A computer is powerful due to its scale. Lots of simple switches joined in unison and working in harmony. The possibilities increase tremendously with a small increase in the number of switches. If you have an upstairs light and a downstairs one you have four possible states, (both on, both off or one on one off). With three lightbulbs, you have eight possibilities. As the number of switches increases the permutations go through the roof. All the graphics, sound and information on the computer are stored and processed by vast numbers of basic on/off switches. Whether you use two state, tri-state or quad-state like DNA does, complex machines can be formed that accomplish amazing tasks yet built on basic building blocks.

Whilst it is obvious that an intelligent force was behind the development of technology, it nevertheless provides a clear example of how something simple namely millions of basic switches can be linked together to produce something remarkable. Once the know how has been established it takes hold and spreads rapidly. An organism that can operate reliably with a viable successful design/arrangement will propagate quickly and relentlessly. Drop a few algae organisms into a pond and within days the whole surface is covered. Progress is only quick once something devised works. Each stage of enhancement takes a long time, testing all the dead ends.

Will to form

There is a will to form and organise brought about the inherent propensity of molecules to bind and combine to make complex items. There is no outside guiding force that pushes things to make certain structures. It is an inherent part of the smaller particles. If certain chemicals get into contact with each other, reactions will occur. Bigger and bigger compounds form. The shift from pure chemistry to biology is significant but inevitable. Whenever the pressures and temperatures are such, more complicated structures build. There needs to be a relatively stable availability of light and energy for long enough else it all goes in reverse. Think again of snow, if it is too warm or too cold or if there is not the right amount of moisture the flakes will not form.

There are a number of things that whilst having extraordinary complexity are not alive. Each snowflake is unique and wondrously structured. They form automatically. Comparable autonomous characteristics are found in primitive bacterium and viruses, leading to insects then to bigger creatures. Whilst snow only forms if there is water present at the right temperature and pressure, life is similar but uses a multitude of elements and compounds. Both quickly assemble in to beautiful configurations and will do so without any prompting.

The idea that each species is distinct and that one animal doesn't seem to mutate and change into a different one can bring about confusion. The more complex the animal, the greater the time required for a significant change. Small organisms like viruses and bacteria do change dramatically in a relatively short space of time though. Creatures will evolve in small steps over a number of generations. A jump from one species to another will involve a significant number of steps over many millennia rather than within a few decades or centuries. A mutation from a cat to a pigeon won't be likely in a single step, but over many thousands of years a change in species will take place. Many changes will take place in the 'leaves' and eventually the 'twigs' of biological change. The main branches, which can represent the species, change only after a long period of time.

If you imagine evolving a car to a helicopter you can see that it will be an extensive process. You would need to remove the wheels, increase the performance of the engine, alter the body, adjust all the controls and add a rotary wing before the car could fly. An off-road vehicle may evolve from a standard car more quickly and as only small changes to the gearbox and tyres are required. This is akin to the little changes seen in animal evolution.

Similarly, if you wanted to build a computer from a new glass material for example, you would not attempt to swap the billions of transistors within the microprocessor all in one go. If you tried this, it would more than likely fail. You would go back to the beginning and build a single transistor out of glass, get the functionality of that right first. Then gradually string more and more together until a new improved one is created. The bulk of evolution gets stuck; you can't go back a number of steps and still have something viable. Each new design must work in its own right or it dies out.

Accidental progress

A huge number of discoveries were brought about by chance and from unintended results from research. Serendipity. There have been many scientists that have worked towards a particular objective and on the way found some unexpected properties within the things they were toying with. In such cases, they would divert their attention to a new cause. This is akin to the way in which new and varied forms of species progress, where the accidentally improved varieties thrive in the environment they inhabit.

This accidental progress has created other animals in the past. Although these designs would have resulted in them having significantly different capabilities, it appears that they didn't have the same ability to thrive as the ones we see today. The progress made has not been orchestrated or manipulated, but it is simply that the viable types have prospered because of the characteristics that they have. Not enough food then it dies out. For every species that is around today a thousand have come and gone.

Viruses mutate and change quickly and each one is like a key trying to get through various locks. The ones that open the pathways spread and multiply. The ones that are barred simply fade away. If one out of the thousands of variants happens upon the right combination through 'luck' they will then go on to multiply further, breaking all the defences in the process. They are not consciously clever. There is no objective or purpose behind evolution. Each mutation changes the species slightly, giving it a different prospect of flourishing. The virus doesn't care about making you ill nor does it try to, it is just a toxin that exists in a more elaborate form than a whole bunch of chemical nasties. Destruction and annoyance are part and parcel of the bigger system and vital to its continuance.

Speak your way to the top

Some question our superiority claiming that dolphins, pigs and chimpanzees are more intelligent than we give them credit for. Even the humble house cat has an ability to be grumpy when it senses we are packing for another holiday. Chimpanzees will use sex like us to get attention, with their privates glowing bright red, legs wide open, laying partially back between the branches of the tree. Such use of power along with the frequent scolding and teaching the infants put them on par with us. They understand one another quite well, but have not been seen writing about it.

Language can be intentionally ambiguous or stiff and clear. It can be abstract or based on reality. The bigoted assume that only those that can arrange neat prose are able to convey concepts from one mind to another.

There needs to be space for animals to evolve and there is not much of that to foster another equivalent species whilst we hog everything. Would it make a difference to your world view if there were more than one human equivalent around? What if the

Neanderthals lived side by side with us the homo sapiens. What if there were three other species with pretty much the same capabilities as each other. Or are they? We might simply assume we are all the same. Only by pure misfortune, a minor string of events lead to this one species being one that stands out.

Man monkied about for ages before they began to distance themselves as top primate. To make real headway a lot of force, violence and quashing of uncertainty is needed to get the bulk to fall in line with the leaders.

A termite went to see the toppity termite to get approval for a new construction. Yes, you can, go ahead but make sure you create plenty of parking for the disabled and allocate a few levels for the underprivileged. Also, I want to see that it doesn't cast a shadow over the ant's nest over there. The power of being able to talk to one another is not to be underestimated. You can't even think without language. Wrong. Picture an object and rotate it and work out what will fit and where it will reside. Some people can't do this, that is true. There are those with limited or no visualisation capabilities. Can you count without saying 1,2,3.. in your head? Picture an apple, think of a pair of pillar boxes, a trio of rings and a table with four legs. Now move from one image to another.

Not alone

It is quite likely that on planets some way away other life forms will evolve too. Communicating with them won't be easy, by the time a message is sent back and forth one or another will be in decline. Will it send the religious into a tailspin? Quite the opposite. Suddenly a long-forgotten scroll will be unearthed and upon it will be a severe message; God has given two sets of people a chance to prove their devotion, the ones who manage to convince every living soul to hold absolute belief and are abiding by certain instructions will be saved. Ideologies are cunning and are adaptable when needed.

Animal Machine

Many baulk at the idea of being considered as an animal let alone as some fancy self-repairing machine. On the animal front the notion that we are some higher order super species prevails in many quarters. We give birth to live young, eat, defecate and have a whole host of features in common with the other species. So, what separates us? We are not the only ones with self-awareness. Other animals can plan too. We might be judged to have the most intelligence potential, but in other areas we are not as capable. We can't run as quick as a cheetah, swim as well as a dolphin and obviously flapping our arms produces no flight. Instead the combination of deftness, excellent language skills and useful extra intelligence give us a crucial edge. How you view this relatively small margin of superiority is not that important, but taking a look at the human from a machine point of view is quite revealing.

There are lot of ideas out there that propose amazing things, but there is nothing quite the same as having something to test yourself on your self. An examination into how you work takes a little grit, yet is nothing much more than paying attention to your attention. Firstly, you need to come to terms with the fact that you can only attend to one thing at time. We can multitask, we can do more than one thing at a time but we can't pay attention to two things simultaneously. We can switch the attention between a number of things quite quickly, but have to dwell for some time on each item one after the other. I have heard a few say that women are better at multi-tasking than men, well some have been shown to be good at talking and moaning simultaneously but that is the worst example of a difference between the sexes possible. Neither is it true. It appears as though we are doing two things at a time but you can only make active adjustments to one thing at a time.

There are numerous tests you can try to watch your attention flick from one thing to another. Walking and talking is a prime candidate. Watch a group of people when out walking and they encounter a gate or have steep steps to climb. The talking will stop briefly whilst they negotiate the obstacle. Anything that is new or unfamiliar will cause an interruption to the flow causing you to stop, work out what to do before proceeding. We can drive and chat, but again we pause speaking when something in the road diverts us. Much of what we do uses autonomy. We examine the procedure then follow it through using the sub-conscious without needing to pay much attention to it.

When we are learning a new skill such as driving we focus on all the aspects of handling the vehicle. Once we pass our test and have driven a car for a long time, we can drive places with little thought or consideration of how we do so. Sometimes we take the wrong turn as we follow a regular route, one that has been firmly imprinted. We can let go of paying attention when it is something what we are familiar with.

During any given day, our attention will flip between a range of things, each switch precedes a period of time that we call a moment. Sometimes our attention will dwell for twenty seconds or longer. At other times it is much more fleeting, very brief. The attention will get drawn away from the present item by something, an interrupt, maybe a loud noise, a knock on the door, the phone ringing or something moving that catches our eye.

The process of revealing your mechanical workings is a matter of perpetually observing each and every change of attention. You need to be alert to your every action to become aware of what each event really consists of. All through the day you can probe the countless moments and the physicality of your actions. It is hard to describe and even harder to get under the skin of it straightway. It is doing something distinct from the notion of deep trances and mediation which might seem like opening a window into the soul. Instead, it is noticing the goings on inside you. Gradually over time you become positively aware of each thing that you are focused on and begin to note everything that distracts you. I found it a little disturbing. It took a few months to 'get in' and unfortunately it took the best part of a year to relinquish the habit and return to a form of normality.

When you blink, your mind shuts off the vision in time to the blink making it kind of disappear from your consciousness. You don't see black flashes every few seconds as the mind fills in the blanks and creates an illusion of continuity. You will notice the blackouts when you pay attention to your blinking though. Your eyes are constantly scanning all over the place yet the same movement by a video camera would create a horrid fast paced jumping about. This again is not how we experience life. Each change of attention is merged and smoothed over unless you start scrutinising it.

Throughout your day you can spot all the autonomy and all the interruptions that you come across. You will notice the messages from your bladder informing you of the need to go to the toilet. A flight of stairs is briefly judged before you climb them without much need to make adjustments. That is unless you bump into someone coming the other way and need to recalculate a new path. Then there is the autonomy like your breathing, which can be controlled to a fair extent, but will work away on its own without any active input from your attention. You can ignore many an interrupt like a rumbling stomach more easily if it is below a certain threshold. As the pertinence of the bodily event rises, the messaging system increases the level and frequency of the reminders alerting you to it. An alarm of some sort, be it a loud noise or strange smell can jolt the attention into a mode for reaction. All of which can be monitored precisely by studying oneself.

The attention is the core of the being, the gateway to all areas of the mind and a key part to the sensation of being a conscious individual. As you can only pay attention to one item at a time various mind modules need to buffer information. Your hearing for example will record a few seconds worth of sound. It will operate in an endless loop over writing the moments prior. If you feel the need to examine the sounds you can pay attention to this area and copy the stream for further examination before you lose it. Many times, you will hear something, particularly a sentence someone has uttered and not be quite sure what they said initially, but after some processing you make it out. Of course, this is error prone and we can often mistake what we heard through bad interpretation of the audio.

The stream of sound that can be buffered is somewhat limited in length hence why a phone number can be recalled easier if said quite quickly as it is not the amount of numbers in total, but rather the amount of numbers heard in a set amount of time. Extracting a person's voice from all the background noise with other people talking is no mean feat. Some struggle with this as the part of the machine in question begins to decline. When in peak condition it can decipher fragmented speech and calculate the most probable bits to string it all together into something coherent. Inventing something to place in the gaps is a native prominent feature of the mind and we get confused by what is invented to fit and what wasn't.

Our minds have a lot to contend with, just to maintain the health of the body. Regulating the metabolism and monitoring many things from the heart to the lungs and other organs, plus it is always alert for pain signals. There is a lot going on around the clock most of which we don't pay attention to and can't do much about. There is a lot we can do without being able to describe how we do it. We just learn how to do it with our conscious mind and then file it away in our sub-conscious, so that we can do it automatically without having to pay any regard to it.

Each mind function runs autonomously at different levels according to need. The process by which the attention flits between them without jarring creates the illusion of consciousness. It is the amalgamation of all the sensory inputs and thought centres, each having their turn acting on the core attention that brings about the feeling of being alive. As there is a seamless transition from one to another and never locking onto one for any great length of time, we get this sense of cognition that we all take as experiencing normal life.

We can set a function a task to do and when it is complete it will let us know by way of bringing it to our attention. We may be working on a problem, cast it to the back of our mind for it then to reappear solved sometime later. Each area can only do one task at a time competently giving rise to conflicts. Doing something with your hands won't detract from working on a solution to a mental problem. However, trying to write and speak at the same time is not feasible as the same language area is being utilised. Trying to look at two things at the same time is equally challenging. Whilst the eye will notice movements using a different schema to the visual processing area, all it can do it bring it to your attention. Quite often it will be set to look out for certain things. Where once tyre repair shops do not stand out, you begin to see them everywhere when you have recently been on the lookout for them because of a puncture.

Place a treat in someone's bedroom. Put it somewhere it can be seen but not too obvious. Sometimes it can be days rather than hours before they notice it. People can be asked to count the number of times a juggler transfers some balls between their hands. In the background a big gorilla moves past and few notice it as they are paying attention to the moving balls. Magic tricksters understand this and will control the focus of their targets using sleight of hand. The thing that they are drawing your attention to is merely a distraction away from what they are hiding from you.

As your vision is far removed from a camera and works by building up a picture, your mind makes up what could potentially fill the gaps. Every time you walk into a room you do not process each and every object as that would take a very long time. Instead you scan around and just identify the important things. What we say we see and remember is far removed from what we actually receive through our eyes.

As you enter an unfamiliar place you will scan the area and spot lots of things that interest you. If you like well-built individuals, you will clock them all even if you are unaware of doing so. Hence why old people literally grey out as the scan skips them completely. Camouflage works so well because to survey an entire scene in front of an animal takes too many mental resources. When you know what to look for and have an idea of the shape it becomes much easier. As a large region of the mind is devoted to the complex task of facial recognition it is hardly surprising that we can see faces in tree bark and clouds as it is always on the go trying to identify them.

Not only does your mind skip, ignore and allow much to pass it by it is very much prone to making errors. What we see and remember is much more about the emotion than anything close to reality. Having an impression of something is a far quicker method of absorption than close scrutiny. This is one area where we differ from mechanical devices which can do laborious analysis with no problem of fatigue. People believe they are right, convinced at times beyond any uncertainty, but in truth they are liable to make significant and frequent mistakes. Our capacity to process information at speed is somewhat limited so our minds cuts corners and approximates a lot.

You can get under the skin of the attention movements caused by pain and sensory alarms. An unusual touch like an itch or bite or a sound above ambient levels and unexpected tastes will be easier to follow than reminder signals though. We set up inbuilt reminder calls for something we had planned to do. These are not quite so straightforward to work into the self-examination process. You can jostle with the itinerary nudge, but you will find the mechanics much harder to relate to compared with other interruptions.

Each of us has different pain thresholds with some being able to tolerate a lot more than others. Some aspects of pain can be enjoyable to some. Pain is change after all. Change feeds the reward system. What you find uncomfortable could be indifferent or pleasurable to other people. A really close analysis gets you to the bottom of where pain is, if something drops on your foot is the pain there or in the mind?

The heart has neurons very similar to those in your head. The heart gets a request to beat harder and faster rather than being controlled directly from above. I suppose saying someone has a good heart is appropriate as it is a separate entity to the spirit in the mind. When something does indeed drop on your foot, go try it with something fairly heavy and notice that the pain is in the foot not your mind, the throbbing is very much there with the cells telling you about it.

You are a collection of parts not a complete object which also hosts a few kilograms of bacteria with their own cooperative agenda. It is not only you that gets hungry. You may even get to appreciate what someone feels when they get pain from a phantom limb, a limb that they no longer have. Life maybe a series of problems but it is also a sequence of interrupts.

The chance of anyone getting this far in the book is pretty remote, let alone bothering to do any real self-examination, so an extensive explanation is quite a waste. If you are in the tiniest of tiny minority that wants something to while away a few weeks of your time keep focusing on your attention. Every action, pumping, inhaling, swallowing. It is all mechanical. It is distinctly different from relaxing, meditating or trying to blank the mind. It is following each and every switch of action, being alert to all changes and constantly consciously observing all the things that divert you from the moment in hand. Nothing will seem the same if you persist with it. The fantasy element during sex is curtailed and replaced by the bodily awareness, the input to the senses replaces the sensuality. If you begin to watch your blinking, you will notice the black / flash but a few minutes later you forget that you forgot you are not noticing it. That's no good. Apply this to the many other things going on and you are on your way. If that is too troublesome, try something more fun. Watch a game of football and keep watching the referee. Ignore the ball and the other players. Just watch the referee for a while.

Special keys

Our life, being a series of moments, a few milliseconds to many seconds long can get disrupted. Load up with one key and it enables you to lock onto a thought path for much longer. This key will reduce the amount the attention twitches. Along with the relaxing effect it can enable you to solve problems that require a lot of thought. The effect can bring about laughter at rather ordinary events, though this diminishes over time as you get accustomed to the way it works on your mind. It is one of the many keys that provide that all important change, change that gives reward and satisfaction.

With the ability to visualize and imagine things, pictures can be brought to the fore with eyes closed or open. Sounds can be replayed. Some keys can interfere with the usual way we manage these inner workings. Some will see this as some kind of spiritual enlightenment rather than the reality of a machine behaving in a non-standard way. When a key unleashes spurious signals, amplifying ones that would normally be ignored and unnoticed the mind stumbles to keep up. Messages tripping over one another. They can hijack many pathways including those from the inner ear which causes rapid head spin and juddering.

Dormant memories can be brought to the fore into this visualisation area. Inverted, distorted and miscoloured. Use of keys need not be restricted to those that want a detraction from the humdrum of existence. Can you use a key and hold the nerve to keep the movements associated with the attention in context. It might help you appreciate your irrelevance and get further under the skin of being an animal machine. Just pray that the key does not jam in the lock.

Nothing Matters

Mankind has achieved a lot, much of it visible like the impressive buildings and transport systems. Other accomplishments are hidden underground; pipes enabling us to flush our waste and cables by which we power things and communicate. All of this and so much more gives us a real sense of being the top dog in the animal kingdom. It also leads us to think that there is a grand plan of some sort.

With lots of people working together, mountains of rock and earth can be moved to build dams diverting colossal amounts of water. We have our thoughts diverted too. Away from our insignificance in the grand scale of the universe towards what we can see around us. It is all too easy to forget that we are on a tiny planet floating in a wide wide sea of space.

Whilst we have the tools to achieve earthly ends we have some serious limitations. Getting to the moon took enormous effort and staying there for any length of time has proved somewhat difficult. The prospect of colonising other planets is highly unlikely. We would not survive any lengthy trip in our current form. Our bodies are suited to this cosy place and would fall apart elsewhere. Even if we were to harness new energy sources in time to aid the journey we are unlikely to do much before the conditions on this planet deteriorate. Mankind is strong and dominant in its domain but futile outside of it.

We live in a relatively thin atmosphere and can't go too far above nor below the surface without encountering problems. Where many go on pilgrimages to distant lands to fulfil obligations, one needs to go somewhere above 14000 ft. to get the experience of how hard it is to walk about and do things there that are ordinary at sea level. If you intend to acclimatise on the way up, go higher to get the same effect. Get a feel of your feebleness.

Some people have the power to upend the lives of millions and change a lot, but they have no control over the destiny of the universe. As a species, we can play no significant part in the running of the universe for we are microbes, truly miniscule on the scale of what is out there. This can invite us to look introspectively on the petty squabbles and desires of day to day living. Some may speculate that as technology progresses we will be capable in the future to do something about a large object hurtling towards the earth. It is hope over reason to assume that a film star will set off with a large explosive and alter its trajectory. More than likely we wouldn't even spot it until it is too late anyway. There are countless doomsday scenarios that are not worth worrying too much about so instead we are more inclined to keep our patch tidy and sort small troubles out.

The earth shields us from the harsh external environment with a magnetic core and a specific atmosphere, for how long it will remain that way we can't be certain. For most people, so long as they are going to be okay and their children will be alright it is not something we feel the need to pay too much attention to.

What happens on the earth is irrelevant to the wider universe. Whether we thrive or not won't make any significant difference, the earth will continue its orbit around the sun however damaged or pristine. The rest of the planets, stars, comets and all the cosmic dust will also follow some course as they have done for some time. If the earth broke up it wouldn't really matter but of course it would be a pity for us living here. All that knowledge, all those talents would be lost and gone forever. If it makes you happy you could archive all of humankind's discoveries and scientific postulations. Store them in multiple vaults and as a further backup fire them off in bright yellow capsules in multiple directions to different galaxies. For surely all this work can't be in vain. Maybe we could pass from this life into a virtual electronic form and float in an ocean of marvelousness. Great idea, but reward is felt through the chemical changes within a body not a change in bit state.

Have you served a higher purpose and have you done enough to qualify? There is nothing but admiration for those who do not fake their belief and have real faith in their god. They understand that the godly force is around us, watching from the side lines waiting to pull aside only the really committed ones. So long as you have picked the correct spiritual entity from the mass of conflicting ones available. Was it reasonable to make the younger ones in your charge follow your lead. Are you comfortable with them feeling guilty if they are not as committed as you? Were they given the chance to check out alternatives?

Some believe that if we all were to obey the orders from up above or form a harmonious bond with one another, all things will come together to form an unbeatable sphere of rectitude. If only the arguments would peter out. Problems make us as much as they break us. If we whittled all the languages down to one and stuck to a solitary belief system, the job will be done. And that will be the point where it is game over for all.

Either way

What you do with your life doesn't matter, what you don't do doesn't matter, nothing really matters. Whatever the outcome you will die at some point regardless. People around us make it feel as though things matter. We care about our lives and care about the things we do and have compassion for others. Things mentioned at the start of this text drive us to care. We are all co-considerationally selfish, we are ridden with curiosity and placated with a reward system. Enlightened, educated, informed or sophisticated, call it aware, we may or may not be. We have our time, we play our game and it only seems to make a difference but ultimately it does not.

The journey

We are spat out at the source of the river. Some manage three heartbeats and become another still born statistic. Others drown or hit the rocks. Those that make it to adulthood are still being swept along by the force of the current. All of us end up in the ocean to meet our maker and reused by those in the lower ranks of the food chain. All the atoms that have been holding us together are then given over for other animals and the plants to use.

Looking at life deeply is akin to swimming to great depths. Some will choose to stay on the surface. Some will explore a little way down and a good few will reach the bottom gaining awareness by touching the river bed. Those swimming down get to see a whole world of intrigue. The metaphorical coral reefs, the unending variety of fish and sea species. On the surface, it is just a limited world view. No matter how far you get or how deep you explore you have to return to the surface to eat and breathe though. An enthralling life still terminates at the graveyard irrespective of how deep you swim. We can't truly escape our human form. No new technology or future advances in science will change that. Emotion needs a whole living body. We will never be able to morph in to something that lives forever.

We as members of the human race participate to varying degrees. Many people have come and gone and lots more should follow. You can only come back as another member not as a particular individual. Memory of a former life is not evident or up for serious discussion. Though you will have made some waves some Interference, connection and disturbance to the soul of all life for sure. A simple act of going into a shop and buying something is enough to make a difference to some else's day, more cash in the till and more stock that needs replenishing. On the brighter side your smile and friendly greeting can boost the morale of the serf counting down the minutes left before going home.

The journey inside yourself, the examination of what and who you are can change your priorities. Many of us will go on holiday and whilst there we get more of a chance to sit and think. We reflect for a while, but return to reality quite quickly once back at home and back at work. There is always that important meeting to attend and project to finish never relenting never ending. What are we working for if we don't balance the financial rewards with inner rewards of a quality of life? The things that seem to be so pertinent and cherished at some point in time end up as waste to contend with. Consumerism is, as was said at the start, just that. Items made and fanned out across the globe percolating down the line to satisfy a fleeting need. You will have a role in some of that. It may have provided something for people to remark upon, enjoyment even, but was the value exaggerated?

If one thing disheartens me more than anything it is the naff comments and retreating demeanour when a conversation gets more involved. In discussions that are a little deeper, people come alive, their body language tells it all. I never ever found it in the least bit depressing. I found it to be the exact opposite. I can appreciate that people have entrenched views and beliefs yet when pushed they can argue their case rather well. Throwaway lines such as "we are putting the world to rights tonight" have the subtext; Nothing we say will make any difference and that we should keep our heads down and remain busy with the business of everyday life. Many people won't need to read a book or study a script to find themselves never being embarrassed, having great confidence and a free nature. Having any form of enlightenment is not a necessity nor is it a worthy aim, but some can see a positive in being more of what they want to be. There is a liberating practical side to philosophy.

Some are born laissez-faire and worry little about anything, but when the onset of financial pressure takes its toll or the prospect of taking possession of a house beckons or a baby comes onto the scene things can change somewhat. People come to the realisation that problems, serious or otherwise can be put to the back of their head until directly faced with them. Then they can be broken down into manageable parts and worked through. It is not about ignoring a car crash that is soon to happen nor procrastinating and sidestepping things that would be good to get resolved. Instead, it is taking the attitude that you will just deal with any problems as and when they arise. Work out the options, select one and get it done. Muddling through is a norm and is alright considering that the last thing people want is to be judged. One does not need to justify their ways for humble individuals can see the greyness where a preacher has distilled things into a black and white, acceptable unacceptable dryness.

Many wish to make the world a better place but at the same time yearn for the simplicity of the past. Progress is not always viewed as positive; we make changes for what we see as good, ignoring the possibility that such alterations have downsides and compromises. We only end up with a few more options a few more choices and slightly quicker alternatives. Some like the changes and others see the alterations as spoiling what was perfectly fine before. Is sex any better now than it was 1000 years ago? Maybe the opportunity to take part has been prolonged into older age with magic pills to maintain the stiffness and sensuality. It could be that plastic aids have replaced wooden or leather ones, but are these really worthy of industrial and technology revolutions and human sacrifices. The next time you walk into a meadow or trot down a valley ask yourself if nature's beauty has been helped or hindered by all our endeavours. You plant this and that and cut back a vivacious species hoping to enforce a balance by killing all the things that were doing just fine.

Things are progressing. We have moved on. However, the excitement for what is around the corner, advancements to come, wanes when you realise that what really matters is pretty constant. Has fashion improved? Not one bit. You may cringe at what you wore 20 years ago, but it was as good as what it is today.

In the past good quality housing, access to information, clean running water and the means to travel were an aspiration. Now they have moved more towards been taken for granted. With ever better medicinal practitioners we also live longer in some nations than before. However, we must not ignore that half of the world live on the equivalent to what the other half might spend on single cup of coffee a day. I doubt compassion and relief for the less well-off will increase to noticeable levels anytime soon. We care if the wealthy perish in a small event but if tens of thousands get washed away or shaken to pieces in an impoverished place it is a case of c'est la vie. Life goes on regardless, often oblivious and there is a limit to what we can do, or are prepared to sacrifice.

We like to think that we make steps forward in the political arenas and that we have more freedoms now than before. However, the governments simply get better at creating an illusion of this and harden their stance. More and more disruptive technologies are changing the way we do business. This has sparked new ventures not possible previously. From making fire to cook, to using fire to generate steam, disruption is nothing new. They are all however progressing at the expense of something else, not always adding to the sum of all things. We have to do more, learn more and consider more just to tread water. Where some risks have been eliminated others have emerged. For a good few, life today has the potential to be more rewarding, for others little has changed. The subjects we talk about change, but the joy of talking to one another is always the same. Of course there have been outstanding improvements but some things get lost in this process of change.

Preoccupation

The overwhelming majority of people become so preoccupied with their day to day existence that they never stop to consider what it is all about. It helps if you aren't in a stressful difficult situation maybe with money concerns or having to care for people in poor health. Then we have the myriad of distractions where we can't even use the loo without something to read or play with. This is not a major issue as the ignorance paradox takes in people that explore, people that ignore, people that shy away from difficult subjects, all people and the only difference between one that thinks they know more is a bit of smugness. In other words, in makes not one jot of difference how much you know at the final reckoning. People living in so-called ignorance can be as happy as anyone else and be as fulfilled as the next man. Where do you draw the line, how much knowledge is enough? Ignorance of the facts, ignorance due to lack of understanding and ignorance less to do with stupidity but not even knowing what you don't know. Many live a whole life in hardship never discovering the riches close to hand.

We all know we can't take our wealth with us but some might be glad to leave any debts behind. Many build a tomb and have their treasure buried with them spiting those that could have made use of it. When you die, your skills, knowledge and years of learning evaporate. All that mastery and structure of your soul is no more. That is the real loss.

Did you make a contribution? Was it one that nobody else could have managed. Was it one nobody would have made at some later point. Will the world stop when you do or will it carry on quite fine without you? Will you be missed? Maybe briefly and you come to the fore in a few people's mind from time to time until they pass away too. Empires that you build crumble either quite quickly after you die or at some stage later on. The changes you made get changed again and all traces of you gets gradually wiped away to leave not much more than a name in a register or footnote in history.

It is not uncommon for some to initially proclaim that they are going to change the world. Then lower their sights on making a big difference to their country. As time passes this gets reduced to a more realistic aim of making a small mark on their immediate locality. From aspiring to rid the world of all diseases to getting a hole on the village hall roof fixed.

One high achievement in its own right is to get through to the end unscathed. To avoid being stabbed, shot, injured or debilitated by the plethora of traps and to be left unscarred by the losses of loved ones especially those that you were helpless to help is a big thing. It only takes one tiny body part, a gland, valve, a seemingly insignificant bit of your anatomy to go awry changing an outlook from heavenly to hellish in an instant.

The optimism of finding a definitive explanation for matters of life and living fade over one's lifetime. So much ends with a conclusion that wasn't quite what was hoped for. You begin to see that there are at least two sides to each equation and we have to work out which to use in each scenario. Each judgement has to be made in context and nothing is quite as simple as we first thought. The early bird catches the worm, hence a worm does well to have a lie in. Writing this heap of words is like a policeman hunting a suspect for years on end, to finally find out the culprit has died long ago. Never getting the chance to apprehend nor comprehend the waste of effort. All the policeman really set out to do was change a few neurons in their head. Case open to case closed.

There is a vain hope that when it ends you will be given the answers. All will be revealed. If only that were so. You will get your vindication. You will be proven correct and only small details of where you erred will be filled in. The only blunder is having this belief and as the whiteness turns to dark you will not even be conscious of you own expiration. Another precious life completed. The world is no more as far as you are concerned. You die every night in effect and there will be no exciting beautiful fun unreal real dreams as an interlude. If you perish in a big calamity, blown up, smashed to pulp in an instant you won't even get the last fun ride, the hallucinogenic peace making dreamy last few minutes of ultimate bliss.

People may stare at the stars and wonder at our insignificance, whereas others will have no such interest. They may deem subjects like astronomy as really dull and irrelevant. The whys and wherefores of existence have no relevance to what they are doing. You may wish to explore avenues of thought but others won't, they 'have' to get up in the morning and go to work. They have more pressing things on their mind that 'must' get done. The trap, the illusion, the compulsion to conform, the urge to fit in, the need, the greed, the want for more, the guilt, the toil, the fun, the pleasure. We will be doing it for ever and ever until the day we realise 'our time is now' is no longer.

Many people are looking for the meaning of life without realising that there is none. Some will treasure the connections with one another, friendships, kinships, relationships and shared experiences and see that as the most immutable important currency. If you were hoping for a happy ending or some guidance as to what to do, here you will be disappointed. The ignorance paradox doesn't tell you what you should do, there is no lesson to be learnt it is just a feature of life. And if you should be confused or fail to get the riddle just reread the beginning and once a few pages in again you will see it no doubt. Any down heartedness turns to an uplifting sense of freedom. Maybe, but then why bother, we already have our own personal worthy aim.

Great but not impressed say you. It is a correct observation to see anyone challenging you as a type that is just pretentious. Nothing more than crystallising stuff we already half know. Your problem is that you have not got a problem, that is what it seems. Neither a stumbling block nor self-doubt. You have day to day issues and mountains of things to contend with, problems of sorts, but your life is running swimmingly. You retain the idea of heading towards a day where you have even greater self-esteem. To be even more revered. In fact, you think of yourself as the wise one, the one people come to for help and a leg up. Scores to settle, points to prove with your peers, people nearly as rich or with more wealth, people with more influence or greater notoriety. The great guru the one who saw through the mess and picked wisely. The top chump who looks at the zookeeper with disdain. Everything will be done at a time of my choosing, everything is in control. I will work out what, to whom and when I will give my assets away. My life is sorted. The sleepwalker. Mr zookeeper knows they themselves are not superior. They aren't looking down their nose at others. They are not laughing at them. They are not trying to change them, but they do like to instil some self-doubt in those around them.

Maybe it is me that has all these daft conjectures and everyone else is going along just fine. Nope, there are funerals every day, people retiring, people changing direction after pursuing schemes for ages. Let's not rock the boat and stop challenging people.

We see those that are sleepwalking, those that dabble a bit, plenty that plan their life, many self-assured, the completely uninterested and all those that are a mix of all these. Some will find meaning in life through what they are doing, but some are adamant that there is no ultimate meaning whatsoever. The thing that bothered me the most was how to justify saying that there is no meaning to life. How to put it into perspective?

We have those that are totally sure they are doing what they should be and will be making sure everyone else is following too. They are the ones lots of people look up to for reassurance that they are on the right path. The similarity to these groups of people and an ant colony is remarkable. There will be soldier ants on hand to guard against invaders, but also to keep the worker ants in check. Any ant that deviates from doing as they are told is quashed. Some will be inspired by the group effort seeing it for the good of all, however, it is in principle for the benefit of the king master ant the most.

The dabblers explore quite a lot and feel semi-satisfied that on aggregate they have lived a virtuous life and need not worry about political or social problems that are too complex and too numerous. Plus, there is no point fussing day and night over things that are out of their control anyway. They meddle with a few bits and pieces to 'expand their horizons' and with a little bit of charity work and a little bit of community involvement they are quite content.

The planners find an objective and do what is necessary to achieve it. They will have their long-term goals and set themselves a few side tasks. Getting to where they want to be is what it is all about for them. A university qualification, job upgrade, better house, faster car to developing an item/system that will transform life as we know it. It is all part of the distraction technique of being busy enough to feel it is unnecessary to consider deep meanings. Those that are the most occupied are the least interested in the underlying why.

It is all about degrees, degrees of merit. Take a look at a dog, it can be fairly content with its lot. They don't have the pressure of dog school and all the exams at the end of it, although some do get house trained and learn a few tricks. Any dog that goes on regular walks, has a balanced diet and receives love and attention is seen as getting a fulfilling life. Lower down the scale we could point to a mouse. It will have a fun time running up and down the pipes in your home and live a while before running out of steam. Does it have meaning in its short life with its heart beating many times quicker than yours.

Standing beside a stream I watched an insect swoop down to get a drink and got caught up in the flow. As it meandered down heading towards a stick, I was expecting it to grab onto it, get out and dry off before flying away. It was swirled about by the eddies and arrived near the bit of wood then, floosh, gobbled and gone by a crafty fish in wait for passing fodder. What meaning did that insect have in its life? Pare down to the bacteria then to the virus and you get living things with ever shorter life cycles. We as humans propose that because we are much more advanced that there must be more to life than being born, fidgeting about a bit, then succumbing to some illness or dying in an accident. Having a greater thinking capacity gives us the illusion and delusion of being more than the dog, mouse, bacterium and lump of wood.

I look at some people and wonder what makes them tick. I know the drives now, but to see an old codger, senile, plodding at a snail's pace on a mission to fetch a simple loaf of bread with day after day of aimless aims, what am I not seeing? Their close cousin is the retard, the slow in mind, fast in unusual body movements with a gurning grin, docile manner and fruitlessness than makes us look the other way. Painted nails and plastic fantastic, fake, fudged and self-consumed is thee that lays upon a cheap bed in the sun. Catering for this lovely one is the eternal slave sauntering along to open up, get things ready once again, knowing it is futile to even imagine anything more. The prim and proper, all tidy and discreet getting made up for another big event. To others it is an excuse to have a drink and be merry, for these it is a chance to demonstrate their class. A class act in a class of impressers. Who is here, who has been de-ranked and who has been up to no good in the eyes of those that make the rules.

What then makes people tick aside from each having a different clock and different objectives in the time available, not a lot. In a desert, we see a mirage and amble towards it, in life we think we see greater relevance in our life than in others. It is so hard to shed the notion that we have not just a purpose, but are on the way to making some kind of achievement that makes all the effort so worthwhile.

Open a tap and fill a bowl with water then me, you, anyone can stare at the reflection and see that a life is as transient as that image. Tap the bowl and watch the shimmering, your waves of beavering, busy, idle interaction that alters but changes nothing in the end. Equally valid and equally worthless are we. It is a name, a number, a mark in the sand with nothing tangible of us left behind. It is all one big con. Think, ponder, postulate for as long as you like until the light in your head goes out and the chemicals stop flowing. No more curiosity, no more reward and no more self.

Why bring people down to earth? Once an appreciation of the ultimate futility is understood and becomes a feature of a person's core, they can then find a firmer ladder to climb. After which a product of utility for all might manifest itself.

Illustrations

The original concept was a simple box with four doors, something that wouldn't take too long to make. It offered up a chance to do something away from the mundane work work work for money routine.

As things went along it got considerably more involved and time eating. Basic doors evolved into shutters and sliders. Getting each mechanism to work without interfering with one another created lots of issues to solve.

The problem side of things was a big part of the fun; finding solutions the most rewarding. Computer aided design would have made the process much easier as you can see what fits before you make anything. By doing it all by hand, make, fit and test it leans much more towards art rather than a pure engineering project. That is what I like to think anyway. Nevertheless, I feel that it was only by holding, feeling, shaping and meddling with the metal, could I really come up with an end product of my liking. I do not think that one can expand an initial idea so much when working at the computer screen.

It has absolutely no utility whatsoever, it is not a clock or some handy device, but it may provide a trifling amount of amusement and encapsulates the "what's inside?" vibe.

Making the 4 doors, five mechanisms and frame gave me an insight into using a lathe, milling machine and casting. The hope was to make a near perfect solid silver square box frame. I tried to cast in one go. By using some aluminium angles and casting sand I made a mould. As the frame was to be only 4mm thick I was not able to get a good enough pour to fill the entire mould. After a few attempts another strategy was needed. Maybe if I just get four strips of silver and a sheet I could silver solder it all together. What I didn't take into account is that as you heat the metal to solder it, it expands. It is going to be hard to get all five pieces at the same temperature to avoid any gaps and buckling. Alternatively, a jig to hold it in place is equally awkward to set up.

Screwing it all together seemed unsatisfactory as the thickness didn't seem to be adequate to take the screws. The other problem was that when you buy silver sheet you expect it to be flat. Each piece is far from flat as the stockist use a guillotine to cut it thus putting an annoying bend in it.

So back to casting again, this time I tried to make four side pieces with a couple of nubbles on each to screw into. Being smaller than a whole frame the casting would not need any vacuum assisted pouring. I managed the first one. It was far from anything a competent foundryman would deliver but it was machinable to my required specifications. The next pour resulted in an explosion probably because the sand was too wet. After picking hundreds of globules of silver of the floor and putting back into the crucible I thought about pouring into an open mould. The resulting apparition, the return from the dead showing their face arms belly and so forth lead me to reconsider the perfect box shape.

Another side was made by heating the silver in situ until it flowed, then running a piece of wood quickly across to get it to flatten adequately. Molten silver doesn't run like water does, instead it has a tendency to form globules and misbehave. Nevertheless, whilst using more silver than simple sheets the result is fine.

After endless hours on the milling machine I sized each piece to fit the top sheet.

When it breaks it is a good thing. (sometimes)

For the third time in three weeks something has broken and the after-effect has been quite positive. Silver is quite malleable and doesn't welcome being milled. Unlike brass, which flakes of nicely it has a propensity to snarl up, smudge rather than machine away. The vibration and noise was gradually increasing, the amount I was trying to mill (depth) decreased yet still no encouraging result.

You can enter one code to move the mill slowly and anther code to move it quickly to another spot. Put the wrong code in when the end mill is too low and it will fly across and snap instantly. Entering G0 rather than G1 and another expensive carbide bit destroyed. However, with a new bit in the milling was wonderful. Obviously the one I was using was getting blunt and not cutting at all well. Breaking it solved the problem and saved a lot of time figuring out the next move.

I broke a ticket barrier in China the once and missed the train as the police wanted me to pay for it. (I noticed that there was a chip in the perspex and perhaps it was faulty hence they should pay me instead for delaying my journey. This kind of worked as they reduced the settlement to a third.) On the other train we met someone who showed us an unbelievably useful item which we bought at our destination and used during our visit.

I broke my tablet and was so disgusted by the internal build, penny pinching components, that I decided that I would buy another type altogether. This lead to a different way of working whilst away, one which has become far less painful and increased the time sightseeing halving the time not. So, serendipity is found in miniature disasters.

Mechanisms

A slider was easy just a grove and spring to shut. The small door opener was not too difficult either as it is a simple sprung pull rod.

However, the door catch was not so straightforward. In theory it is just a translation of the up-down pressure to in-out to hold the door. However, with the limited room and problem of it sticking, it was not quick to get right.

The shutter proved rather frustrating. A simple scheme, but it was far too willing to jam particularly if you pushed it at one side. The square shaped bars bunch up and interlock slightly, randomly and create deep dissatisfaction. The cure was found by opening the curve runner somewhat.

The shutter mechanism needs to both keep the shutter up and close it. Here one learns the imperative of getting the brass pieces set to tight tolerances. Even a fraction of a millimetre off and it doesn't work. Initially I had the shutter winding over a roller with the aim of tensioning the roller to provide the up and down force. I settled for a less elegant wing device instead.

The main heavy silver door needs to be stay open. The point of action would be outside the box. Using the same principle as the other door meant extra work was needed.

Gears seemed the obvious solution. In a factory a gear can be churned out in seconds. On a milling machine it is a harder task. There is most likely software already available that will spew out g-code to direct the mill, but I chose to write my own as the maths would be fun, or so I thought. It didn't take that long once I worked out a scheme and it was gratifying to see the gear emerge after the mill had done its work.

I attempted to mill a logo on a platinum piece using a very fine bit (0.2mm). It worked in principle but each time the mill snapped it was hard to set it back off again from the same place. The assay office kindly laser engraved it instead for a pretty reasonable token sum. The issue of who really made an artwork question reared its head. Great works which sell for large sums of money are quite often actually made by students and helpers. People will impart large fortunes for something because the name attributed to it is big. The value placed on it can also depend upon to who has owned it previously. Art galleries have vast vaults with thousands of fine paintings that don't see the light of day. Millions of songs have been written but most are rarely heard because luck and notoriety was lacking. This is neither a grand piece nor has it been made to sell and pragmatic decisions have to be made.

A sapphire held in a white gold setting and a diamond/red stone rudimentarily set on the lever provide a little distraction.

After some buffing and polishing the item was ready to photograph. Taking a picture of a mirrored surface was unexpectedly troublesome. A front on picture means you can see the camera and the person taking the picture. Even poking the camera through a sheet of white paper doesn't eradicate the problem.

A craftsman could have made something like this with a better finish and in half the time, but an average result is enough at times. For each part in the finished element at least 3 others were made and scrapped. One could copy and reproduce this fairly quickly. However, it is not the making but the devising that shines.

The only way model

Simple item made to illustrate the idea. Milled and drilled, taped and screwed in place. Engraved deep to allow selenium to be melted into the channels. Finding a metal that is black and has a lower melting point than the brass was not forthcoming hence this element with its unappealing odour that lingers in the workroom for days on end was an alternative.

Should illustration

On completion of this little 'art' work I realised that not only am I never going to make anything of any real note, but the process is just a way for me to demystify certain processes that others handle with great aplomb. It is nice to take things to experts to have made, but also to work through the issues wrapped up in doing it yourself. Four days to engrave the little badge. Oh, it would have been so easy to get a stencil made and quickly sandblast it on. Instead coding to drive the engraving machine and fruitless attempts to get it to work. As always it is knowing how, in this case that the carbide bit need only breathe on the glass to get the marking neat and uniform. Too much depth caused the mill to burn out and fail half way round. Any attempt to restart just created more mess. Ten sheets later this was worked out and just .01 mm on the Z axis makes all the difference in the world.

The ability to cut glass and do the lead work is bound to come in useful later and at the second go it became satisfactory. Just hard work figuring out how to bend the lead into a nice curved shape around the glass. Simply forming across ever thinner brass rods proved better than any mechanical device devised.

The glass stringers were quickly bent and fused at their ends. Lampworking, bead making and glass sculpting is easy to get into and maybe after many years of practice would produce items of much greater significance, but this is sufficient for this illustration.

Cover

I thought I would have another go at some casting. A simple plate that anyone who knows about this kind of thing could easily complete in a few days. I understand that the procedure for casting items goes back thousands of years and it seemed to take us about that long to get even marginally acceptable results. Paying someone else to do it is not only ten times cheaper, but would have produced something far better. All the gear and no idea. Sand casting just never came close. Mixing sand and plaster of Paris showed promise, but even ignoring the odd mould exploding, created never ending pitting and cast defects.

So on to using molochite. It all looks so straightforward, but just getting a wax copy to start with can take days. There are so many types of wax to waste time on. You can use a machine to make a master then use some resin to make an inverse copy. Then you pour some hot wax into this resin mould. Frustratingly, it will then either curl up or hundreds of bubbles will form. So, you put in a kiln and then sweep all the bubbles out whilst still inside. Then take out and put some weight on top allowing it to cool. There will always be one letter that is just not right. Carving wax, green lost wax, paraffin candle wax, bees wax on it goes till I hit on microcrystalline wax which is the least difficult one to use for this application.

What I did learn from all the failed use of various types of moulds including the very expensive delft clay, is that the gate system is bountiful. A cone and a gate system with a counter intuitive thinness makes for a nice metal run and reduces the probability of surface defects. Watching others add a simple hook to the end to hang the item to dry between coats is yet one more example of how an obvious problem can be addressed. These moulds with or without wax in are fragile until the metal is poured in and has cooled. I would stand them up but even after a few were knocked over the solution didn't register.

The actual part where you pour the metal is quite straightforward. Having some nice lifting and pouring tools is great. Paying for all the things needed is the easy part. Exactly the same at the dentists, handing the money over, an amount some people find quite high is the simple bit. I would pay double if you could skip the part where you have to sit in the chair. Whack a spoon full of borax and a load of slag coagulant once molten and get someone to help lift the crucible out of the furnace into your holder.

I was asked why I just didn't machine the thing out of a flat brass block. That was a possibility and although it would have taken a long time, maybe a week or two it was far better to spend the best part of a year doing it this way as I just wanted to 'master' casting. Why gold plate it when you can just use a spray can? Well why not do it the way we want to, you do. When telling people about using a furnace outside some asked if can you do it indoors. Well you could but not if you like to keep somewhere to live. It is all about making incremental improvements (changes)_and keeping at it.